# MORE THAN STORIES

# MORE THAN STORIES

*the range of children's writing*

Thomas Newkirk

*University of New Hampshire*

HEINEMANN

*Portsmouth, New Hampshire*

**HEINEMANN EDUCATIONAL BOOKS, INC.**
70 Court Street Portsmouth, NH 03801
*Offices and agents throughout the world*



The author and publisher wish to thank the following for permission to reprint material appearing in this book:

A shorter version of Chapter 1 appeared in *Language Arts* 62 (1985): 593–603.

Figures 2–1 through 2–6, 2–8 through 2–10, 2–14 and 2–15, and 2–17 through 2–20 are from Marlene Lindberg, "The Development and Field Testing of a Kindergarten Writing Assessment Procedure," Ph. D. dissertation (1988), Department of Psychology, University of Hawaii, Honolulu, Hawaii, and are reprinted by permission of Marlene Lindberg.

The quote on p. 40 is from Catherine Snow, "Literacy and Language: Relationships during the Preschool Year," *Harvard Educational Review* 53 (1983): 165–89, and is reprinted by permission.

The quote on p.41 is from Gordon Wells, *The Meaning Makers: Children Learning Language and Using Language to Learn* (Portsmouth, N.H.: Heinemann, 1986), pp. 96–97, and is reprinted by permission.

The quote on pp. 57–58 and Figure 2–16 are from Susan Bridge, "Squeezing from the Middle of the Tube," in *Understanding Writing: Ways of Observing, Learning, and Teaching*, 2nd ed., edited by Thomas Newkirk and Nancie Atwell (Portsmouth, N.H.: Heinemann, 1988), pp. 85–87, and are reprinted by permission.

Much of Chapter 3 appeared in Thomas Newkirk, "The Non-narrative Writing of Young Children," *Research in the Teaching of English* 21, no. 1 (May 1987): 121–44.

The letter from Harry Allard on pp. 111–12 is reprinted by permission of the author.

The quote on pp. 139–40 is from Jerome Bruner, *Child's Talk* (New York: Norton, 1983), pp. 110–11, and is reprinted by permission.

The quote on pp. 141 is from Thomas Newkirk, "Young Writers as Critical Readers," in *Understanding Writing: Ways of Observing, Learning, and Teaching*, 2nd ed., edited by Thomas Newkirk and Nancie Atwell (Portsmouth, N.H.: Heinemann, 1988), pp. 156–57, and is reprinted by permission.



**Library of Congress Cataloging-in-Publication Data**

Newkirk, Thomas.
More than stories: the range of children's writing/Thomas Newkirk.
p. cm.
Bibliography: p.
Includes index.
ISBN 0–435–08490–9
1. English language—Composition and exercises. 2. Language arts (Primary) 3. Children—Language. I. Title
LB1528.N42 1989
372.6—dc19 88–26067
CIP

Designed by Wladislaw Finne.
Printed in the United States of America.

OPI Docutech 2005

*to Maurice*
*and Ruth*

# Contents

# Acknowledgments

In writing this book, I have, like Blanche Dubois, depended on the kindness of others. I have received the generous cooperation of several teachers, who have allowed me to spend time in their classrooms to gather data. So, special thanks to Anna Sumida (Kamehameha Elementary School, Honolulu, Hawaii), Florence Damon (Mast Way Elementary School, Lee, New Hampshire), Pat McLure (Mast Way Elementary School, Lee, New Hampshire), Kathy Matthews (George B. White School, Deerfield, New Hampshire), and Ellen Blackburn Karelitz (formerly, Great Falls School, Somersworth, New Hampshire).

This book was made possible by a Visiting Professorship at the University of Hawaii during the 1985–86 school year. During that year, I was able to get a real start on the writing. I want to thank Tom Hilgers for extending the invitation, and I'd like to express my appreciation to the wonderful "writing group" that was there that year: Bill Strong, Russel Durst, Suzanne Jacobs, LaRene Despain, Roger Whitlock, Joy Marsella, and, of course, Tom Hilgers. I also want to thank Roland Tharp and Marlene Lindberg of the Center for the Development of Early Education, a research unit of the Kamehameha schools, for their extraordinary cooperation.

Closer to home, I've always received support, encouragement, and inspiration from Donald Murray of the University of New Hampshire's English Department. Don believed in me (on the scantest evidence), and, for that confidence, I'll always be grateful. Donald Graves of the UNH Education Department has also been centrally important in this and other projects. I'll never forget my first trip to Atkinson, New Hampshire, in 1979 to see the research project he had begun; I realized that day that things would never be the same in the field of children's writing. Don Graves has done more than anyone I know to show what children can do.

I've also drawn encouragement from my partners in the New Hampshire Writing Program: Jane Kearns, Paula Flemming, Jack Wilde, Ellen Blackburn Karelitz, Terry Moher, Sue Bridge—people I've worked with for the past ten years. Many of the ideas in the book came from the discussions we've had. Jane Hansen, another partner in the New Hampshire Writing Program, has been a wonderful colleague, teaching me a great deal about the ways in which reading and writing can intersect. I also want to thank my collaborator and friend, Nancie Atwell, who has given me such encouragement and useful advice on this and other projects.

I want to thank the Central University Fund of the University of New Hampshire for a grant that helped in the data collection for Chapter 3, and I want to thank Stuart Palmer, Dean of the College of Liberal Arts, for the grant from his office, which helped during the preparation of Chapter 6.

I received considerable assistance from two graduate students. Nancy Krygowski recorded and transcribed the group shares that appear in Chapter 6. Elizabeth Chiseri Strater helped collect many of the pieces of children's writing that appear in Chapter 3. For this and innumerable other contributions, I thank her.

Working with Heinemann Educational Books was, as always, a real pleasure. Special thanks to Philippa Stratton for her helpful guidance, to the various readers for their reactions and advice along the way, and to Donna Bouvier and her staff for their work on the production end of the process.

Finally, this is a book about a family. Thanks to my wife Beth, not simply for her patience with me while I worked on this book (the standard enduring-wife acknowledgment), but for her insights on literacy, gained from working with our children. Thanks also to these children—Abby, Andy, and especially Sarah for teaching me so much about writing. The lessons I learned in writing this book I learned primarily from her.

At the end of *Huckleberry Finn*, Huck, the narrator, says, "If I'd a knowed what a trouble it was to make a book I wouldn't a tackled it, and ain't a going to no more." I can't say I feel that way, but writing a book surely makes it clear how much you don't know. When writing a single chapter or an essay, you can always plead the limitation of space to account for not following certain threads of analysis or not citing certain sources. There are fewer excuses for such oversights in a book. Or perhaps the most appropriate is the excuse given by Samuel Johnson when asked why he completely misidentified a term in his dictionary: "Ignorance, madame, pure ignorance." There's a fair portion of that in this book as well. And for those lapses I take full credit.

# Introduction

This book began for me with an image. I had taken my five-year-old daughter to the city's pool, and, after some playing around in the water, she decided to get out. She went over to a poster listing the pool rules and tried to read it. It was winter, the air chilly, and she was shivering. But she stood there, her head tipped back, trying to read the rules for what seemed to me an uncomfortably long time. Why the fascination with rules?

As I thought about the poster, I began to realize why it seemed to her such a fascinating and powerful piece of writing. Here we were, about fifty swimmers in all, seemingly controlled by the words written on this poster, words that would, among other things, keep her out of the sauna bath until near the twenty-first century. Small wonder that a child would be fascinated—these words represented the power that written language could hold.

I was also surprised because, at the time, I associated learning to read with learning to read stories—imaginative literature seemed the natural starting point, with interest in the analytic or functional uses of language coming later. The Romantic poet William Taylor Coleridge argued at the end of the eighteenth century that children lack "the comparing power," or the ability to make judgments, and that educators should therefore "address [themselves] to those faculties of the child's mind, which are first awakened by nature, and consequently admit of cultivation, that is to say the memory and the imagination" ([1918] 1950, 401). Many developmental models of learning reflect this view: analysis and evaluation regularly are thought of as higher-order thinking, while remembering and storytelling are lower-order thinking. Taller people (older people) do higher-level thinking; shorter (and younger) people do lower-level thinking. Adolescents and adults can reason; children tell stories.

In this book, I will take what might be called a semiotic position on development. While not denying the obvious fact that children develop, I will argue that traditional conceptions of development are inadequate because they overstate the differences between the young and the older language learner. Coleridge, for example, viewed judgment as a late-blooming intellectual faculty, rather than an evolving competence with links all the way back to the consistent preferences of the infant. Traditional theories, too, tend to treat language development as a type of biological growth, a "natural" unfolding of human potential along a predetermined path. By contrast, the semiotic position, while acknowledging the importance of biological maturation, considers the course of development to be strongly influenced by the child's culture, particularly the "ways with words" of adults in that culture. This new perspective provides a messier but ultimately more accurate and less reductive view of the learner.

Semiotics itself is the frequently obscure science of signs, originated by the enigmatic and nearly impenetrable Charles Pierce. Yet several of the basic assumptions of semiotics offer powerful insights into the ways we know and communicate. Semioticians reject the positivist view that meaning resides in the external world to be perceived by the learner. Rather, we as*sign* meaning; we treat objects, gestures, statements as *signs*. If I extend my hand to someone to whom I have been introduced, that extended hand is interpreted as a kind of "glad to meet you." Yet there is nothing inherent in the act to suggest that meaning; an extended hand can as easily signal the beginning of an assault. But the context of an introduction suggests the first interpretation. In assigning meaning, we bring to bear both personal and cultural knowledge. For example, the meaning I now might assign to a story about the death of a child is different from the one that I would have assigned before I had children of my own. But, because I also operate within a culture (or many cultures) where I share interpretive strategies with others, interpretation does not break down into purely individualistic responses. When a story begins "Once upon a time," we expect a fairy tale of some kind and are confused, at least momentarily, if the story goes on to tell about something that actually happened.

Long before they enter school, children are already master semioticians—they can read situations and act appropriately. Even their lapses are instructive. One day, my younger daughter, age four, was playing with her friend Thomas. With the timing children are known for, Thomas had to go to the toilet while his mother was showering, and he needed his mother's help. As negotiations were proceeding in the bathroom, my daughter hovered at the door watching. As she got out of the shower, the mother turned to my daughter and said, "Abby, would you mind closing the door?" Abby did as she was told, closing the door, but stayed *inside* the bathroom to watch. Abby interpreted the words correctly in a literal sense—she closed the door—but she failed to interpret their implicit message—would you please leave me alone while I take care of this mess. What's striking, though, is how regularly even young children read situations correctly and act accordingly.

From the semiotic perspective, then, learning to read and write are extensions of the social abilities that the child has already developed. Frank Smith's metaphor of the "club" (1983) is useful here. Smith sees proficient language users as members of a club that children seek to join. Club members cannot tell children explicitly how to join, but they can provide demonstrations—by making available examples of the club's writing, by allowing children to watch members writing, and, perhaps most importantly, by treating children as club members even as they master the conditions for entry. It's the Pygmalion effect; treated as writers or readers, children begin to pretend their way into literacy.

The children portrayed by semioticians like Jerome Harste and Frank Smith are immersed in the adult literate culture and anxious to master the forms that will allow them entry. Among these forms is, to be sure, the story, but there are many others: grocery lists, signs, letters, junk mail of all sorts, questionnaires, quizzes, jokes, riddles, badges, party invitations. The child is not pictured in the garden, close to nature and still unbound by the inevitable yoke of adult life; more likely, the child is tagging along behind Mom in the supermarket, reading labels—a member of the can-readers club.

Where traditional research on development has tended to be "deficiency driven," the semiotic approach is "competency driven": It begins with the assumption that children are skillful language learners, adept at many of the social routines of the adult culture. Take, for example, this "Tooth Lady" letter written by Abby at age seven. It was bedtime, and she had just pulled out a loose front tooth. She decided to write a note and put it in her special tooth pillow (which had a slot for such letters). The note originally read:

*dere toth lady*

*I lost a toth will you gev me some monny I was strong. Ples tell alittle bit [about] you*

---

---

---

Abby folded the note, tucked it into the pillow, and crawled back into bed. A few minutes later, she asked, "What if the Tooth Fairy takes my little pillow? I think I better say something about not taking my pillow." I tried to assure her that the Tooth Fairy wouldn't take her pillow, but she insisted on adding a line to her note. She got up and wrote:

*don't tak the pelo its in*

With the note refolded and back in the pillow, Abby said, "You know why I didn't say, 'Please don't take the pillow'? Because if you say please the Tooth Fairy could decide to take it."

While some developmentalists might view this letter as evidence of a stage when Abby accepted fictions like the Tooth Fairy, the semiotician will view it as evidence of her knowledge of language conventions. The letter contains a statement, which justifies the succeeding request, which is in turn followed by a back-up reason. It begins with the main business —asking for money—and then shifts into something more gossipy, a pattern basic to letter writing. Finally, the letter shows that Abby understands that requests imply possible refusal in a way that demands do not.

Another advantage of the semiotic position is that it opens up the curriculum to a variety of language forms. By forms, I do not mean rigid organizational patterns that are chosen once a writer has found the meaning to be conveyed. Form and meaning are intertwined closely in the composing process; we don't think formless thoughts—thoughts have shapes, and these shapes are, to a considerable degree, determined by the genres offered up by our culture. Donald Murray ([1978] 1982) writes:

*Most writers view the world as a fiction writer, a reporter, a poet, or a historian. The writer sees experience as a plot or a lyric poem or a news story or a chronicle. The writer uses such literary traditions to see and understand life. (36)*

But, because any way of seeing is also a way of *not* seeing, Murray emphasizes that genres can become habitual and even stereotypical ways of looking at life:

*Genre is a powerful but dangerous lens. It both clarifies and limits. The writer and student must be careful not to see life merely in the stereotyped form with which he or she is most familiar but to look at life with all of the possibilities of the genre in mind and to attempt to look at life through different genre. (36)*

It would follow that a child who has mastered a repertoire of genres has a number of lenses with which to view experience: genres, while constraining, are also cognitive instruments for making sense of the world. It would also follow that any system of education that limits children to one genre, even one as powerful as the fictional story, may also limit the vantage points that children might assume.

The exclusive emphasis on story writing can be limiting in another way: It assumes that one type of writing or reading is congenial (or natural) for all children. But is that the case? On what grounds do we say that an informational book on dinosaurs is less meaningful than *Where the Wild Things Are?* My own work in elementary classes suggests that children differ considerably in the forms of writing they excel at (and the kinds of reading they prefer). A child who writes dull, conventional stories may write excellent descriptions of science displays. Others may exhibit a fluency in their letter writing that is missing from other types of writing. All of which argues for an elementary-school classroom where a range of possibilities is open to students.

Romantic assumptions about language learning also lead to what might be called the Great Divide approach to literacy. When children leave elementary school, they often leave behind them the "creative" discourse forms. They may never write a poem, a play, or a story in secondary school (although they will read these genres). Arthur Applebee has observed that "the high school years are a time of transition from reliance on primarily time-ordered or descriptive modes of presentation toward more analytic modes of presentation" (1984, 185). To borrow a phrase from First Corinthians, high school is a place to "put aside childish things."

I contend that this Great Divide approach is flawed in two major ways. First, secondary students do not get enough opportunities to write the kind of discourse that they read and are thus denied the insights into reading that writing can provide.

And, second, there is evidence that students do not make the transition to these analytic modes. National surveys of student writing ability suggest that secondary students find analytic writing extremely difficult. The National Assessment of Educational Progress (1981) found that only 3 percent of the high-school students tested could write a competent argumentative essay. Even if we acknowledge that the NAEP tests are highly artificial (there is no real audience, assigned content, grading, and so on), these results are disquieting. Colleges regularly bemoan the fact that students come unprepared for the analytic writing that will be required of them.

It would be churlish (and unjust) to assign the blame for this problem to elementary schools. But it is at least possible that the Great Divide assumptions upon which writing instruction rests may not be serving us well. The transition in high school is too abrupt. Students are suddenly expected to write extended discourse in non-narrative modes when no groundwork has been laid for this new demand. Students must write extended expositions, themes, without ever having created smaller pieces of analysis. The result, I feel, is a reliance on formulas such as the five-paragraph theme that enable students to produce extended expositions but only by turning writing into a kind of slotting, an advanced version of fill-in-the-blanks only with bigger blanks.

The Great Divide approach also causes teachers at the elementary and secondary levels to see themselves as working for different—even opposing—ends. I remember one beginning curriculum director who thought it would be a good idea to have regular meetings between the elementary and secondary teachers in his district. There was one meeting. The secondary teachers criticized the elementary teachers for spending all their time on "creative" writing while ignoring correctness and "proper form." The elementary teachers responded that the high-school teachers sacrificed the interests and imaginations of their students at the altar of correct form. Such disagreement may be the inevitable result of the isolation between the two levels, but it also may derive from the ideology of distinctiveness that claims that the interests and abilities of young children differ fundamentally from those of older students.

There is an alternative to this view of writing development. Skill at exposition might be understood not as something that "happens later," but as an evolving competence, beginning, perhaps, with the first label that a child attaches to a picture. Susan Sowers, in an important paper on writing development

(1985b), found that young writers often produce "attribute books," lists of facts or feelings about a topic. How does a student develop beyond writing these lists? What increments of progress might we document? What is the connection between the literate forms of the home (for example, letters, signs, invitations) and school writing? This book will focus on these and related questions.

To uncover the steps that children take in achieving competence in non-narrative modes, we must describe the intermediary forms that they create. In effect, we lack a vocabulary to describe this development. I was reminded of this lack recently when I was consulting with a state department that was specifying grade-level goals. One of the second-grade goals was to have students write a paragraph. I remember saying something like, "I've never seen a child that age write a real paragraph." And yet children of that age do achieve organization in their writing—it is not a random collection of information. But how do we identify and name the patterns they create? The only descriptive language I had for exposition was that appropriate for mature expository writing—and it didn't fit.

I open the book with a theoretical examination of long-standing assumptions about language development that seem to me increasingly untenable, particularly as they attempt to claim that analytic writing is a late-blooming competence. Chapters 2 through 5 examine specific kinds of expository writing that children attempt: Chapter 2 looks at the labelling of pictures; Chapter 3 at lists; Chapter 4 at persuasive writing; and Chapter 5 at letters. In the next two chapters, the emphasis shifts from kinds of writing to classroom instruction. In Chapter 6, I focus on sharing sessions in one kindergarten and one first-grade classroom in order to examine the relationship between talk and writing. And Chapter 7 presents a conversation with Kathy Matthews, a second-grade teacher; her words show one way in which a classroom can be organized to provide children with a variety of writing opportunities. In the final chapter, I return to a major theoretical issue—what is the writing process?—and try to demonstrate how effectively John Dewey's concept of experience can be used to understand classrooms like Kathy Matthews'.

Finally, a word about the writing samples that are examined in this book. One primary source of data is the writing done by my daughter Sarah between the ages of four and seven years four months—a collection of several hundred signs, letters, lists, quizzes, jokes, certificates, song lyrics, and recipes. The other writing was collected in three schools: Mast Way Elementary School in Lee, New Hampshire; Oyster River Elementary School in Durham, New Hampshire; and Kamehameha Elementary School in Honolulu, Hawaii. In most cases I have corrected the invented spelling so that the reader doesn't have to be constantly deciphering. I have, however, retained the original spelling in places to give readers a sense of the children's actual work. In all three schools, children wrote regularly and received responses to their writing. The hum of the ditto machine was stilled.

Clearly, this sample is not representative of schoolchildren in general; in fact, I can make little claim that my methodology, if it can be called that, is at all designed to assure that the hunches, speculations, and patterns I describe in this book fit some mythical average child. As much as possible, I will try to use multiple examples to illustrate my points, but, of course, each reader must decide whether my observations have any wider validity. I'm sure I will be wrong as often as I'm right. But what matters most—and what may be generalizable—is not the result of this examination but the point of view, the way of looking at children's writing.

For me, research has always been more a way of seeing than a way of proving. My father is an entomologist, and every summer during my childhood, he would grab his army knapsack filled with empty peanut-butter jars, call for our dog (who would leave a meal to join him), and head for the woods. Sometimes, I would go along. We would walk into the darker parts of the woods where the sunlight barely made its way through the trees, and, at some point, my father would motion me to stop.

"Look there," he'd say, pointing.

"Where?"

"On that blackberry bush, near the top." My eyes would have barely adjusted to the dark. But my father was able to see the end of every twig on any bush, instantly, effortlessly.

He'd move closer to the blackberry bush and point again. Still nothing. Finally, I'd see what he saw, perhaps a robber fly, about three-quarters of an inch long, suspended from the end of a leaf. "Look at his hind legs. Bet it's a diptera." I would edge even closer and see the robber fly's feet wrapped around a tiny fly. Slowly, my father would open a peanut-butter jar, then, in one motion, close it around the robber fly, give the jar a shake until the robber fly released its dead victim, and then let it go. After a couple of hours in the woods, he would walk over to his office at the college, examine the insects in his jars, and identify them by genus—wonderful names like "lepidoptera," "hymenoptera," "coleoptera."

One of his favorite science writers was the French entomologist J. Henri Fabre, author of *The Insect World* ([1913] 1964). I was aware of this book when I was young, but I read it only recently at the suggestion of Donald Graves. In the introduction, Fabre justifies his unwillingness to write in the dry academic style of official science, even invoking the insects themselves to testify on his behalf:

*Come here, one and all of you—you, the stingbearers, and you, the wing-cased armour-clads—take up my defence and bear witness in my favour. Tell of the intimate terms on which I live with you, of the patience with which I observe you, of the care with which I record your actions. Your evidence is unanimous: yes, my pages, though they bristle not with hollow formulas and learned smatterings, are the exact narrative of facts observed, neither more nor less. . . . (17)*

And, Fabre continues, if the insects cannot convince the reader, he will say to his academic critics:

*You rip up the animal and I study it alive; you turn it into an object of horror and pity; whereas I cause it to be loved; you labor in the torture chamber and dissecting room, I make my observations under the blue sky to the song of Cicadas. (17)*

I now know why my father loves Fabre.

While the children's writing in this book was not done to the sound of cicadas, it did occur in supportive contexts, both at home and in school, where writing served real purposes for real readers (if, of course, we consider Tooth Fairies to be real readers). Both traditional instruction and traditional experimental research isolate the child from such contexts; the student is given a task and expected to complete it independently. This model of intellectual activity seems to be drawn from the big-money quiz shows of the fifties. I remember how contestants were placed in glass isolation booths so that, when they were asked questions, not a whisper of sound would disturb their concentration. I also remember the tension of the fifteen or so seconds when the contestant was actually thinking. Brows would furrow. Eyes would look momentarily puzzled. And all of us watching felt that we were in the presence of immense intellectual activity. But, most of all, I remember the music, a repeating six-note tune that I still associate with thinking.

Writing doesn't work that way. Even as we work alone, we are members of a collaborative community. And even the most traditional of researchers, those who place their subjects in modern-day isolation booths, usually end their articles with words of thanks to colleagues who helped them. Apparently, they are unwilling to work under the conditions that they impose on their subjects.

There are no isolation booths in this study.

There are examples of children participating in the literate communities that surround them and include them. There are examples of children appropriating the forms of discourse that these communities offer. A five-year-old shivering as she reads the pool rules, trying to figure out how society uses language to regulate behavior. Thinking, perhaps, that one day she will help to write the rules.

# DEVELOPMENT

# 1 The hedgehog or the fox: The dilemma of writing development

*The fox knows many things, but*
*the hedgehog knows one*
*big thing.*

ARCHILOCHUS

In many U.S. school systems, there is a curriculum director whose job is to puzzle out what a curriculum is. The etymology of the word is promising: it comes from the Latin word *currere*, 'to run,' and is closely related to the word *curricle*, a two-horse chariot used for short races. Presumably, curricles went around in circles just as curricular trends do in this country, the only difference being that curricle drivers knew they were always going over the same ground, and we often don't. The curriculum director, and those who specialize in this murky science in colleges of education, generally tries to keep the chariots moving in the same direction at roughly the same pace.

Yet the very order suggested by the word "curriculum"—that fixed track upon which the race occurs—seems antithetical to schooling that acknowledges the individual interests and abilities of students. Too often, decisions about what students do at what age are purely arbitrary, and claims by publishers that their work is developmentally sound are only promotional hype. The organization of instruction often shades into regimentation, an interminable forced march through exercises and worksheets. Any missed step, the teacher's manuals imply, might lead to serious problems—like those of the ducklings who didn't learn how to follow their mother at the right time and ended up following the zoo keeper instead.

But even supporters of child-centered education must recognize the necessity of some general ordering principles. While any curriculum hopes to engage the interests of children, none can be defined solely by those interests. Dewey recognized this problem when he wrote in 1902:

*It will do harm if child-study leaves in the popular mind the impression that a child of a given age has a positive equipment of purposes and interests to be cultivated as they stand. Interests in reality are but attitudes toward possible experiences; they are not achievements; their worth is in the leverage they afford, not in the accomplishment they represent. ([1902] 1956, 15)*

The teacher, according to Dewey, has the clear responsibility to establish the environment of the children, so that they can engage in activities that promote growth, and thus "by indirection to direct" (31). Later in his career, as Dewey saw the excesses of child-centered education, he argued more sharply:

*As the most mature member of the group, [the teacher] has a particular responsibility for the conduct of the interactions and intercommunications which are the very life of a group as community. That the children are individuals whose freedom must be respected while the more mature person should have no such freedom is an idea too absurd to require refutation. The tendency to exclude the teacher from a positive leading share in the direction of the activities of the community of which he is a member is another instance of reaction from one extreme to another. ([1938] 1963, 59)*

Dewey's position presupposes that the teacher understands human development and can plan experiences that are appropriate for students at various points in their development. But, until fairly recently, no one had mapped out lines of development in the area of writing that might inform the curricular decisions of the child-centered teacher. James Moffett's *Teaching the Universe of Discourse* (1968) was the first, and is still the most comprehensive, attempt to provide such a map.

Moffett set himself an enormous task—to develop guidelines for a language-arts curriculum that were consistent with theories of cognitive development. Drawing on the Piagetian concept of decentering, Moffett claims that students develop along two major dimensions. The first, the referential dimension, concerns the writer's relation to the subject matter. Initially, the writer cannot go beyond the immediate—what is happening. But, progressively, the writer is able to abstract from immediate experience—through memory, generalization, and, ultimately, speculation. The second line of development occurs along the rhetorical dimension, the relation of the writer to the audience. At first, the writer is capable of addressing an intimate audience, the self or an audience with a special interest in the writer. As writers mature, they develop the social awareness to be able to address increasingly distant and unfamiliar audiences.

There are strong similarities between Moffett's scheme and that developed by James Britton and his associates (Britton et al., 1975), easily the most influential development model in the field. The Britton team borrowed extensively from Moffett, and their categories of the development of transactional writing are essentially refinements of Moffett's. In addition, both Britton and Moffett see beginning writers as being dependent on the resources of speech; for both, initial writing resembles speech written down. Both, then, see the young writer developing out of a relatively undifferentiated expressive-narrative matrix.

Moffett makes a number of important qualifications in his scheme. Most significantly, he rejects any implication that growth is a unidirectional movement *up* the scale of abstraction; rather, it involves the ability to move expertly among levels. Nevertheless, Moffett clearly feels that movement along these dimensions constitutes the intellectual growth that can inform a language-arts curriculum. And, while he carefully refuses to tie these levels to specific ages or grades, he does claim that they represent the general order of acquisition. In true Piagetian fashion, he and his associate Betty Wagner write:

> *Different students pass through stages at different chronological times. What holds for different people is the* order, *regardless of the timing. So growth descriptions can only say when some learning will occur in relationship to when other learning occurs for the individual. (1983, 29)*

This is, of course, the Piagetian dream of the curriculum maker: the wonderful prospect of a general sequence for all students based on the invariable stages of human development. It is a way out of the dilemma. We can have our cake and eat it, too; we can meet the developing needs of students within a coherent and ordered curriculum.

Moffett's work remains the strongest challenge to date to the arbitrariness of most curriculum building in the language arts. His emphasis on dialogue anticipates (and helped bring about) important instructional innovations—the use of peer groups and the writing conference, to name only two. And he tied language learning plainly and irrevocably to the development of thinking abilities.

Yet any developmental theory needs to be eyed with some skepticism, particularly as it relates to younger children. All developmental theories begin with the assumption that the youngest children in an examined span are *relatively* undeveloped, less capable than the older children being studied. The task of the developmentalist is to uncover these limitations and to show how they disappear progressively as children develop. There can be an underlying pathology to this quest, a deficit hunting, a bias toward disability, that can cause and has caused investigators to underestimate the capabilities of young children.

Moffett's model also deserves critical attention because it embodies certain "commonsense" notions about growth, notions that are accepted as givens in many discussions of student growth. For example, educators regularly refer to thinking as a hierarchy of abilities with various levels of difficulty. Analytic thinking is usually placed at or near the top of these hierarchies and, for that reason, thought to be beyond the range of young children. In sum, Moffett's model embodies the belief that the thinking of children is qualitatively different from that of adults.

In this chapter, I will argue that Moffett's model is flawed because it depicts beginning writers as being far more limited than they actually are. This flaw is due, primarily, to overestimating the dependency of writing on oral language and by failing correspondingly to gauge how reading (and not solely the reading of stories) can expand the repertoire of the young writer. In examining Moffett's model, I will consider three main contentions:

1. Young writers are limited to writing about "what is happening" and generally can put that information only in a narrative form.
2. Beginning writers are limited to an intimate audience and initially have difficulty addressing a more distant audience.

3. There is an invariable order of acquisition in writing development along these dimensions.

I make this challenge as a preliminary to presenting an alternative theory (or at least the beginnings of one) that rejects the hierarchical distinctions upon which Moffett's model is built.

## WRITING ABOUT—THE REFERENTIAL DIMENSION

Moffett refers to his levels of abstraction as a hierarchy; in doing so, he is drawing on a way of thinking about thinking that goes back—at least—to Plato and whose most influential proponent in the United States has been Benjamin Bloom (1956). Bloom's division of the "cognitive domain" into six levels has had a profound effect on reading and questioning pedagogy—in fact, we often speak of "higher" and "lower" levels of thought without considering our reasons for classifying thinking in this way. Unquestionably, it satisfies our need for order to conceive of cognition as a domain within which there are clearly defined levels. Yet, like the Ptolemeic model of the universe, schemes like Bloom's and Moffett's must introduce more and more qualifications and amendments to account for anomalies, eventually reaching a point where the models must be rejected altogether. I will outline some of the anomalies in Bloom's model before moving on to similar problems in Moffett's.

The first problem with Bloom's taxonomy is the hidden ideological bias within it. The question here is whether Bloom's levels are value-free descriptions of cognition—or whether they should be interpreted as statements about the kinds of thinking *valued* in our culture and, particularly, in academic institutions in our culture. When we talk about higher-level or higher-order thinking, I would argue that we are making a statement about values. Such thinking is the culmination, the ultimate aim, of instruction; "higher" shades into "better" or most significant or most worthy. Plato himself, when he ranked the citizens in his imagined republic, placed philosophers at the highest level, with poets (along with teachers) ranked just a notch above tyrants.

In Bloom's hierarchy, and in those that it has spawned, remembering is usually considered to be the lowest level. But, in an oral society, where traditions and rituals are not written down, remembering likely would be considered one of the highest and most important cognitive activities. The survival of such cultures depends on those who can remember and pass on the rites and rituals that sustain the society. In literate cultures, as

Plato foresaw in the *Phaedrus*, the printed word makes memory less important. As a literate culture, particularly one that would rather look to the future than the past, we tend not to value memory, so we place it near the bottom of our hierarchies.

In effect, we are trapped by the spatial metaphor ("domains" and "levels") that promise a neutral mapping of territory where a foot is always a foot, where Boston is always south of Portsmouth. This spatial metaphor obscures the ideological and cultural assumptions behind the models, which generally elevate the thinking valued in the culture. In Aldous Huxley's words, "Every hierarchy culminates in its own particular Pope" ([1931] 1959).

The second problem with Bloom's hierarchy is the "fallacy of misplaced concreteness." Seduced by our own language, we believe that the world fits neatly into categories that we develop to name it. Yet, despite their neatness, Bloom's categories bear little relationship to the way a mind really works. A mind working according to Bloom's taxonomy would be an immobile machine unless evaluation (his highest level) were intertwined in the process of thinking—how else could someone make a conscious decision to progress from one level to the next? After taking in raw information (ludicrously misnamed "knowledge"), one needs to determine whether the information is sufficient to proceed to the next level. At that next level, "summary," the learner needs to reevaluate the information in order to identify the key points to include in the summary. If the learner is summarizing an analytic piece, he or she needs to reenact its analysis. The mental activities that Bloom defines as levels are viewed more appropriately as recursive processes that intertwine in much of our thinking.

Bloom holds his taxonomy together through what philosophers call "implicature." The higher levels like evaluation are defined in such a way that they "imply" completion of some lower-level operation. Defined in this way, evaluation is a more complex, higher-level operation, just as six is a higher number than five. But the price he pays is that his model barely resembles the actual process of thinking. Even the initial act of perception is imbued with our values—we select and judge as we observe. Nothing comes into us raw; as the rhetorician Richard Weaver claimed, "Experience does not tell us what we are experiencing" (1953, 193).

The most basic anomaly in Bloom's taxonomy is that, from the time they begin to talk, children seem to use the entire spectrum of thinking levels, as Halliday (1975) has shown in his careful analysis of his son's language development. I remember taking my own younger daughter to the park at age three, during a period when she was very dependent on her mother. As she was walking along she said, "You know sometimes I miss Mommy and sometimes I don't," clearly, a generalization, important for us both. The child who says "I like this book because it has nice pictures" is performing an act of evaluation—Bloom's highest level. As children develop, the generalizations they make and the evaluative criteria they use change (Hilgers, 1986), but these *kinds* of mental operations are pervasive from the time a child begins to talk. Piaget's great insight into child development was precisely his unwillingness to treat scientific thought as something that happens later; instead, he viewed children of all ages as scientists, capable of speculating about their world.

Bloom recognizes this difficulty, particularly in defining evaluation as his highest level. He tries to justify its elevation by distinguishing "evaluation" from "opinion." (Presumably, "I like it because of the pictures" would not be an evaluation but an opinion.) But this distinction only raises another problem—where does opinion fit in the cognitive domain? What is its relation to evaluation? If forming opinions is a kind of thinking—and it surely is—then it should have a place in a taxonomy that purports to map the cognitive domain. Theories cannot simply wish away the facts they cannot explain.

Bloom's model of the cognitive domain is not explicitly developmental; that is, he does not argue that children pass through these levels sequentially as they become mature language users. Moffett makes this developmental connection. He claims that children have such difficulty with higher-level discourse that they cannot be expected to write at the level of generalization or speculation:

> *Whereas adults differentiate their thought into specialized kinds of discourse such as narrative, generalization, and theory, children must for a long time make narrative do for all. They utter themselves almost entirely through stories—real or invented—and they apprehend what others say through story. The young learner, that is, does not talk and read explicitly about categories and theories of experience; he talks and reads about characters, events, and settings. (1968, 49)*

Moffett's claim, then, is the same claim that Coleridge made 150 years earlier, that the "comparing power, the judgment, is not active" for children and that instruction should focus on those capabilities that flower early—memory and imagination.

But anyone who has ever argued with a three-year-old knows that young children are not limited to stories, that, when provoked, they can bring the universe of discourse to bear on recalcitrant parents. Moffett's attempt to deal with this anomaly is ultimately unsatisfactory. He argues that, while children can generalize and speculate, they do so in very short utterances:

*If asked to create, not paraphrase, an essay of generalization, [children] make it so short that the real issue of continuity does not arise. So although one can claim that they write high level discourses of generalization and even theory, this would be true of utterances so brief as to finesse the basic assumption underlying my whole analysis—that the linguistic capacity to sustain such monologues depends on the cognitive capacity to explicitly interrelate classes and propositions and to embed lower level abstractions, as evidence or examples, into higher orders. (1968, 56)*

Moffett does two things in this passage: he defines discourse as a *sustained* monologue, thereby excluding the brief statements of theory or generalization that children make. And he identifies the distinguishing feature of these high-level monologues as the embedding of lower-level abstractions in higher ones, a capacity he claims young children do not possess.

By treating short statements of generalization or theory as virtual nondiscourse, Moffett diminishes the comprehensiveness of his theory, which should account for what he calls the "universe" of discourse. Yet, consider this letter from a six-year-old:

*Dear Mom,*

*I can't take it any more. I need my own room.*

*Love Margot*

If we accept Moffett's argument that this letter is too brief to be considered a monologue, what is it, and where does it go on his scale? It certainly is not an example of recording or reporting. Nor is it a narrative. A comprehensive theory would incorporate discourse like this letter into the scheme of development, rather than setting limits that, in effect, deny that this kind of writing exists. Like Bloom, Moffett tries to banish unruly evidence.

Even if we accept Moffett's definitions of generalization and theory as the embedding of lower-level abstractions into higher ones, it is still possible to find children's writing that meets his criteria. Surely he is correct when he claims that children cannot produce "essays of generalization," but neither can many students of any age, according to the National Assessment of

Education Progress (1981). And, since young children never read essays of generalization, it is unlikely that they could produce them. But, if one is willing to look beyond the essay of generalization for examples of sustained non-narrative writing, they can be found in abundance, particularly in the signs and letters of beginning writers. This writing often contains the basic elements of the essay, just as children's stories contain the basic elements of the story.

I'll begin by reproducing a series of pieces written by Ben between the ages of six and seven when he was having difficulty adjusting to his stepfather and a new stepsister, Molly. Here is one of Ben's first letters to Molly:

*Mole iLOVE SIDR iWLtakkravU iF UNEDMEiWLBETHRA love Ben*

*Molly I love [you] sister. I will take care of you. If you need me I will be there. Love Ben*

We can see in this letter the beginnings of the multilevel discourse that Moffett claims is beyond the range of young children. The three positions in Ben's letter seem to be arranged in the general-to-specific order that characterizes expository prose. He begins with a general statement of his affection. He then makes two comments indicating the consequences of his affection, the first more general (I will take care of you) and the second indicating more specifically what he will do to take care of his stepsister (If you need me I will be there). To test whether the discourse is merely a random set of statements, we can rearrange its elements to see if any meaning is lost. In this case, rearrangement breaks up the general-to-specific pattern that gives the letter coherence.

Ben uses a similar pattern in an important letter of apology that he wrote to his stepfather:

*Tim ILOV eu UARAGODFATHR IAMSEAE THTisD GOHM LOVE BEN*

*Tim, I love you. You are a good father. I am sorry that I said, "go home." Love, Ben*

Here again is the opening statement of affection, followed by what might be read as a reason for this affection—Tim is a good father. And, because Ben now knows that Tim is a good father, he is sorry that he told him to go home.

I am not suggesting that Ben thought in terms of general-specific or assertion-reason; very likely, he didn't. But he does show, in these early letters, some ability to relate sets of propositions, even if the relationships are not made explicit.

In a piece written about a year later, after Ben had finished first grade, his analytic ability was more evident:

*All tings misistr [my sister] des*

*She gats into the catfood and plas in the toylat [toilet] You can see she is a babe and a hag [hog] But here a sam goo things she das I Like Wen she plasa wme [with me].*

Here we have, in embryonic form, an essay of generalization. Ben is now relating assertions explicitly and providing evidence for his assertions. The structure of his analysis is something like this:

- General Category: Things my sister does.
- Major Division: Good vs. Bad
- Assertion (Bad): She is a hog.
- Evidence: She eats the cat's food.
- Assertion (Bad): She is a baby.
- Evidence: She plays in the toilet.
- Assertion (Good): She does do good things.
- Evidence: She plays with me.

In his early letters, propositions are related only implicitly, but now the relations are explicit. The "you can see" indicates that he will pass judgment on his sister's actions, a judgment with which the reader will agree. The "but" signals the transition from bad to good behavior.

Children are also masters of the excuse, a form of exposition in which a set of reasons is given to persuade another to let the offender off the hook. In one first-grade class where the teacher encouraged note writing, students used notes for a variety of purposes, including the excuse. One day, Shawn wrote his own note explaining why he was late:

*I HR NOW THICS Foor MOM IN THE CLOC WT OFF ON ROG TIM Y WY I M LAT*

*SIN SHAN*

*I [am] here now. [I had to do] things for mom. And the clock went off on the wrong time. [That's] why I am late.*

*Signed Shawn*

Even though the student has considerable difficulty spelling (even misspelling his own name), he is able to give two reasons to justify his tardiness. Even more interesting is the last part of his note, "That's why I am late," a statement that classifies the previous two sentences. So, not only does Shawn provide reasons, he signals to the reader that they are reasons. Shawn also shows himself to be a perceptive "reader" of the school culture by his understanding (or, at least, hope) that his written excuse will carry more weight than would an oral one.

Children's competence in non-narrative writing is also evident in their creation of signs. In her case study of her son Paul, Glenda Bissex (1980) showed that the sign was one of the earliest forms that he tried and that many of the signs were embryonic arguments, usually used to protect territory. The title of her book, *GNYS AT WRK*, is taken from a sign that Paul taped to his door to keep unwanted visitors out of his room:

*DO NAT DSTRB GNYS AT WRK*

*Do Not Disturb. Genius at work. (23)*

In this sign, as in Shawn's note, are the rudiments of the argument: the demand/request for a type of behavior, coupled with a reason why this request is reasonable. In a second sign, written at about the same time, Paul tried another maneuver to keep adults out of his room:

*DO.NAT.KM.IN.ANE.MOR.JST LETL.KES*

*Do not come in any more. Just little kids. (23)*

Here, Paul is using the second statement to qualify the original demand, creating an exception to his original prohibition.

As signs become longer, the arguments in them can become more elaborate. The following sign was written by my daughter Sarah at age six for a booth at a lawn fair where children could make their own pin-on buttons:

*Desin-a-button*

*only 75 cents* *the desin*
*cuck.E.cheese*
*Unicon rainbows*
*and much much more*

*it's a better pric*
*than last year*
*75 cents*

As with Ben's description of his sister's actions, the structure of this sign is fairly complex:

- Major Assertion: Buy a design-a-button (implied)
- Major Reason: Low cost

- Evidence: The cost is seventy-five cents.
- Evidence: The cost is lower than last year.
- Major Reason: The many designs (implied)
- Evidence: Chucky Cheese, unicorns, rainbows, and much, much more.

Again, the rudiments of the extended argument seem to be present.

My intention in examining these pieces of children's writing is not to suggest that exposition should supplant the writing of stories or that children's writing never resembles speech written down. I do want to argue that children can adopt a variety of written forms in addition to the story and that they do so by attending to the demonstrations of written language surrounding them. As educators, we need to look for continuities between an argument as basic as a stop sign to one as complex as a literary essay. I believe that Moffett's model of development fails to account for the range of non-narrative writing that children attempt because he does not recognize the influence of environmental print. But as long as children have access to a variety of non-narrative forms, they will adopt them, just as they adopt other forms of adult behavior. Children join the club. By overlooking this influence, Moffett pictures young children as occupying an overly circumscribed world—storyland. If children make narratives do for all, they may be responding to our own limited vision of the possible.

### WRITING TO: THE RHETORICAL DIMENSION

Moffett seems closer to his Piagetian base when he defines his rhetorical dimension—the relationship between writer and reader. According to Piaget, young children have extreme difficulty taking the perspective of someone else; they are egocentric. Egocentrisim obviously limits the ability of a writer to anticipate the needs and reactions of a reader, particularly one who does not know the writer personally. Moffett therefore claims that early discourse is usually for the self or for an intimate audience (conversation) and only later for a well-known audience that is not immediately present (correspondence). The most distant audience is both unknown and not present.

If Moffett's claims are correct, two predictions follow:

1. Young children (grades 1 and 2) have difficulty writing for an audience other than themselves.
2. These children do not choose to use forms of discourse that reach beyond an immediate audience.

Before examining these predictions, I want to note briefly some of the recent research challenging Piaget's claim about the extreme egocentrism of children. The best known of these challenges is Margaret Donaldson's *Children's Minds* (1978). In this book, Donaldson demonstrates that children—who, according to Piaget, are virtually locked in to their own perspective of distant objects—can imagine the perspective of others if they can see a reason in doing so. Piaget, she argues, failed to uncover this capacity because of the artificiality of his tasks.

In fact, the challenge to Piaget's egocentrism claim had begun well before publication of Donaldson's book. In 1971, Helen Borke demonstrated that children as young as three are capable of responding empathetically to another person's perspective. And, as early as the late 1920s as Piaget's work was being published, the noted British educator Susan Isaacs (1929) felt that Piaget overstated the limitations of young children.

At the time Donaldson's book appeared, I began to visit the site of Donald Graves's research project, where he and his associates were examining writing development in grades 1 through 4. Like many observers at the project site, I was struck by the nonegocentric ways in which even the younger writers went about their business. The children in the classes frequently shared their writing and fielded questions from their classmates about character motivation, sequence, gaps in information, and focus. To be sure, some of the younger children were writing for themselves, but even they seemed to be moving toward audience awareness. Egocentrism did not appear to be nearly the barrier one might have expected it to be.

As children became familiar with the questions that the teacher and students would ask, they began to anticipate them in their writing. To paraphrase the Russian psychologist Lev Vygotsky, a social *inter*personal pattern of questioning seemed to go underground and become an *intra*personal act of composing. This process is evident in the following piece by a first grader:

MY CLASS PLAYS KISS AND CHASE

*Amanda is my friend. I go out at recess. We always play kiss and chase. Who plays? Kristie, Jason, Andrew, Misty, Jaime, Jacqui, Stephanie, Lynn, and Jeff.*

*The girls chase the boys first and the boys chase the girls second.*

*Me and Amanda chase after Jason and Andrew. Stephanie and Kristie chase after Jeff.*

*When the boys kiss the girls, we say, "Yuk." When the girls chase the boys, they say, "Gross."*

*How come we like to play? We like to say, "Naa, naa, naa, naa, you can't catch us."*

*How come I like to play? I have long legs to run. They always get Amanda and Lynn and Kristie. Jason gets them.*

The writer has interjected rhetorical questions ("Who plays?" "How come we like to play?" "How come I like to play?") like those she has heard readers ask in response groups. But, now, they are underground, her own method of exploring her topic.

"Kiss and Chase" was written in a collaborative classroom where the child was well known and knew her readers well. Yet the writing of young children is not directed only to immediate audiences; children can, with some success, address audiences more removed than classmates and teachers. The lawn-fair sign quoted earlier is an example. This expertise can also be shown in the letters that children write. One rainy day, Sarah and her friend Heather decided to write fan letters to Michael Jackson. Sarah wrote:

*Dear Michale Jackson*

*I love yoru songs aspesple your abum thriller. I like to hear you won 8 gramy awards you should feel very proud of yousealf. Congratulation Michale Jacson and again congratulation. I hope I become a famos Ballarena and I can sing bake round music some day. I want to be a famos Girl.*

*Love*

*Sarah Newkirk*

Now, it can be debated whether Michael Jackson is a known audience—he seems fairly mysterious to me. But it is clear, I feel, that the letter uses the conventions of the fan letter appropriately. There is the tone of adulation (never used in letters to family or friends). And the letter begins with references to Jackson's recent achievements and only then moves to information about the writer; reversing this order would have made the writer appear self-centered.

It is unlikely that Sarah composed this letter by transposing her consciousness and imagining how Michael Jackson would react to each sentence. Rather, she seems to be following the conventions that she has picked up from reading letters of congratulations from her grandparents. The Michael Jackson letter illustrates a central confusion and the concept of "audience awareness." Many composition specialists imply that proficient writers have their eyes constantly on potential readers. Writing is a mental tennis game: The writer watches every movement of the reader across the net; failure to do so is grounds for being labelled egocentric. This is truly the heroic ideal of composing.

I suggest that, because writers—even young writers—are (or can become) members of interpretive communities (Frank Smith's clubs), they can use the agreed-upon conventions of the community to do some of this work. These conventions spare us the impossible task of starting from scratch every time we produce a piece of discourse. Conventions cannot dictate to Sarah exactly what information to put in her signs or letters, but, as a reader of these forms, she knows the kind and general order of information for each. She works within these conventions so that her final product is congruent with her readers' expectations. She can move beyond an immediate audience because she has access to the forms for doing so.

I contend, then, that it is misleading to claim that children are limited to immediate audiences or to subjects that mirror their own immediate experiences. Rather, there seems to be a *range of appropriation*, a set of forms that the young writer can use, some to address an immediate audience, others to address audiences that are not immediate. Some are used to narrate what is happening, others to frame arguments or convey information. It would be naive to suggest that this range is as extensive for young children as it is for mature writers; obviously, some cognitive limitations keep young children from mastering certain forms. Furthermore, as Margaret Donaldson (1978) has shown, the child needs to see the purpose for which a kind of discourse is used, and the intent of many discourse forms is not apparent to young children. But the range invariably is underestimated by developmental models that see writing as developing out of a narrow narrative-expressive matrix.

In Moffett's discussion of the rhetorical dimension, we are once again trapped by a spatial metaphor—this time, distance. The learner is viewed as moving from an immediate to a distant, from a known to a relatively unknown, audience. Through an act of cognitive muscularity, the writer is able to transcend the immediate and deal with this distant audience. But, from the semiotic perspective, this continuum does not exist. The writer learns to work within various communities, all of which are puzzling initially. The writer never learns to write for an unknown audience. If we were asked to address a truly unknown audience—say, give a funeral oration at a tribal meeting in the Brazilian rain forests—we wouldn't know where to begin. We would probably do no better than could a seven-year-old. Fortunately, experienced writers don't write for unknown audiences;

they are familiar with their audiences because they understand the conventions of the forms that these audiences read. Indeed, many experienced writers say that they don't need to consider their audience—they claim to write for themselves. But the self for whom they write shares the expectations of the intended readers. From this semiotic perspective, then, many of the difficulties experienced by writer are due not to the inherent cognitive difficulty of the tasks that they attempt, but to their lack of familiarity with the conventions of that discourse.

Ann Berthoff (1984) made precisely this point when commenting on the difficulty that many students have with argumentation and on her dissatisfaction with attempts to attribute this difficulty to students' stages of cognitive development (see, for example, Lunsford, 1978). What can you expect, Berthoff asks, when virtually the only examples of persuasion (hardly argumentation) are television commercials? For students living in an earlier age, the difficulties were not nearly so great:

*You may be sure that pre-pubescent Presbyterians in the eighteenth century were capable of composing arguments on natural depravity, while pre-pubescent Baptists were writing on the grace unto the chief of sinners, and little Methodists were writing on topics like "Must the drunkard be an unhappy man?" My advanced composition students find almost intolerably difficult Huxley's "On a Piece of Chalk," a public lecture which a century ago enthralled workers with no secondary education. But Huxley's audience had heard two or three sermons each week of their lives. (754)*

The capacity to handle disputation, she concludes, is a culture-bound skill that is not predetermined by neurobiological stages of development or, at least, not as determined as cognitive models of writing development would have us believe.

This environmental explanation has particular force when one examines students' difficulty with non-narrative writing. While reading instruction in the colonial period did include numerous non-narrative texts, particularly the catechism and psalter, the reading fare in elementary-school readers has been mostly narrative, though the purposes of the narratives have changed over the years. The stories in the McGuffey readers often had the didactic purpose of illustrating right behavior (Ronald Reagan is a master at using stories in a similar way). So, while the form is narrative, the story is often seen as an instance of someone acting honorably.

But, around the 1920s, the intent of the stories shifted from moral enlightenment to entertainment, and sometimes even the entertainment function was subordinated to reading instruction (the birth of the controlled reader). The few speeches and persuasive pieces included in the McGuffey reader had also disappeared by the 1920s. Nila Banton Smith (1965), in her history of reading instruction in the United States, found no examples of informative or persuasive writing among the 1,219 selections in the ten most commonly used readers. Reading specialist Richard Vanezsky estimated that 95 percent of the selections in basal readers were narratives (quoted in Stotsky, 1984).

Not unreasonably, then, we might attribute some of the difficulties that students experience with exposition to the virtual exclusion of this writing from the books that they must read. I suspect that, in some research studies on report or persuasive writing, children are being asked to write a kind of discourse *that they have never read.* Little wonder that they have trouble. But it is simplistic—or at least premature—to claim that this difficulty derives from the inherent difficulty of exposition or argumentation or in the inherent limitations of students.

Even in high school, when students are expected to cross the Great Divide and produce exposition, they are limited by the fact that most, if not all, of their reading is in textbooks or literature anthologies. They are expected to write essays—but they don't read essays. As a result, when they meet with writing different from their previous reading—say, Martin Luther King, Jr.'s "Letter from a Birmingham Jail"—many will refer to it as a "story."

## INFLEXIBLE ORDERS

Now to the curricle's track. Does any sequence invariably describe the growth of the writer? Intensive research over the past decade suggests that there may be sequences in the very early years when children are first learning the conventions of print. For example, most children around the age of three explore the mandala (a circle bisected by a line), a form that contains key elements of the letters and drawings that will come later (Kellogg 1970). But attempts to find fixed sequences for writers in the school years have come up empty. In fact, one of the most significant results of this research is what *hasn't* been discovered.

The most widely publicized of these studies has been Donald Graves's two-year longitudinal project examining the composing processes of children in grades 1 through 4. It is illuminating to compare the original expectations stated in his grant proposal with the conclusions in his final report. Graves clearly expected to find invariable sequences of development that were analogous to the stages defined by Piaget. Graves wrote in 1978:

*The work of Jean Piaget suggests specific sequences in the child's growing understanding of logic, number, time, and space. The preliminary data (Graves, 1973) strongly suggest that children use specific problem-solving strategies at different stages of development in the writing process. . . . We are at last at the point of asking intelligent questions that will* lead us *to identify variables along developmental lines. . . .(23)*

In his final report, Graves identifies some tentative sequences, but, in discussing the implications of his work, there is no more talk of "stages of development." In 1982, he wrote:

*Many similarities were seen among the children when they wrote, but as the study progressed, individual exceptions to the data increased in dominance. In short, every child had behavioral characteristics that applied to that child alone. It is our contention that such variability demands a waiting responsive type of teaching. (29)*

And it should be remembered that Graves and his associates were working in one school with a fairly uniform approach to teaching writing. Had a variety of schools with a variety of approaches been studied, this variability undoubtedly would have been even more dominant.

Graves's reservations about fixed sequences have been echoed by other researchers. Carl Bereiter (1980) has identified six skill systems (transcription, social cognition, and the conventions of language, to name three) that must be integrated in a fully skilled act of composing. But, like Graves, he does not claim that these must be mastered in any particular order or that they are yoked to the Piagetian stages of cognitive development. Working in a different research paradigm, Jerome Harste and his associates (1984) similarly have rejected the notion that there is a fixed order to the kinds of discourse that children attempt:

*There is no sequence to the order in which demonstrations are inherently learned. Which demonstration is learned is a function of which demonstration is highlighted. The context in which literacy occurs affects the nature and direction of literacy learning. (195)*

There is, then, no fixed path for the curricle to follow.

This skepticism about universal schemes of writing development is related to a more general skepticism about fixed schemes of development. For example, Lawrence Kohlberg's model of moral development (1977) has been challenged by Carol Gilligan

(1982) on the grounds that it fails to value the moral decision making of women. Many of the women that Gilligan interviewed did not base decisions on abstract moral principles (according to Kohlberg, the highest moral stage) but on more immediate and pragmatic concerns. Kohlberg's model can be regarded as an ideological statement about morality but hardly as a value-free statement on human development. Robert Coles (1981), who has spent a lifetime observing children in crisis, contends that Kohlberg's model underestimates children's capacity for truly moral behavior.

There is a shift, then, from unified theories of development to theories that allow for considerable variability—from what Howard Gardner (1983) calls the "hedgehog" approach to the "fox" approach (and here I end the suspense about the chapter title). Gardner takes his terms from an aphorism of the Greek poet Archilochus—"The fox knows many things, but the hedgehog knows one big thing"—by way of Isaiah Berlin's brilliant essay on Leo Tolstoy (1970). According to Berlin, Tolstoy was torn between the "fox" and the "hedgehog" views of history:

> *His genius lay in the perception of specific properties, the almost inexpressible individual quality in virtue of which the given object is uniquely different from all others. Nevertheless, he longed for a universal explanatory principle; that is, the perception of resemblances or common origins, or single purpose, or the unity in the apparent variety of mutually exclusive bits and pieces which composed the furniture of his world. (36–37)*

This is also the dilemma of educators, the one with which we began the chapter.

If models of writing development are to be viable, they must be more complex, more foxlike, than those currently accepted, particularly as they describe young writers. Any model of development claiming that beginning writers are limited to a single kind of discourse, be it recording (Moffett) or expressive writing (Britton), fails to account for the diversity, even the virtuosity, of beginning writing. Such models do not acknowledge adequately the capacity of children to understand and appropriate a diverse set of discourse forms that can be used for a variety of purposes. Expository writing should not be seen as developing *out of* narrative writing or expressive writing, for the simple reason that beginning writers can attempt exposition as well.

Berlin's book is entitled *The Hedgehog and the Fox*, and that might be a better title for this chapter. The hedgehog and the fox are not alternatives but terms in a dialectic; we must accept both views. We must be capable of believing two contradictory ideas: We must understand that individuals are distinctive, with particular abilities and interests, living out their lives in environments that are also unique, yet we must also act upon general understandings of human behavior and growth—we need to identify patterns, categories, and principles that transcend individual instances. If writing development were purely a function of context, as Harste seems to suggest, we might ask why we should look at development at all, since no two contexts are the same. But, if we propose a unified model of development for all children in all learning situations, we undoubtedly underestimate the variability that so overwhelmed Graves when he wrote his final report.

In the next chapters in this book, I will try to walk this tightrope. I will analyze several kinds of non-narrative writing and suggest ways in which children move from basic embryonic forms to writing that increasingly approximates mature expository prose. Yet I will not claim that any sequence is invariable or that it is age specific or that it is fully inclusive. I hope that this analysis will serve to open discussion of a question that is far more important than any answer I can provide: How do children develop their ability to write exposition?

# REPERTOIRE

# 2
# Draw me a word—write me a picture

It was writing time in Anna Sumida's first-grade classroom, and, as usual, Jason, Gregg, and Alan were drawing. Each had drawn a space-age tank that was being assaulted by varieties of spacecraft. Laser beams threaded through the sky. At first glance, the three pictures seemed distinct—that is, until Jason showed me the hinge at the end of each paper that attached the three drawings. At times, they would swap papers because each child specialized in a particular type of plane; Gregg, for example, was a master at drawing small jets. All the while as they were drawing, the three kept up a running commentary, complete with explosive sound effects, elaborating the story of the ongoing battle. I watched as Gregg created a magnetic field (a series of wavelike lines) that sucked one of the bigger planes into the hold of his tank. When the alarm clock rang indicating the end of writing period, Jason quickly wrote "Spac Invadrs" at the top of his paper.

I asked permission to photocopy the three papers and enthusiastically explained their complexity to a teacher standing by the machine. "Yes," she sighed. "Now, if we could only get them to write that."

In a way, this teacher's observation is right. Schools are far more concerned about verbal competence than graphic competence. In fact, it is easy to feel impatient with students like Jason, Gregg, or Alan who spend their time drawing when they could be writing, who clearly view the written message as marginal. School culture is word centered; while we might admire the drawings of young children, we're not terribly concerned (as a culture) when the interest in drawing gives way to an interest in print.

Fortunately, early research on the writing processes of young children has confirmed the interrelationship of writing and drawing. Donald Graves and his associates have shown that when children draw before they write, the drawing helps them to discover what they would like to write. According to Graves (1983), the drawing serves as a "rehearsal" for the writing. But when I think of Jason, Gregg, and Alan, I have difficulty thinking of their drawing as a rehearsal for the minimal message that Jason eventually (and grudgingly) wrote. The drawing-as-rehearsal concept seems to me to be inadequate for three reasons:

- It gets the priorities wrong. A rehearsal is a preliminary to the more important performance and has significance because it prepares the actor for that performance. But, for many children, the drawing is more important, taking up most of the paper, with the writing squeezed into any free space.
- It suggests a greater separation between drawing and writing than the children actually intend. When you ask a child to show you his or her "writing," the child will display both the picture and the caption or label. The "writing" is the whole production, text and picture—even the running commentary is part of it. To be sure, as writers mature, the writing becomes more self-sufficient or, as David Olson (1977) terms it, more "autonomous." But this view of writing as text, separate from pictures and oral commentary, is too stripped down for the beginning writer.
- The word "rehearsal" suggests that the drawing is a cognitive crutch to help students find things to write about. But students actually may be working within a genre that they know well—the picture book. They interpret the request to "write" as a request to reproduce the "writing" that they've seen before. I've noticed that, when young children change genre—for example, when they write birthday announcements or letters—they tend not to give the drawing the central position. Their desire to draw before writing in

school may show their understanding of the picture-book genre rather than their cognitive need to produce a picture so that they can find something to write.

The idea of drawing-as-rehearsal is just one more example of the word-centered view that reigns in our educational system. The child's drawing is reduced to a preliminary, a kind of pre-writing, rather than being accepted as an important communicative symbol system in its own right. Of course, a host of researchers have taken children's drawing seriously—among them, Rhoda Kellogg (1970), Jacqueline Goodnow (1977), and Howard Gardner (1980)—but usually as it represents the development of artistic abilities. Less frequently explored is the relationship between drawing and the development of literate ability. To borrow Ann Dyson's beautiful expression, children like Jason, Gregg, and Alan are "symbol-weaving" (1986), constantly shifting among mutually supporting systems of representation—talking, drawing, and, in a minimal way, producing written text. Their "writing" is a fabric formed of all these strands.

While symbol-weaving may describe more satisfactorily the relationship between drawing and emerging print literacy, it is also considerably more complex than regarding drawing as rehearsal. I first thought one could begin to analyze this weaving process by looking at the writing and drawing (and talking) that children did during writing time in school. Yet because children seemed so primed to use writing to label pictures, I began to wonder how their early experience of learning to talk and, particularly, learning to talk about picture books set the stage for learning to read and write. Labelling pictures is not new for most schoolchildren; it has solid roots in early language-learning interactions with parents. So, in the first part of this chapter, I will look at the way this early learning prepares the way for literacy learning.

Next, I will address the question of genre. In the last chapter, I argued that the dominant theories of writing development underestimate the *range* of children's writing; even beginning writers seem able to appropriate a variety of non-narrative forms. Can the same be said of their pictures? Do children draw narrative pictures and expository pictures, that is, pictures that show a frozen moment in a series of ongoing actions (a narrative picture) and static pictures that seem to be graphic lists, perhaps showing the members of the child's family in a family portrait (an expository picture)?

Finally, I will examine how children allocate informativeness among the symbol systems available. The written text, the picture, and the oral commentary each make their own contribution to the woven fabric. What guides the child's choice of pattern?

## THE ACHIEVEMENT OF LABELLING

Anyone who has read Helen Keller's autobiography or seen *The Miracle Worker* remembers the scene where Annie Sullivan takes six-year-old Helen to the water pump, runs water over one of her hands, and signs "water" into the other. Suddenly Helen understands that words name things, and her chaotic world stabilizes. Like Adam, she gains dominion over her new world by *naming* it. The linguist Ernst Cassirer (1984) has written eloquently about the importance of this discovery:

*By learning to name things a child does not simply add a list of artificial signs to his previous knowledge of ready-made empirical objects. He learns rather to form concepts of those objects, to come to terms with the objective world. Henceforth the child stands on firmer ground. His vague, uncertain, fluctuating perceptions, and his dim feelings begin to assume a new shape. They may be said to crystallize around the name as a fixed center, a focus of thought. Without the help of the name every new advance made in the process of objectification would always run the risk of being lost again in the next moment. (110)*

So readily—indeed, voraciously—do children around the age of two take to naming objects that it is tempting to view this development as a natural unfolding of linguistic ability. Yet, as Jerome Bruner (1983) put it, parents provide a "Language Acquisition Support System," a regularized pattern of interaction that helps children learn to label, although, as parents, we are often unaware of our systematic assistance.

While we might consider labelling to be fairly straightforward, a fundamental ambiguity exists. Suppose I point to my telephone and ask, "What's that?" A number of answers are possible—"dial," "numbers," "letters"—in addition to "telephone." For you to answer the question, we must first agree on whether we are referring to a part (e.g., the dial) or a whole (e.g., the telephone). It is even possible to answer by stating the *type* of object to which I am referring (e.g., a "nuisance" or "means of communication"), although children are unlikely to err in this direction. Bruner's colleague, Anat Ninio (1980), demonstrated that labelling can only proceed under a tacit agreement about the level of specification required, furnishing convincing evidence of this systematic agreement.

Studying forty mother-infant pairs, Ninio found that parents consistently elicited a label for the whole and that, if they asked for an attribute label, they consistently did so after the whole had been identified. For example, the mother might say, "Do you see a baby? A baby, yes. What else? Shoes. The baby wears shoes." Scollon and Scollon (1979) have called this kind of interaction a "vertical buildup." The main name is elicited first, and, next, an attribute of that whole is requested. A child might be asked to identify an animal and then to describe the sound that the animal makes. There is nothing inevitable about this order; it could as easily move from parts to a whole. But parents act, in Bruner's words (1983), as "agents of the culture," where discourse regularly moves from whole to parts, from assertions to reasons, from terms to definitions, from generalizations to specifics. And this education begins not too far from the crib.

Once children learn that things have names, they often want to name everything, pointing to anything in a room and asking "whazat?" Yet, in many homes, picture books play a special role in the achievement of labelling. First, we point to a picture and say something like, "Do you see the bunny? Point to the bunny." As the child builds a vocabulary of labels, we shift more of the burden to him or her; reversing roles, *we* ask the "whazat?" questions. Again, much of this instruction seems natural and unpremeditated. Yet Ninio and Bruner (1978) argue that this simple act of identifying a picture may be more complex than it first appears:

*Pictures, being two-dimensional representations of three-dimensional objects, have special visual properties: they can be perceived both as a two-dimensional object AND as representing a three-dimensional visual scene. This poses a conflict for the child, one which he solves increasingly by assigning a privileged, autonomous status to pictures as visual objects. There is steadily less evidence of the child trying to manipulate, grasp, or scratch pictured objects on the page. This process might be one of the stepping stones to grasping the arbitrary symbolic representation in language, since visual representations are themselves arbitrary in the sense of a crucial property, i.e. graspability is missing. (5)*

In other words, children who can accept the fiction that a two-dimensional picture of a telephone can represent the actual object may be on their way to accepting the fiction that the word "telephone" can represent the object as well.

Children not only learn routines for talking about pictures in books, they soon begin to develop hypotheses about the relationship of the print to the pictures or objects connected to the print. A number of researchers (Ferreiro and Teberosky, 1982; Harste, Woodward, and Burke, 1984; Snow, 1983) have shown that children initially tend to view all print as a label for an object. Snow offers the following example of Nathaniel, age thirty-one months, who often played with a toy cargo truck with the initials KLM (for the airline) on the side of it. The toy regularly was referred to as "the airport truck." One day, Nathaniel decided that he could read the letters on the side of the truck:

NATHANIEL [*pointing to KLM on toy truck*]: That say airport truck.
MOTHER: No, that says KLM.
NATHANIEL [*insistently*]: That says de airport truck.
MOTHER: KLM cargo.
NATHANIEL [*more insistently*]: That says airport truck.
MOTHER [*patiently*]: In the airport the trucks have to carry cargo from the planes to other planes, or into the city and that's what this truck does.
NATHANIEL [*pointing to KLM*]: Who's this?
MOTHER: Where?
NATHANIEL: That says. . .de airport. . .
MOTHER [*interrupting*]: KLM, Nathaniel, this says KLM. (176)

Nathaniel clearly prefers a straightforward relationship in which words label objects and resists his mother's attempts to suggest that the letters may not represent his choice for the truck's label. The mother's role in this exchange is also interesting. After correcting him twice, she shifts to the identification-plus-attribute pattern that we have seen before. In this case, she explains the function of the truck. But Nathaniel's not buying because he doesn't accept the notion that an object may have more than one designation.

Labelling, and talking about labels, comes so easily to most children who have been read to regularly that we underestimate the difficulty of apparently simple "what?" questions for children with no book-reading experience. Gordon Wells (1986) provides a painful instance of this difficulty in his case study of Rosie. Rosie had virtually no experience with books in her home, so, when asked the simple "what?" question in school, she seemed to be at a loss. In the following excerpt from a transcript, Rosie is in nursery school making a calendar from a Christmas card showing Santa Claus skiing down a hill. The teacher is attempting to get Rosie to identify elements of the picture on the card and is interrupted several times in the process:

CHILD: Miss, I done it.
TEACHER [*to Rosie*]: Will you put it at the top?
CHILD: Miss, I done it, look.
[*Several seconds' pause*]
TEACHER [*to Rosie, pointing with finger at card*]: What are those things?
CHILD: Miss, I done it. Miss, I done it.
[*Rosie drops something, then picks it up.*]
TEACHER [*to Rosie*]: What are those things?
CHILD: Miss, I done it.
TEACHER [*referring to skis in picture*]: D'you know what they're called? [*Rosie shakes her head.*] What d'you think he uses them for? [*Rosie looks at the card. The teacher turns to the other child's calendar.*] It's very nice. After play, we'll put some ribbons at the top.
CHILD: What?
TEACHER: Ribbon at the top to hang them up by. Would you put all the cards together now? Put the cards together.
CHILD: Oh.
TEACHER [*to Rosie, pointing at the skis on the card*]: What's—what are those? [*Rosie looks blank.*] What d'you think he uses them for?
ROSIE [*rubbing her eye with the back of her hand*]: Go down.
TEACHER: Go down—yes, you're right; go on. [*Rosie rubs both of her eyes with the backs of her hands.*] What's the rest of it? [*Puts down card*] You have a little think and I'll get—er, get the little calendar for you. . . . (96–97)

Children like Rosie are generally described as nonverbal or even linguistically deprived, but these terms really say very little. Why does this exchange go so badly? In part, because the teacher is distracted and consequently listens poorly to what Rosie is saying. She insists that Rosie indentify the skis even after Rosie says she doesn't know that word. But, surely, Rosie's bafflement is due to more than her ignorance of this single label.

Because Rosie is unfamiliar with the rituals associated with talking about pictures, she is probably confused by the entire pattern of questioning, beginning with the opening question, "What are those things?" To answer this question, Rosie would have to understand that, for the purposes of this question, the picture is the thing—the expected answer is "skis" and not "pictures," "lines," "colors," or "calendar," which to Rosie may be as reasonable.

Rosie may also be wondering why the teacher is asking the question in the first place: Surely, this woman towering above her *knows* the answer to the question she is asking? The most perplexing moment probably comes when the teacher says "go on." What can this mean? Rosie knows she should say something—but what? The teacher's "go on" presumes that Rosie is familiar with the talk that usually goes on at reading time when a child is asked to elaborate on the original identification (Heath, 1982). Rosie could have responded to the teacher's request for elaboration by giving more specific information about the skis, identifying other things in the picture, predicting what will happen to Santa Claus as he skis down the hill, or, depending on the flexibility of the teacher, by offering personal reactions or associations that might relate to the picture. That is what the request minimally coded in "go on" asks for. And that is what more "verbal" children would do, not simply because they have bigger vocabularies or are more talkative, but because they are familiar with the routines for labelling pictures and providing elaborative information about the labels. Shirley Brice Heath (1982) claims that familiarity with these routines gives some children a powerful advantage in school:

*Close analysis of how mainstream school-oriented children come to learn to take from books at home suggests that such children learn not only how to take meaning from books, but also how to talk about it. In doing the latter, they repeatedly practice routines which parallel those of classroom interaction. By the time they enter school, they have had continuous experience as information-givers; they have learned how to perform in those interactions which surround literate sources throughout school. They have had years of practice in interaction situations that are the heart of reading—both learning to read and reading to learn in school. (56)*

For Rosie, who never had those encounters, these routines remain a mystery.

Heath's essay is entitled "What No Bedtime Story Means: Narrative Skills at Home and School." It is clear, though, that she believes these encounters with books promote more than narrative skills. In effect, the bedtime story becomes a staging area, where the child engages in book talk. When my daughter and I read *Miss Nelson Is Back*, I might pause to comment on the inept principal, Mr. Blandsford: "Don't you think Blandsford is dumb?" And Sarah might say, "Yeah, him and his dumb ball-point pen collection." This kind of exchange is a precursor to more extended character evaluation. In the next chapter, I will show how the label-plus-attribute request (which Rosie failed to understand) anticipates the early informative writing that children attempt. These early routines help students learn what to "go on" means.

Thus, it is hardly surprising that, when children begin to write, they often do so by attaching labels to the pictures that they draw—not because they need the drawings to rehearse for the writings, but because they have often had thousands of literacy experiences that centered around pictures. Children have mastered routines that they apply to school situations. The psychologist Larry Gross (1974) has also commented on the importance of these routines:

*One achieves competence in a medium by slowly building on the routines which have been performed over and over until they have become tacit and habitual. This basic repetitious activity can be easily seen in children who derive enormous satisfaction from performing over and over some action which results in a predictable effect. The feeling of efficacy. . . is the basic and initial form of satisfaction in competence. It is on the basis of a repertoire of often repeated actions that the child can begin to introduce and perceive slight variations and thus extend the range of his perceptual-intellectual competence to more complex forms of organized behavior. (73)*

The beginning writer seems to rely on the routine of labelling and then extending labels by explaining attributes.

Heath's work (1982), in particular, suggests that a modification should be made to the speech-dependency model of literacy learning that claims that the development of literacy skills is built on a foundation of oral language ability (see, in particular, Moffett and Wagner, 1983). If, for example, early writing is talk written down, one would expect that a child who talks fluently would be well prepared for writing. The problem with this position is that it fails to account for the difficulty many talkative, expressive children have with literacy learning in school settings. Heath describes in wonderful detail the rich oral culture of a working-class black community in the Piedmont mountains. Yet, when she followed children from this community into schools, she found that they had problems, not because they were not expressive, but because they did not have access to certain literate routines that had become habitual to the mainstream or middle-class children. It all relates to the request made to Rosie to "go on," which was not simply a request for her to keep talking but to keep talking in a certain way—a game that she did not know how to play. Similarly, I would argue that children do not begin to write by working outside literate tradition, writing down preformal speech. They are working within literate traditions, even before they begin to draw, even as they learn to talk around books.

## THE DRAWING AS GENRE

One day I was reading to my younger daughter (age five years, five months at the time) from an informational book on trucks. Each page pictured different categories of trucks—those that carried things, those that helped in emergencies, and so on. On one page was a picture of a logging truck with "Logging Truck" printed below it. "What do you think this says?" I asked. Abby thought a minute and then said, "I bet it says 'carrying.'"

Her answer surprised me because I had expected the object label. As I thought about my question, I realized that I had asked for more than a simple identification. Abby had the option of determining whether the picture focused on ongoing action or on the identification of the object in the picture. As it turned out, she was drawn to the ongoing action—to the implied verb rather than the implied noun. She read the picture as a narrative (as action), not as a description.

I realize that, in using "narrative" and "description," I am applying verbal terms to something graphic and visual. This is intentional. In this section, I will argue that the written forms that children use—both narrative and expositional—have clear counterparts in the drawings that they attempt. They can emphasize the continuity of action, in effect, drawing one frame of a reel of film, but, if they are skillful and resourceful, a frame that suggests what went on before and what will follow. Or children can emphasize permanence, capturing a timeless moment—a family portrait, for example—that seems to be extracted from the onward flow of events. Each option poses its own graphic challenge and the narrative, in particular, requires the child to suggest many pictures with one.

I will also look at the minimal writing that often accompanies these pictures. These short messages usually are referred to indiscriminately as "labels," as many indeed are. But some of these messages more appropriately are called "captions" because they focus on the action of the picture: I expected a label from Abby, and she responded with a caption.

### *Narrative pictures*

The young writer/artist who wants to draw action immediately confronts a problem—a picture cannot move. Movement must be suggested by the child so that the observer can infer the action. This section will examine how children circumvent the immobility of the picture. Most of the drawings reproduced were done by kindergarten children in Hawaiian schools (Lindberg, 1988). As a result, this sample may have a regional flavor, but most of the drawings will, I believe, seem quite familiar—even Hawaiian children draw houses with smoke coming out of slanted chimneys.

*Strategy 1: The initiating state.* When selecting which slice of the action to depict, a child may choose the opening moment. For example, the child's family may be shown standing outside a house, ready to take a trip. Such a picture represents the starting point of the commentary that accompanies it. The advantage of this strategy is that the child does not have to deal with the graphic challenge of depicting action. The commentary, written or oral, suggests the narrative.

Figure 2–1 is a fairly typical portrait of a family at the moment before the action is about to begin. The child, when asked to tell about the picture, said, "I at the beach. My brothers and sisters went with me. We going swimming." Similarly, Figure 2–2 shows the author-artist and friend Gaylene facing us directly beneath five clouds. The child explained the

FIGURE 2–1 *Initiating state. "I at the beach. My brothers and sisters went with me. We going swimming."*

FIGURE 2–2 *Initiating state. "Gaylene and me going to the pool and then shopping at Pay-n-Save. Then back home."*

picture: "Gaylene and me going to the pool and then shopping at Pay-n-Save. Then back home."

*Strategy 2: The midaction picture.* While strategy 1 yields drawings that seem static, the midaction picture is dynamic; the author-artist has found a visual language to suggest ongoing action. One method might be called the "gravity technique." Because objects cannot remain aloft permanently, we mentally complete the action of an object's return to earth when we see it in midair. It's for this reason that we find pictures of people falling so terrifying. In Figure 2–3, the fish in midair adds a sense of movement to the picture. In Figure 2–4, the ball in midair suggests the activity of the catcher because we mentally complete the ball's flight. This figure also uses wavy lines to denote action, a technique that will be discussed later.

Children can also create dynamic tension between objects or people in their pictures; from this tension, we infer action, imagining the effect that one thing might have on another. If, for example, we see someone with an uplifted knife standing behind an unsuspecting victim, we mentally complete the action. Many of the Hawaiian children experimented with this kind of action picture soon after they saw the Bigfoot show at Aloha Stadium. Bigfoot was a huge truck with wheels about seven feet in diameter. The highlight of the show was when Bigfoot drove

FIGURE 2–3 *Midaction state: Gravity technique—fish in midair*

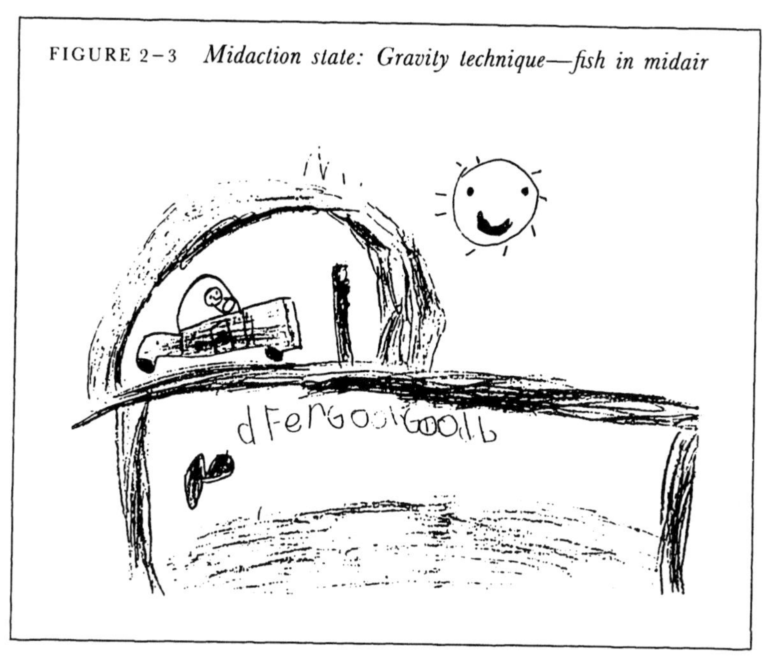

FIGURE 2–4 *Midaction state: Gravity technique—ball in midair*

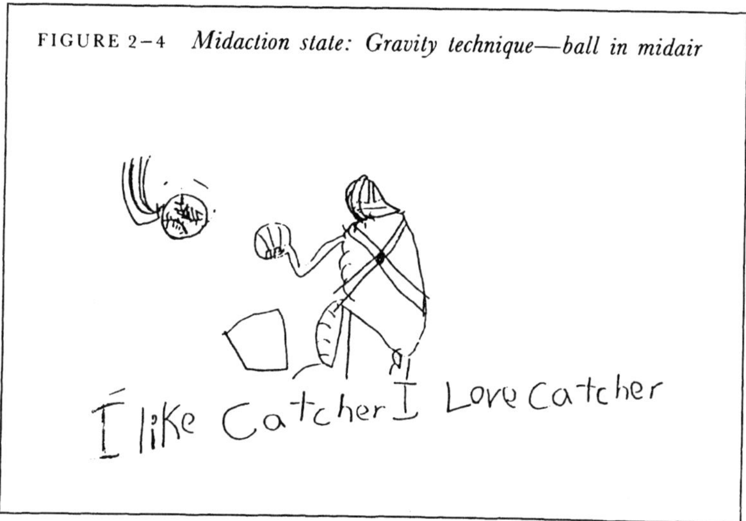


over a series of cars—a delicious power fantasy for many of the boys. In their drawings, the author-artists often successfully created the illusion of action by showing the results of Bigfoot's power. In several drawings, we see Bigfoot on top of a car crushed so thoroughly that it is little more than a shadow. (See Figure 2–5.) In Figure 2–6, we also anticipate action because of what we know about dogs. The child has drawn himself

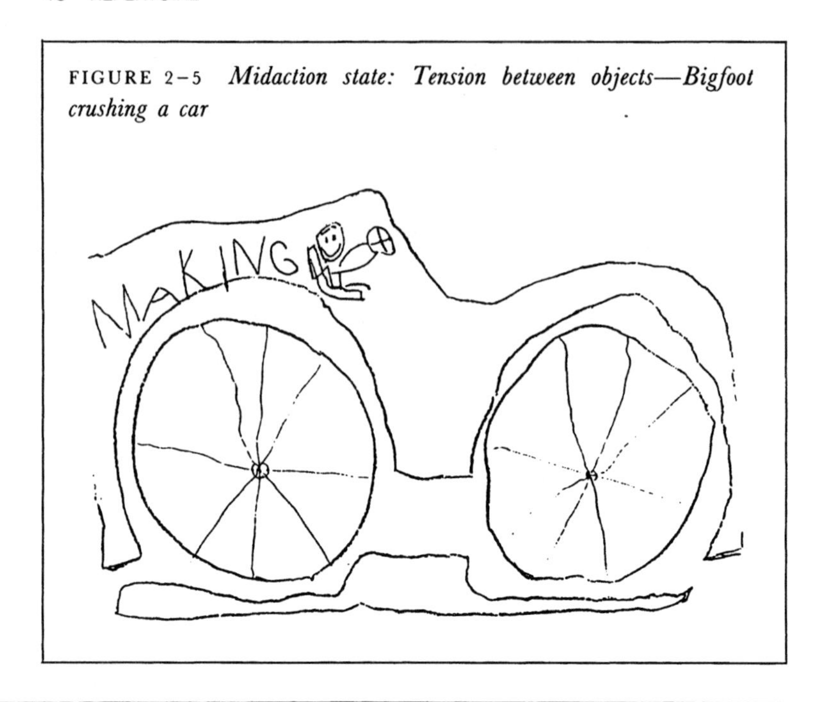


FIGURE 2–5 *Midaction state: Tension between objects—Bigfoot crushing a car*

FIGURE 2–6 *Midaction state: Tension between objects—child and dog*

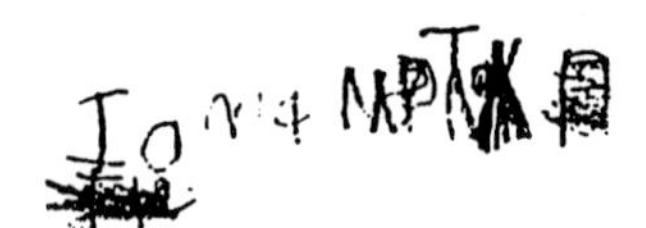

pulling his dog's tail, and we mentally complete the action by imagining the dog turning toward the child.

One difficulty that children face in showing people interacting is the problem of profile. Children almost invariably draw human figures facing forward, looking at us, the viewers, and not at each other. To create a sense of dramatic interaction, however, it is often necessary to break out of this face-forward pattern and show the figures in profile so that we see only the side of the face (Sowers, 1985b). We get some sense of this possibility in Figure 2–4, where the catcher is clearly facing away from us. We also see the effect of profile drawing in Figure 2–7, where the bride and groom are looking toward the ring-bearer, who in turn is watching them. The effect is considerably more dynamic than a face-forward presentation.

Another way to create the illusion of action is to use wavy lines to show dirt flying, wind blowing, firecrackers exploding. The author-artist of Figure 2–8 clearly wants to suggest as much action as he can. He describes his picture: "One motorcycle and fire on the motorcycle. All wind coming blowing—all dark. This all my three smokes." Figure 2–9 was drawn just after the

FIGURE 2–7 *Wedding scene: Figures in profile*

FIGURE 2–8 *Midaction state: Action lines. "One motorcycle and fire on the motorcycle. All wind coming blowing—all dark. This all my three smokes."*

New Year's celebration in Honolulu, when fireworks crackled throughout the city (there were about fifty fires in the city that night). The author uses wavy lines to show the trajectories and explosions of the fireworks.

These examples of action demonstrate the children's awareness of graphic conventions—or codes—that allow an observer mentally to transform something static into something active. Hubbard (1988) claims that devices like action lines are used commonly in Western culture to indicate action. By contrast, non-Western cultures do not denote action in the same way. Hubbard cites an experiment conducted by Duncan, Gourlay, and Hudson (1973), which involved showing the same cartoon picture of a dog to rural Zulus and Western subjects in South Africa. Two drops of saliva are suspended below the dog's visible tongue, action lines trail behind each paw, and a small cloud of dust hovers behind the hind paws. Seventy-five percent of the Western subjects knew the dog was supposed to be moving, as compared to only 1 percent of the Zulus.

*Strategy 3: The postaction picture.* The author-artist may choose to show the concluding frame of the narrative, although this option seemed to be less popular among the Hawaiian sample than the

FIGURE 2–9 *Midaction state: Action lines—fireworks*

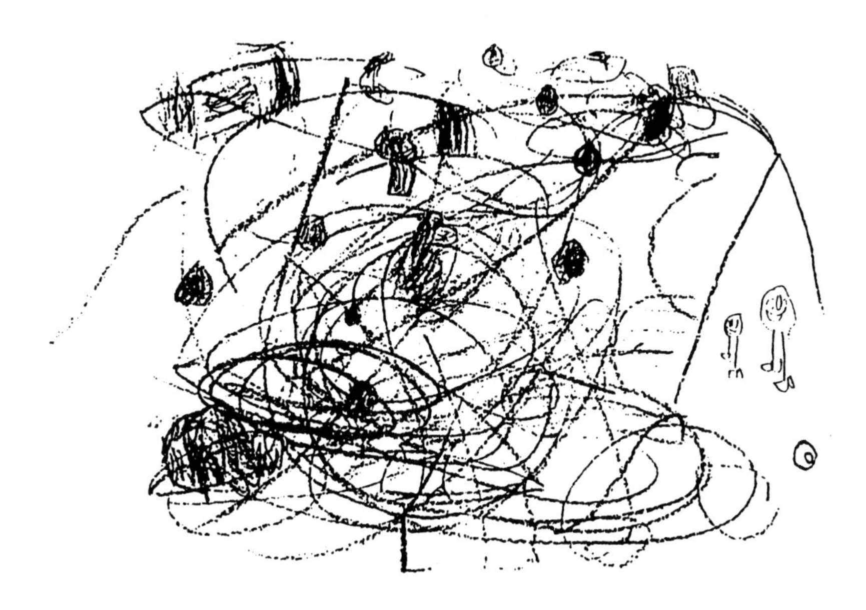

previous two strategies. The most notable example showed a monster all in red (Figure 2–10). The child's commentary: "Monster. It has bloody eyes. Red ears. It has blood right there. It has a bloody nose. It has blood right there too. It got bloody eating little kids."

*Strategy 4: Multiple frames.* A fourth way to subvert the static quality of the picture is to use more than one picture to show what happens over a period of time. A child may show the movement of a kicked soccer ball by drawing a series of balls along the line of trajectory. Children also reinvent the cartoon, using a series of pictures to create the effect of a narrative.

Two teachers at Mast Way School in Lee, New Hampshire, Florence Damon and Pat McLure, began to encourage children to use multiple frames to show a sequence of actions. Children regularly are asked to sequence someone else's pictures but rarely to draw their own. I borrowed the idea and asked Abby (then age six) to try it. She drew nine frames (Figure 2–11) showing a bird building a nest, then feeding a baby bird in the final frame. In fact, there is yet another time sequence in her early frames, which show the tree losing its leaves and becoming bare.

FIGURE 2–10 *Postaction picture. "Monster. It has bloody eyes. Red ears. It has blood right there. It has a bloody nose. It has blood right there too. It got bloody eating little kids."*

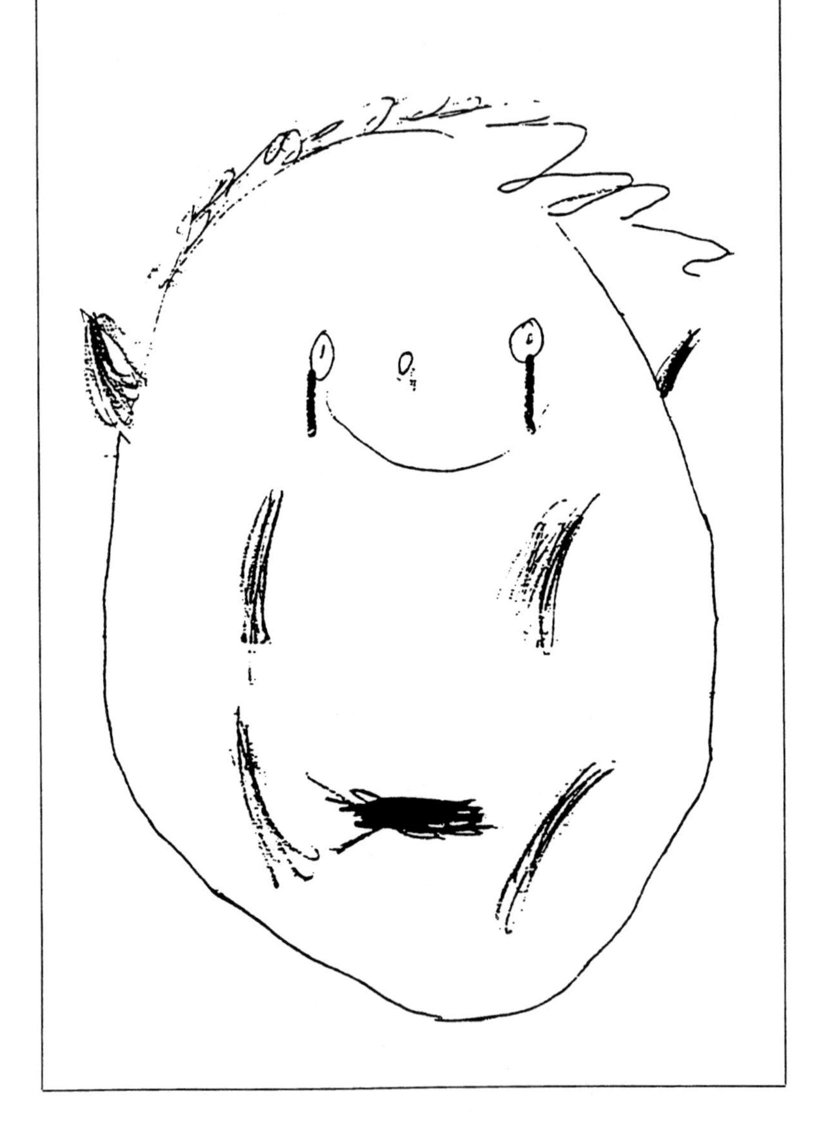

FIGURE 2–11 *Multiple frames: Building a bird's nest*

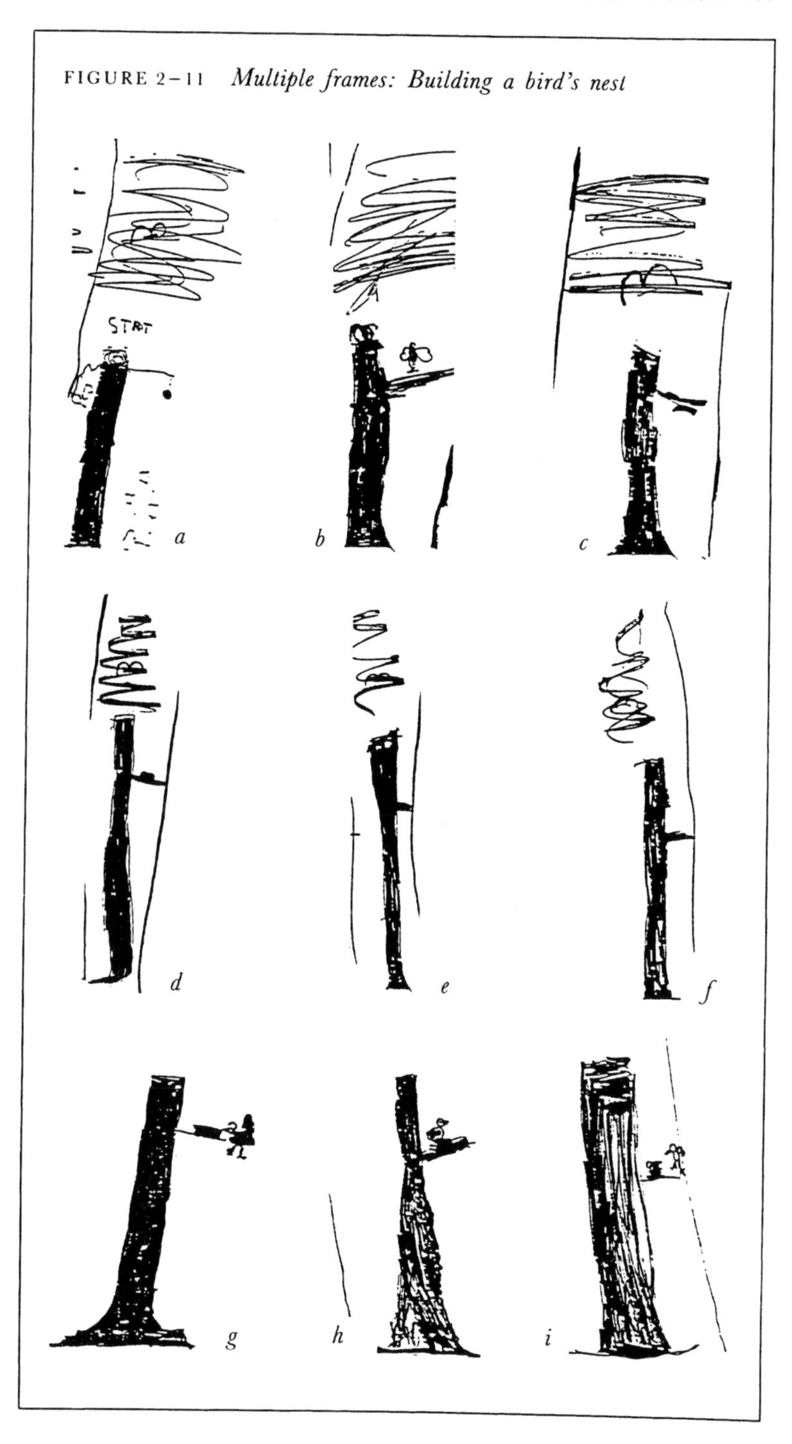

As Hubbard (1987) has noted, there are several variations on this technique. In Figure 2–12, Abby attempts to show the back-and-forth movement of a Christmas tree ornament by indicating the central position with firm lines and using lighter lines to illustrate the ornament's position as it sways back and forth. Figure 2–13, the Happy Puppy Machine, is another attempt to show a process that occurs over time. Here she drew a long conveyer tube that processed the raw material—undifferentiated trapezoids—into happy puppies.

*Expository pictures*

Whereas the narrative picture stresses the continuity of action, the expository picture examines the child's world removed from the stream of events. The emphasis is on what is, not on what happens. Where the commentary on narrative pictures invariably includes an action verb, the verb used for expository pictures is a form of *to be* or *to have*—"this is," "these are," "I have," and so on. It could even be argued that the simple one-word label includes an understood "this is." The *label*, then, can be defined

FIGURE 2–12 *Moving ornament*

as a "to be" statement; the *caption* (which has the same root as *capture*) seizes a moment in a series of actions.

In the expository pictures, we see children confronting two graphic challenges that have clear counterparts in expository writing: inclusiveness and specificity. Probably the best example of inclusiveness in drawing are the many Richard Scarry books, which I did not enjoy reading, although they were favorites of all my children. Mem Fox (1988), the best-selling Australian children's author, says that she needs to throw in a few "winks" to parents to keep their attention. The Scarry books did not cast any winks my way; the story lines seem weak, unimaginative, and utterly predictable. Their phenomenal popularity arises, I believe, from the almost encyclopedic completeness of the illustrations. The books play to the child's love of lists, though the lists are primarily visual. Some children's drawings aim for this kind of inclusiveness.

The most common visual lists were the many family portraits. Crystal's picture (Figure 2–14) is typical. The text reads, "My family. I have three sister and I have one brother in my house." She also names each of the figures: "My mommy

FIGURE 2–13 *Steps in a process: The Happy Puppy Machine*

FIGURE 2–14 *Expository picture: Family portrait*

and me. Pani and Joy." In Figure 2–15, we have something that approaches the Richard Scarry formula: the child suggests action with the caption "I'm playing at my house" but also labels, Scarry style, the elements in the picture.

One decision that the child makes when drawing expository pictures is whether to concentrate on inclusiveness (getting everybody or everything into the picture) or specificity (creating detail within the picture). It's the difference between a wide-angle and a telephoto lens.

Teachers can promote pictorial exposition by nudging students in the two directions that I have indicated. We can encourage the child to add more elements—for example, by asking "Who else is in your family?" "What other pets do you have?" "What other things do you have in your yard?" Or we can prompt the child to add details, asking "How big is your father?" "Does he wear glasses?" Susan Bridge (1988) offers the following example

FIGURE 2–15 *Expository picture: Richard Scarry technique*

of an elaborating conference with her three-year-old nephew. Kevin has already drawn one mask and appears to be starting another (Figure 2–16a).

KEVIN [*drawing, begins to laugh*]: It's a funny face. It's MY face! [*Quickly he draws a tadpole body, revising the mask*—Figure 2–16b]. That's me! [*Pointing to the picture.*] That's my shirt! [*Pointing to the body he has drawn. He looks down at his own shirt, touches the fabric.*] I have stripes on it. [*Makes stripes on the shirt—Figure 2–16c—pats stripes he has just made.*] That's part of him. [*Without hesitation he draws the arms, adding four fingers to each*—Figure 2–16d.] I don't know where the feet are. There's no room. [*Directed toward me—he had drawn the figure close to the bottom of the page.*]

SUSAN: What do you think you could do if there's no more room?

KEVIN: Put it down here. [*Draws two straight lines from the tadpole body to the end of the paper—Figure 2–16e.*] Feet! [*At this point Kevin appears to be finished.*]

FIGURE 2–16 *Expository sequence: Focus on detail—Kevin's self-portrait (from Bridge 1988, 87)*

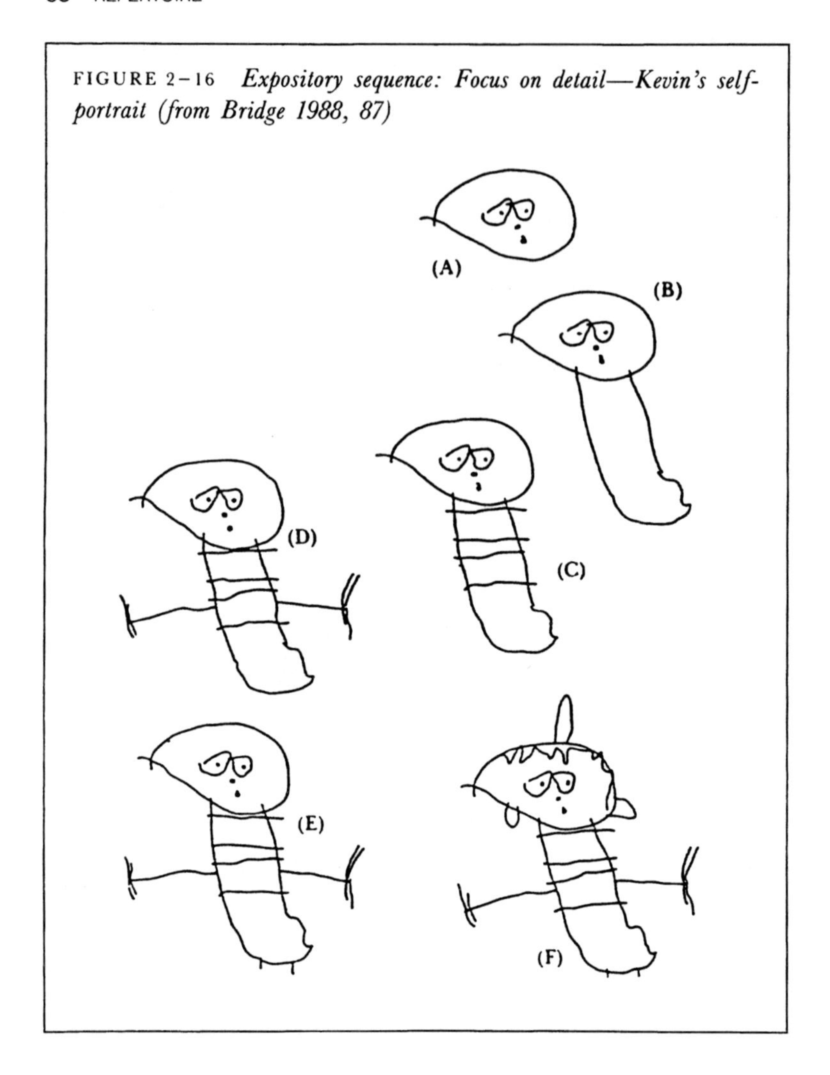


SUSAN: Tell me about your drawing.

KEVIN: It's me!

SUSAN: It *is* you! I can see your face, and your arms—here are your fingers, and your shirt with stripes on it, and your feet. It certainly looks like you. Is there anything else you want to add to make it look just like Kevin?

KEVIN [*Looks at his picture, puts his hand up and touches his ears*]: Ears. [*Draws ears. Puts hand on the top of his head.*] Point. [*Draws a point on top of the head, making a quick motion. Touches his head again.*] Hair. [*Draws hair carefully. Looks at picture, appearing satisfied—Figure 2–16f.*] (85–87)

Bridge's comments urge Kevin to add specific details to his picture. She carefully acknowledges what he has done and then asks the question that sparks that last round of elaboration—"Is there anything else you want to add to make it look just like Kevin?" Another time, she might have pushed him toward inclusiveness by asking, "Are you by yourself in this picture or are you with somebody?"—a question that might encourage him to include other figures.

## THE RELATIONSHIP OF PICTURE TO TEXT

Imagine that written language and drawing are both sources of information. What options does a child have when facing a blank piece of paper? How many different ways can text and drawing relate? There are at least seven:

1. Text only. The text carries the only message, with no accompanying picture.
2. Picture only. The picture, unaided by text, represents the event, person, or object.
3. Picture and text—redundant. The text duplicates what is in the picture.
4. Imbalance—pictorial. The picture is far more specific and informative than the written text.
5. Complementary. Both text and drawing supply specific information, but the child decides which medium provides which information.
6. Imbalance—textual. The text provides most of the information.
7. General-specific relationship. The text identifies a general category, and the picture shows specific items in that category. For example, a child could draw a candy bar and label it "candy bar" (what I would call a redundant relationship) or he or she could call it "junk" ( a general-specific relationship).

I'm sure that this list underestimates the options, but it does suggest the range of choices available to children and, indirectly, to teachers, once they step outside a word-centered mindset.

The problem inherent in dealing with children's drawing-writing is determining which option the child has chosen. I remember one first-grade conference where the child, a reticent boy, had drawn a picture and written a two-word label. The child began, somewhat reluctantly, to explain the story represented in the picture. The teacher would ask, "Where did you put that?" (meaning "where did you write that?"), and the boy would point to his picture to answer the questions. As far as he could see, it was all there *in the picture*. The teacher, however, was expecting the text-picture relationship at least to be redundant, an expectation that probably mystified the boy.

The expectation that meaning will be explicit in the text is both understandable and, in the long run, desirable. But exclusive focus on the text may not be a good short-term strategy, because it assumes, perhaps incorrectly, that a child is adopting a particular view of written language. Moreover, it tends to ignore the work that the child has done in his preferred system of representation—drawing. The teacher in this conference might have worked more effectively within the intent of the child if she had urged an even *greater* imbalance by asking the child to talk about and maybe elaborate on the drawing. If we are to encourage decision making in the writing classroom, we need to view writing in the broadest possible way, as the interweaving of various symbol systems, which is how children tend to see it.

*Picture only*

Some children (like Jason, Gregg, and Alan, or the boy discussed above) develop such skill at drawing that a written commentary seems almost superfluous. Ironically, *because* of their skill, these children may resist the idea that text and picture can be coequal, because making them coequal would take time and energy away from their drawing and require considerable text—more than they would feel comfortable producing—to do any kind of justice to their drawing. Figure 2–17 is an impressive example of an explicit picture. At the center front of the picture is a clown, to the right of him a lion tamer; in the air are four performers, two on the trapezes and two waiting on the platform. Below the trapeze is a net. At the far left of the picture, a man is setting off a cannon, and we can trace the trail of a cannonball across the page. The child has "written" nothing, and indeed one wonders how children with such drawing ability view the implied request to attach written labels to creations such as this.

*Picture and text—redundant*

Sometimes, the written message seems to convey exactly the same information as the picture. Children's drawing often is schematic, with no attempt to be individually explicit. The child's house is the standard house (with the chimney perpendicular to the slant of the roof). The sun that shines in the

FIGURE 2–17 *Picture without written text*

pictures is not the sun that children see in the sky, but a circle radiating lines. The children do not seem to draw reality and then label or describe it; rather, they use two sets of conventionalized symbols (words and schematic drawings), one to label the other. This is the impression we get from Figure 2–18, where the child has drawn virtually the same schematic drawing—the person drawing—to represent Shanna, her mother, her father, and her cousin. The fish are the conventional circle-plus-triangle fish, the sun the conventional sun, and so on. The picture is adequate to identify each referent—we recognize the sun as a sun—but it conveys no more information than that.

*Imbalance—pictorial*

If we contrast Figure 2–18 with Figure 2–19, we notice a shift toward a more fully informative picture. The text, "I see a Rock Foot," serves as a general label, but the picture is more than a conventionalized schema. We can also see carefully drawn fire (red in the original) coming out of the rear of the train and

FIGURE 2–18 *Picture and text—redundant*

FIGURE 2–19 *Imbalance—pictorial*

smoke (blue) coming out of the top stack. The door has a clearly drawn handle and what look like rivets in the smokestack are drawn at painstaking right angles. I have found that children who produce these kinds of drawings, like the children in our first category, also often resist implied requests to extend their written descriptions, although they will gladly add visual detail until the picture is virtually clogged with it. They're not particularly interested in quitting while they're ahead, because, for them, it is the activity of drawing and not the final product that matters most.

*Complementary*

Maurice Sendak, the noted children's author, claims that "you must never illustrate exactly what is written. You must find a space in the text so that the pictures can do the work. Then you must let the words take over where words do it best" (quoted in Hubbard, 1987, 60). In Figure 2–20 we see an example of a complementary relationship where the text does not duplicate what is in the picture. From the picture, we learn several things that the text does not tell us: We see how long the "funny thing's" tail is, we see that the man fed him outside his house

FIGURE 2–20 *Complementary text-picture. "I like when the funny thing had a long tail. The man fed him plenty times. That's my favorite part."*

under a tree, we see the inside of the man's house. The man is shown at two points in the action: inside the house getting the food and outside the house feeding the animal. And from the expressions on their faces, we know that both the man and the funny thing are happy. From the text, however, we learn something that would have been very difficult to illustrate—that the man fed the funny thing plenty of times. Thus, we learn that the action in the picture was repeated several times.

*Imbalance—textual*

Often, near the end of first grade or the beginning of second grade, several forces work to minimize the importance of the drawing and shift attention to the written text. The child becomes more fluent; letter formation is easier and fewer words need to be sounded out. Sometimes this fluency is pushed to an extreme—students compete to see who can write the longest books, books as long as the ones they read. At the same time, children can become self-conscious about their illustrations. Second grade, after all, has been called the adolescence of elementary school. How one appears to others becomes suddenly important. As Gardner (1980) has shown, children begin to ask if their drawings are realistic representations—do they look right? This newfound fluency—combined with a more critical perspective on artwork, combined with a newly developed fear of appearing childish, combined with the pressure from the school to attend more to written elaboration and less to artistic elaboration—inevitably shifts the order of priorities. The writing, now, is completed first. The lined paper provides only a small space at the top for the illustration. Written language does the work.

*General-specific relationship*

Another way in which texts come to do more than duplicate pictures is through the introduction of more general terms, with pictures used to provide instances or examples. (I have been using illustrations this way in this chapter). In one such drawing, my daughter Sarah drew a schematic whale above a small fish, with the inevitable sun in the upper right-hand corner of the page. The drawing was fairly typical, but the text was not: "Whales are mammals and they are big. They live in the water. They eat all the fish." With the word "mammal," the child introduced a superordinate noun that names the class of animals to which whales belong. While "whale" is drawable, "mammal" is not.

We cannot draw a mammal, only an example of a mammal. In another drawing that Sarah, age six, did at about this age, she wrote "Junk" at the top of her page and then drew several examples of junk—candy bars, gum, and so on. These clearly are early explorations of the genus-species relationship.

Of course, we want children to become skilled at producing explicit written texts. We want writing to be more than a hurried formality completed quickly at the end of writing period. But, as teachers and parents, we dismiss too easily the value and complexity of the children's drawing. Although we pay lip service to the idea that a picture is worth a thousand words, we don't really believe it. It's the thousand words that really interest us. Once the golden age of drawing has passed (around the second or third grade), art gives way to a predominantly, if not exclusively, word-centered school culture, and children no longer allocate informativeness between the two systems.

One question worth asking, though, is whether word-centeredness reflects the absolute superiority of written language as a system of representation or, instead, outmoded assumptions about the difficulty of including pictures in texts. For most of printing history, pictures included in books had to be engraved, a process far more time-consuming and costly than setting type. In other words, there was an *economic* advantage to being print-centered. But the advent of photographic printing (as opposed to letterpress) makes chapters like this one, which intersperses drawing with text, relatively easy to do. Computer technology has increased our capacity for integrating graphics and text. Newspapers like *USA Today* look radically different from their predecessors in part because the visual and the verbal are so interwoven. I'm suggesting then that an exclusively word-centered view of literacy may not prepare students for the graphic and design opportunities that will be available to them. Ironically, we all may need to alter our view of "writing" to include these opportunities. We may need to think of composing more as the children in this chapter do—as symbol-weaving.

But there's an even more basic reason not to neglect the contribution that drawing can make to the development of language learners. Drawing can help develop perceptual ability—the ability to make refined observations, which is useful for more than artwork. Consider the story about Louis Agassiz's anatomy class, where, for the first three days, he asked his students to look at a fish and draw what they saw. Elliot Eisner (1983) elaborates on this connection:

*Art education and art educators in particular have a special interest in differentiating the sensory abilities of individuals. When those abilities—call them sensory intelligence if you like—are well differentiated, the qualities to be experienced available, and an interest in experiencing those qualities high, the amount of new information an individual is able to secure from the world is increased. (23)*

My own experience with artists convinces me that Eisner is right. My neighbor is an artist, and, sometimes, when we sit outside at dusk and admire the way the light hits the buildings flush, I know that she is seeing something more complex and differentiated than I am. She might make some comment about shadows or lines or textures that I don't even see until she points them out. For I am one of those who never progressed beyond the schematic house and tree and cloud—though my chimneys no longer slant off the roof.

# 3
# Cataloging the world's contents

In March of 1887, Helen Keller made the dramatic connection between words and things at the water pump near her home. Four months later, at the age of seven years, four months, she wrote the following letter to the "blind girls" at the Perkins Institute in Boston:

*dear little blind girls*

*I will write you a letter I thank you for pretty desk I did write to mother in Memphis on it mother and mildred came home wednesday mother brought me a pretty new dress and hat and papa did go to huntsville he brought me apples and candy I and teacher will come to Boston to see you nancy is my doll she does cry I do rock nancy to sleep Mildred is sick doctor will give her medicine to make her well. . . . I will hug and kiss little blind girls Mr. Anagnos will come see me.*

*good-by*

*Helen*

*(1954, 100)*

Despite the remarkable events of the previous four months, this sounds like the letter of a seven-year-old, although the language is a bit stiff. It appears to be an inventory of important occurrences, and, at first reading, the order seems random, an example of what Carl

Bereiter and Marlene Scardamalia (1979) call the "what next" strategy. The letter's contents seem to follow the order of the associations that she makes in her mind rather than an overall plan.

But, on rereading Helen's letter, we can see that it breaks down into several definable units: the opening, the thank-you for the desk, the list of gifts, information about her doll, information about the church (a section not quoted above), and a closing. While not writing in adult paragraphs, Helen clustered information into thematically related units. Like many children her age, Helen had discovered an intermediary form that begins to approximate adult exposition.

This form of exposition is built on the list. Helen's earlier letters were even more obvious lists of things she had done:

*Helen does play with dogs  Helen does ride on horseback with teacher Helen does give handee grass in hand  teacher does whip handee to go fast  helen is blind  Helen will put letter in envelop for blind girls. (100)*

This enumeration parallels the process of cataloging knowledge and experience in which all young children take delight. Yet the central role of lists in the evolution of children's writing usually is not recognized. Too frequently, lists are not considered to be real writing.

When I first began collecting my daughter Sarah's writing, I, too, held this view. I dutifully filed away her lists but otherwise paid them little attention. I justified this by reasoning that, while they might be a step toward sustained writing, they didn't seem all that interesting in themselves. Without knowing it, I may have been acting on that constant reminder in elementary school to answer questions "in complete sentences." Single-word answers, as I remember, were no better than no answers. To write meant to write in sentences.

Yet, even when the "real" writing began to appear, Sarah continued to make lists. When I stopped to tally the types of writing that she had tried by the age of six years, three months, I found that, next to the letter, the list was the most common form of writing that she attempted. I counted fifty-five lists distributed among eleven categories:

- Name lists 19
- Letter lists 14
- Number lists 6
- Christmas lists 4
- Age lists 3

- Accomplishments lists 3
- Word lists 2
- Grocery lists 1
- Shapes lists 1
- Money lists 1
- Food-order lists (imaginary restaurant) 1

Even her "real" writing was listlike, similar to the Helen Keller letters quoted above. I knew that children discover early what Marie Clay has called the "inventory principle" (1975), but I was surprised by the persistence of the form. Why would children choose to write lists when they could be writing stories? There are several possible answers.

*The list as a pervasive writing form.* The walls of most early-elementary classrooms are covered with lists—of sight words, work assignments, vocabulary words, children's names, number names. The letters of the alphabet are invariably present in both upper- and lowercase. In one first-grade classroom, I counted twenty-two lists on the walls alone. And in workbooks, readers, and textbooks, lists are so prevalent that psychologists Michael Cole and Roy Andrade claim that "schooling perpetuates the dream that Man could get a catalogue of all the world's contents, which, when properly classified and memorized, would represent full knowledge of the world" (1982, 24).

The list is no less common in homes. Shirley Brice Heath (1983) studied the frequency of various kinds of writing in "mainstream" and working-class homes. She found that, in both, writing was used most often as a memory aid: grocery lists, notes in photo albums, lists of things to do, reminder notes, lists of telephone numbers and appointments. Often these lists are superimposed on another list—the calendar. We look up phone numbers in the huge list in the phone book. We prepare food according to recipes—lists—which are themselves listed by the score in cookbooks. Many of the other books we buy, particularly self-help and diet books, are elaborated lists. And what child is not fascinated by one of the greatest lists of all: the Sears catalog.

*The list as an aid to thinking.* Jack Goody, in his book, *The Domestication of the Savage Mind* (1977), claims that the list permits a way of thinking—or arranging words into classes—that is impossible in connected written prose or in speech. Lists, according to Goody, "increase the visibility and definiteness of classes [and] make it easier for the individual to engage in chunking, more particularly in the hierarchical ordering of information which is critical to recall" (111). The list has a special power: By freeing the word from the sentence, it allows various combinations and categorizations to be considered. It is for this reason that many prewriting strategies—brainstorming, outlining, webbing—are variations on the list (see, for example, Murray, 1984).

Goody examines the early uses of alphabetic writing and concludes that its first function was not to reproduce speech but to label and inventory. The first known appearance of writing is on possession labels tied to property to indicate ownership. As governments became more centralized, the need for systematic record keeping grew. One of the most complete collections of early writing, recovered from a Canaanite site (in present-day Syria), dates from 2,000 B.C. It contains 508 documents, two-thirds of which are lists. One hundred twenty-seven are quotas containing information on taxes, supplies, conscription, or rations; fifty-nine are lists of personal or geographic names; and fifty-two are lists of professions. Goody's point is that the initial purposes for writing differed significantly from the uses of oral language—writing did *not* develop to make speech permanent.

As civilizations developed, official lists evolved into more complex and detailed categorizations. Lists of important dates evolved into chronicles and then histories. Lists of plant and animal names evolved into the biological classifications (genus, order, species) that we know today. Lists of words evolved into dictionaries. Goody maintains that writing systems made possible these increasingly complex systems of classification, thereby facilitating a way of thinking that we call modern.

Children may continue to write lists because they sense the power of the form. Like the ancient Canaanites, they understand that listing and categorizing are powerful tools for gaining dominion over the world.

*Lists as an externalization of expertise.* I doubt if anyone has ever finished writing a resume and then set it aside without admiring it. We admire our resumes for the same reason that we spend time in front of the mirror—to look at ourselves, what we are, what we've done. I suspect that the pharaohs, who had the major events of their reigns carved into stone, did not do so simply to provide a record for posterity; rather, listing these events made them more real, impressive, objectified.

Children gain the same gratification from listing. In Figure 3–1, a second grader demonstrates his knowledge of the different moves in breakdancing, while Figure 3–2 records

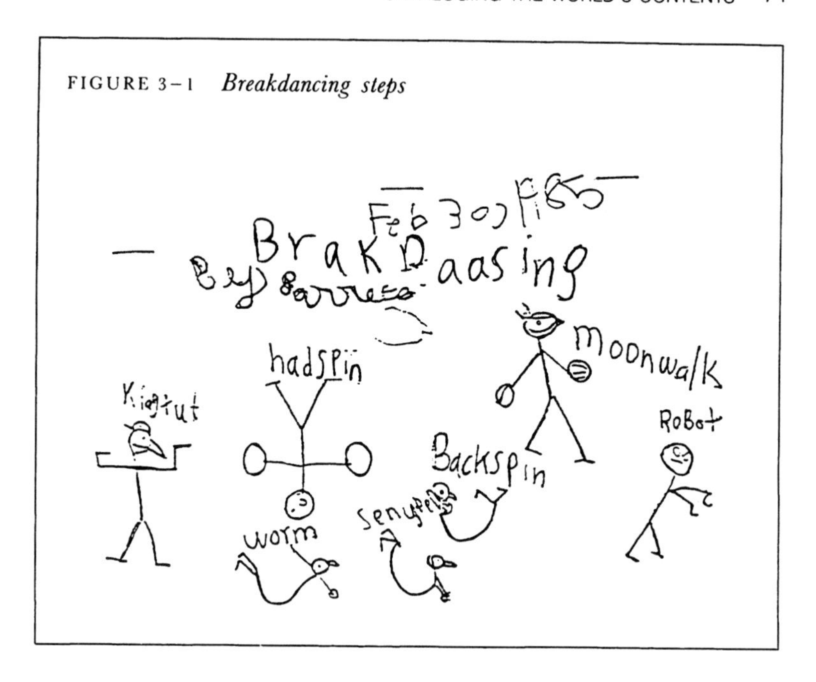


FIGURE 3–1 *Breakdancing steps*

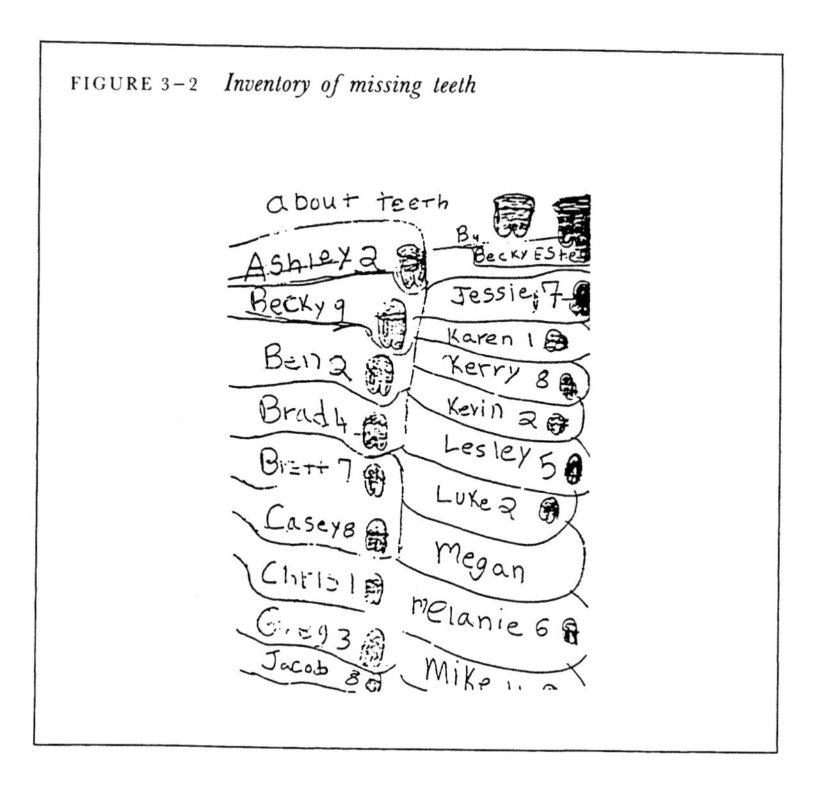


FIGURE 3–2 *Inventory of missing teeth*

information on missing teeth in one second-grade class. At age six, Sarah showed off her knowledge of food groups:

*Dare—Che's [cheese] Mike [milk]*
*Juke [junk]—pizz [pizza]*
*Frut and Vagas—carat Apple*
*Gran—Bred*
*Mete—Fish and Ham*

And she listed the "polite words" that she knew:

LIST OF WOED THAT ARE PLITE
*Ples*
*take you*
*yur's wakecome*
*Esgous me*

Lists are a way to demonstrate mastery, to hold up a mirror to one's knowledge.

Lists' appeal to children has been documented widely (Bissex, 1980; Clay, 1975; Harste, Woodward, and Burke, 1984). But the critical question—at least for schooling—is how list making leads into writing that is more demonstrably expository. I contend that schools let this ability wither as students are expected to write stories exclusively. Schooling, for many children, does not expand the range of possible written forms—it constricts it.

In this chapter, I will chart a rough progression that students seem to follow as they develop expository abilities in the early grades. The forms that I identify should not be considered as stages that students must go through in a specific order; rather, I hope that they will help teachers to note potential changes in student writing. As more attention is paid to students' expository writing, this admittedly crude system will need to be refined and modified.

Central to my scheme of development is the concept of intermediary forms. Children approach proficiency with complex exposition by attempting forms that have some features of adult exposition. This viewpoint contrasts with the traditional "deficit" approach in which children's exposition is seen as deficient adult writing (see, for example, Scardamalia, 1981). A swimming analogy may clarify the difference. Most children learn to swim the crawl stroke by attempting an intermediary form, the dog paddle. The dog paddle is not a failed version of the crawl stroke, but a reasonably effective way of swimming that does not require the child to coordinate stroking and breathing. Similarly, children's exposition is not failed adult exposition; rather, children acting as semioticians attempt various forms that exist in the culture, many of which approximate what we consider to be expository writing. The list is not flawed expository writing; it is a form, used widely in our culture, that engages the child in some of the cognitive activities necessary for writing exposition, particularly ordering information into categories, while not requiring others, such as forming explicit generalizations about that information. By working within these forms, the child gains what Larry Gross has called the "feeling of efficacy" (1974, 73).

## GROWTH IN EXPOSITION

Before defining these intermediary forms, I needed to identify the features of children's writing that I wanted to examine. The first was coherence. In exposition, statements are connected to other statements both explicitly and implicitly. If a child writes "My dog is friendly. She wags her tail," we read the second sentence as an example of the dog's friendliness. Statements can be connected in a variety of ways: specification, definition, illustration, contrast, cause-effect, statement-reason. One of my hypotheses was that, as children become more experienced writers, they build in more of these logical connectives. The work of Walter Loban (1976) on the development of sentence structure, although it does not include writing samples from grades 1 and 2, predicts this line of development.

My second hypothesis concerned overall structure. I speculated that, as students develop, they categorize their information more precisely into hierarchies. The main topic may be divided into subtopics or component topics.

These dimensions—coherence and hierarchical structure—can be made more tangible if they are applied to a piece of children's writing, such as the following report by a third grader on Ralph, the class mouse:

*Ralph likes to eat Skippy peanut butter. Ralph is in a cage. He has a spinning wheel. He has a motorcycle. It's red. He has a toilet. The first time Ralph was in the classroom Ralph stepped into a box. Ralph likes to climb to the top of the cage. Ralph has two tiny teeth. Everytime Ralph gets down he cleans himself. His tongue is one centimeter long. . . .*

The writer seems to be recording information as it comes to her. We can almost trace the pattern of associations. Reporting that Ralph stepped into the box triggered a memory of another action, his climbing to the top of his cage. The sentence about his teeth triggers the next about his cleaning himself. Yet, despite the associative quality of the report, a cluster of four statements describes one aspect of the topic—what Ralph has in his cage ("He has a spinning wheel. He has a motorcycle. It's red. He has a toilet."). Another cluster is about Ralph's mouth and what he does with it. For the most part, information in these clusters could be reordered without any loss of meaning. But one pair of statements fits the identification-plus-attribute pattern noted in the previous chapter ("He has a motorcycle. It's red"). There are also two complex sentences in the report that connect two pieces of information—when something happened and what happened.

My next step was to draw diagrams that would show how pieces are structured. I first divided texts into clause units and then categorized the ways in which individual units were related. Sometimes, particularly in the writing of very young children, units seemed to be randomly related:

*My dog is black. I like my dog.*

These two statements make just as much sense in reverse order. So, to indicate the lack of coherence, I diagrammed the relationship as follows:

If statements were in a chronological sequence ("I fed my dog. Then I put her to bed"), an arrow indicates the relationship:

Dog

o → o

If statements were related in a logical way—defined as any nonchronological order—the relationship was indicated with a two-way arrow. The sequence "I like my dog because he is black" would be indicated with a two-way arrow.

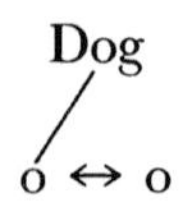

In longer pieces, like the report on Ralph the mouse, information is often divided into clusters. To indicate these clusters, I introduced intermediary nodes on the diagram. The diagram for "Ralph the mouse" would look like this:

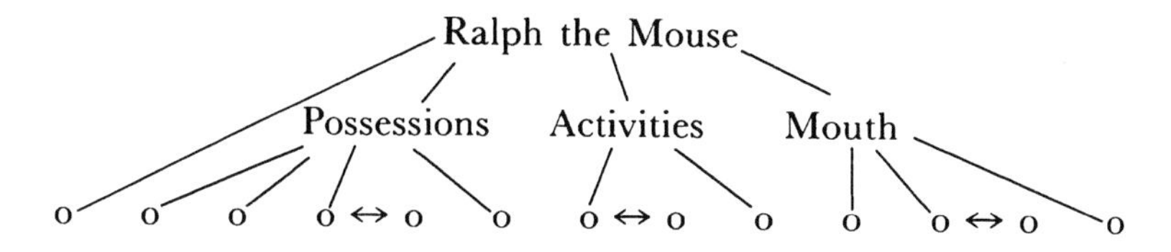


To test this system, I drew diagrams for 170 pieces of exposition written by students in grades 1, 2, and 3 (for a more complete reporting of this research, see Newkirk, 1987). These diagrams revealed that students regularly attempted several basic forms.

*The label*

The first and most significant labels that children write are their names. Much of their early writing, as shown in the previous chapter, consists of labels and captions for pictures. A label implies a "this is" type of statement, while a caption summarizes or anticipates the action in the picture. The label, then, is an initial form of exposition, because it examines objects and people removed from ongoing activity.

The structure for the label is as follows:

Topic (picture)
|
o

The label usually begins as a single word; the child knows that a word under or near a picture will be understood as an identifying label containing an implied "this is." Initially, particularly when the child is working with unlined paper, the label is often written near the object, in much the same way that Richard Scarry (1971) labels objects in his books. Scarry, in fact, provides two models for text about pictures: In his books, some text is in its own separate space, and some is allowed to attach itself to the object being labelled. I suspect that, when children are encouraged to use paper with lines on the bottom, they interpret this as a request to assign distinct text spaces and picture spaces.

*The list—basic*

One of the earliest forms of extended writing is the list of single words that fit into a stated or implied category. The structure of the basic list might look like this:

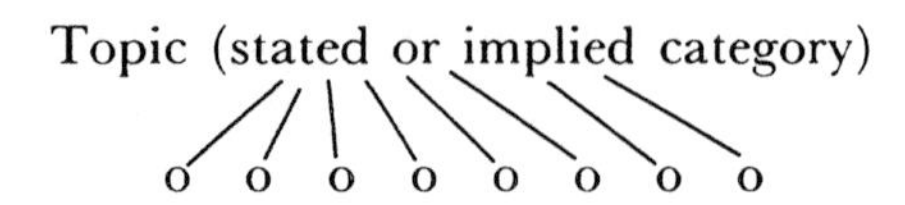


Sarah's first list was a shopping list, written when she was one month shy of five:

*BACN*
*DOg FOOD*
*s.h.n.POO*
*BRAD*
*GM*
*MET*
*TE*
*MEKBOBS [milkbones]*
*UNDRWAR*

This is a single-category list; that is, there is only one principle of categorization—things to buy at the store. In later lists, Sarah set up subcategories within the major category. At age six years, two months, she began writing lists of possible names for the baby that was to be born. In one, she classified the names by sex:

| GIRLS | BOYS |
|---|---|
| *Gina* | *Joseph* |
| *Rachel* | *Joey* |
| *Christie* | *Lowlin* |
| *Sunshine* | *James* |
| | *William* |
| | *Billy* |

Anticipating the birth of the baby, she tried another form of double-category list, in which there was classification *within* the major category. In this list, she noted the names of the children in reverse order of arrival:

*the third* ________
*the second Abby*
*the first me*

A Christmas list written at about the same time was a different sort of double-category list. She ranked her requests in order of preference:

*1. Tape recorder*
*2. Baton*
*3. Speaker*
*4. Calculator with Cover*

Children in one second grade began to use double-category lists to do research in their classrooms. Bradley polled his classmates to see in which months their birthdays fell. Rebecca polled students to see how many teeth each had lost and recorded the results on a chart (Figure 3–2).

These children have discovered the peculiar power of written language to catalog information, to sort it into categories and subcategories. This power is also exploited in the next form to be discussed, the attribute series.

*The attribute series*

In her study of adult-child interactions at reading time, Heath (1982) notes that the parent often expands the child's identification of a picture with a question about an attribute. The parent might first ask, "What's that?" The next question might be "What does the doggie say?" or "What color is the ball?" A similar progression seems to occur in children's writing. The name of an object (or an animal or a person) is followed by a listing of attributes.

At first glance, these attributes seemed to be put down in almost any order; the structure of the attribute series appeared similar to that of the single-category list. But the more I looked at children's attribute series, the more organized they appeared. In fact, it was fairly difficult to locate completely random attribute series where individual statements could be shuffled with no effect on meaning. Susan Sowers (1985b), who first identified this form in children's writing, provides the following example:

*Whales are black and some are gray.*
*Whales are big. They can eat you in one bite.*
*There are brown whales and there are black whales too.*
*There are white whales.*
*There are killer whales. (73)*

Much of this information can be shuffled around, but the child has set up two main categories of information (color and size). The piece could be diagrammed as follows.

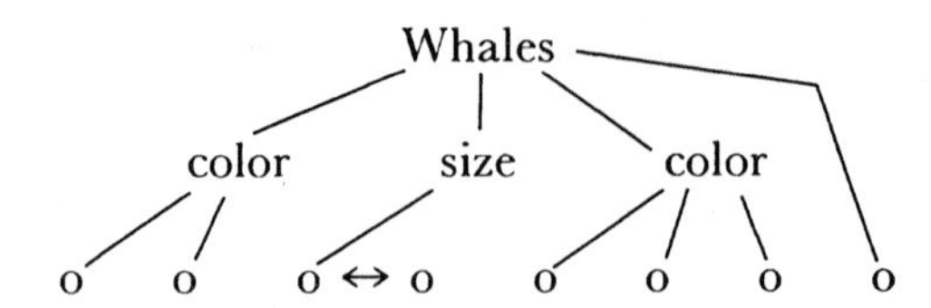


In addition, as the double arrow indicates, the statements "Whales are big. They can eat you in one bite" are logically connected, with the second sentence providing an illustrative example to support the claim made in the first.

In my sample, the following piece on animals was as close to random as any that I collected, but it, too, contains come coherent multiclause units:

*i like birds, cats, dogs, cubs, and some bears. Some water animals are nice to me. I like them and I think that they are very, very cute. Sharks are fish, if you didn't know that now you know that. The whale shark is very harmless to people. A shark does not have any bones. Baby sharks are called pups. The largest fish in the ocean is the whale shark. It can weigh more than an elephant. It's very long. White sharks are the most dangerous sharks of all. When scientists want to learn more about sharks they get close to them.*

In this mostly random listing of facts, the writer has built at least two coherent units:

*Sharks are fish, if you didn't know that now you know that.*
*The largest fish in the ocean is the whale shark. It can weigh more than an elephant. It's very long.*

In the second unit, the child used the same pattern as did the writer of the piece on whales. There is an assertion about the size of the whale shark, followed by two more specific statements about its size.

Writers of nonfiction for young children also use the attribute series. The text for Gyo Fujiawa's *Baby Animals* (1978) is a list of animal characteristics. It begins:

*Baby animals come big and small.*

*They are very young so they like to be petted and snuggled. . .gently.*

*Puppies are fat and funny. Bow! Wow!*

Fujiawa listed attributes, clustered into general categories: The first group of statements describes how young animals look and feel, and the second, how they move. Within each cluster, the order is seemingly random, just as it is random in much of children's early expository writing.

In the pieces on whales and sharks, the children break out of the pure list through the use of what might be called couplets, pairs of statements in which the second is an elaboration—an attribute, a reason, an example—of the first. One major type of couplet is the identification-plus-attribute pattern that seems to be a logical extension of the early labelling that children do. A first grader attempted this pattern in his short report on knives:

[p. 1] *This is my knife.*
[p. 2] *My knife is sharp.*
[p. 3] *This is my Bowie knife.*
[p. 4] *My Bowie knifes are sharp.*

In the next two pieces, we see a more extended use of the identification-plus-attribute pattern:

*This is pluto. It is the furthest planet away from the sun. They thought it was neptunes's moon but it wasn't.*

*This is neptune. It is the second farthest planet away from the sun.*

*This is saturn. It has 10 moons. It has the most rings in the solar system.*

(FIRST GRADER)

LOTS OF HOCKEY EQUIPMENT

*This is a pair of shoulder pads they protect your chest and your shoulders.*

*This is a hockey helmut the bars across your face are for when someone hits you the rest of it is just for your brain.*

*These are knee and shin guards they go under the sox*

*This is a girdle it goes under the long kind of pants like showed on top [arrow to another picture]*

(SECOND GRADER, EXCERPT)

This progression beyond the identifying label to the inclusion of elaborative information is an unmistakable movement toward mature expository prose.

*The initial paragraph*

I classified as an initial paragraph any cluster of three clauses that were coherently related in a nonchronological fashion. Predictably, these clusters first appeared in "hybrid" pieces also containing some single attribute statements and some couplets. The following is an example:

MY DOG

[p. 1] *My dog is black.*
[p. 2] *My dog bites my sister and me when she is excited but she isn't trained.*

[p. 3] *My dog is not all mine. It is my sister's too.*
[p. 4] *My dog's name is Casseopia but we call her Cass for short. Casseopia is a constellation in the sky. You can see it sometimes at night. It is a big "W."*
[p. 5] *We got her at the Dover SPCA.*

(SECOND GRADER, EXCERPT)

Many initial paragraphs begin with a variation of the identification-plus-elaboration pattern of the couplet. In the next example, the writer identifies his gang and then goes on to explain what the gang does:

*The oranutang gang is three boys. Their names are Jaime and Mike and Taylor. We work at recess. If we see a fight We break it up. But if they fight back we tell the teacher.*

(SECOND GRADER, EXCERPT)

A few second graders and many third graders in the sample introduced their initial paragraphs with superordinate terms—words or phrases that name the intent or the idea behind the paragraph. These terms establish an anticipatory frame that helps the reader to understand the information to follow. In adult exposition, these terms are critical ingredients of the openings to paragraphs. One second grader used the terms "ceremony" and "regular" to frame her description of a Brownie meeting:

*We are having a ceremony. This ceremony is not a regular ceremony. It is a ceremony that you light a candle. Then you get a pin and then you do a puppet show. Then we will do flags. Then the troop wile go home.*

Third graders used these terms more frequently and variously. In the next piece, the opening sentence signals the intent of the paragraph. On the previous page, the writer had told about receiving a stuffed Heathcliff for Christmas. She continued:

*Here's a* description. *He is orange with black with stripes and bulging eyes. He has a big black nose and a tongue sticking out the right side as if he is licking his chops. . . .*

Here, the writer used a term to specify the rhetorical intent of the discourse to come. Experienced writers frequently use this technique, relying on terms like "illustration," "example," "reason", "comparison," and "alternative," which function as a language to talk about language, signalling to the reader what comes next.

In another third-grade piece, the writer used the word "tips" to indicate the intent of a paragraph on building a model-train collection:

*Here's some* tips *at keeping your set good. When not in use put a piece of plastic over the set. When your engine is not in use, put the engine in a clean place and set it upside down because if you don't the wheels will be pushed into the engine and jam up and the gears won't work.*

The use of superordinate terms seems to be part of a more general attempt by many third graders to consider the reader:

*Since our story is about a meet, we will tell you what one is. . . .*

*Hi! My name is Robert and I have come to tell you about my Christmas presents. . . .*

In pieces like these, the writer assumes the role of tour guide, ready to take the reader through the information.

Not only do many third graders begin to signal their intentions, they also start to move beyond identification-plus-elaboration to build coherence in a variety of ways. They clarify terms that might be confusing, as in this account of horseback riding:

*Then on my second lesson we started to trot. We had to go on a lunge line.* A lunge line is like a really long leash and you attach the reins to the line. That will take care of steering the horse.

They extend their work through exemplification:

*The best way to start a coin collection is to find lots of pennies. Then you get cardboard folders marked Lincoln pennies at a hobby shop.* Let's say the date is 1964. You look for the hole with the date 1964 under it. You push the penny until you hear the click. Then you do the same with the other pennies.

They extend by providing reasons:

*Melissa and Champion are my cows. I raise beef cattle to show. I love to show cows.* The reason I named Melissa Melissa is that I have a good friend named Melissa. She has beef cattle and taught me everything I know about beef cattle.

They extend by explaining cause and effect:

*We used to have two rabbits but they got away.* Here's how they got away. My sisters opened the cages because she wanted to play with the rabbits, and they got away.

And they extend through specification:

*I learned a lot from doing this report.* I learned different types of cows and behavior and breeds. I learned that cows used to roam wild. I learned what cows are useful for.

The analysis of the sample indicated that, in the first grade, only 16 percent of the pieces were predominantly initial paragraphs. By second grade, this proportion had grown to 34 percent, and, in third grade, to 70 percent.

*Ordered initial paragraphs*

Initial paragraphs often could be reordered without any loss of meaning—there may be no compelling reason why a section on feeding a pet should precede a section on why the pet bites the mailman. Unordered initial paragraphs would be diagrammed as follows:

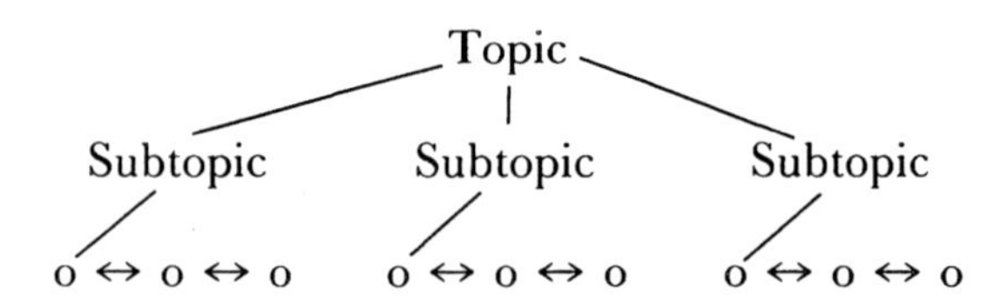


In a few cases, though, the writer was able to relate not only the statements in the initial paragraphs, but the initial paragraphs as well. This piece on the advantages and disadvantages of the writer's brothers is a clear example:

*It's kind of hard to play Tommy's games but he doesn't play for long. Usually Tommy is screaming because his teeth hurt or he is sleeping or eating or he is busy chewing on something. But you can still get him interested in a better game. Or you can read to him.*

*My big brother is hard to play with also because he is either playing at D and D (Dungeons and Dragons) or he is at Robert's house working at the computer or at Funspot which is his favorite place to be. It's hard to play with him. But maybe you can make an appointment. Sometimes I like to go to Funspot with my big brother or play Crossbows and Catapults which is a game.*

*I have some advantages in having an older brother. Like having someone who has the kind of homework that is neat. I get to help Andy a little. Another advantage is when Andy and I get a little older and Andy can take me places if he'll let me drive with him. I think that will be neat. One advantage of having my little brother is I'll have someone to boss around.*

(THIRD GRADER, EXCERPT)

Not only are the initial paragraphs coherent, but the entire piece is built on a pair of contrasts: younger/older brother and advantages/disadvantages. The writer used the connective "also" in the opening to the second paragraph to link it to the first paragraph. The word "advantages" functions as a key connective; it indicates that the shift from the "disadvantages" mentioned in the first two paragraphs and helps the reader anticipate and interpret the information included in the third. Yet, despite its complexity, I believe that it is possible to view this excerpt as an extended and elaborated list.

## CASE STUDY—BEAU

Do the categories just described really characterize the path taken by beginning writers? To answer that question (or, at least, to begin to answer it), I selected the writing folder of one first grader, Beau Lee, to examine in more detail. Beau attended first grade at Kamehameha Elementary School and was placed in the "upper middle" reading group. Until January, students worked on their writing in the morning, when the teacher was occupied primarily with reading instruction and children rotated every twenty minutes. After the New Year, writing was shifted to the forty-five-minute period following the lunch hour.

Beau was one of several students who preferred to write informational pieces. Before the New Year shift, little distinguished his work from that of the other boys; they all wrote about the giant car-crushing vehicles, Bigfoot and The Animal (see illustration in the previous chapter). While Beau did produce some labels early in the year, he generally extended his writing beyond the label. On November 8, he wrote under the inevitable picture of Bigfoot, "I have a truck named Bigfoot and he is big and blue." In December, he produced another identification-plus-attribute combination—"This is a Turbo-Animal and he is bigger than Bigfoot." In a more extensive example of this form, Beau wrote on two consecutive pages:

[p. 1] *I have a toy named the animal.*
[p. 2] *The animal can go up a mountain with his big claws.*

Beau also wrote about movies that he had seen, developing a consistent pattern for these reviews: a) identify movie; b) state your reaction; and c) tell something about what happened. He used this formula twice:

*I saw a Ninja movie and it was fun to see The good guys was fighting the bad guys*

*I saw the movie Breaking and it was bad I saw ozn[?] and todr[?] and they was breaking.*

During this Bigfoot period, I can remember thinking that Beau and his fellow enthusiasts were not making much progress because they always wrote on the same topic. Only after reviewing his folder did I see that he was not standing still during this period; as Hilliker (1988) demonstrated in her study of kindergarten students, Beau was experimenting within his chosen theme, exploring ways of going beyond the identifying label, and setting the stage for the great burst that was to come in the New Year.

In January, along with a longer writing period, the children had access to a different kind of paper. Instead of paper lined only in the bottom half, they now could use paper that was entirely lined. This seemed to make a difference. Beau and his classmates, I believe, took this as a cue to write more, to fill up all the lines, to experience the satisfaction of producing a long piece of writing. Beau changed in another way as well: he began to write more nonfiction, focusing particularly on what his parents bought him. In February, he wrote "My Two Posters":

*I have two posters. One is a checkerboard and one is a turbo and the turbo one has the years. The one that I like the best is the checkerboard one because it is pink and black. The turbo poster is almost like the checkerboard and my dad brought it for me. My dad bought it at Mexico. It is nice.*

This production, juxtaposing the descriptions of two posters, is considerably more complex than his earlier pieces. But we can still see the same general-to-specific pattern that Beau applied in his Bigfoot pieces. He moves from mentioning that he received two posters, to identifying them, then to giving information about each.

Attempting a double description in another of his longer pieces, written in March, Beau created an incredible circumlocution to avoid repetition:

*I watched wheel warriors this morning and it was good. I have a wheel warrior and its name is Armefors and it's gray and black and gold. And the other day I got another wheel warrior and its name is saw warrior and the one that I told before after I told the name was the color the color was the same. My dad bought it for me.*

Beau appealed to the reader to return to the earlier text to retrieve information needed to describe the second road warrior.

Beau's most extensive piece of writing that year was a self-assigned report on humpback whales. The structure of this piece is similar to the hybrid pieces mentioned in the previous section:

*These are humpback whales and they live way out in the sea. They have lines on the bottom. They weigh 100 pounds. Their color is gray. They eat krill and little things. In the earliest winter they get babies and December is when they get babys. They live in the atlantic ocean. No other animal is bigger than a whale. I know that when the water is getting hot the whale goes to colder waters and when the water gets cold they go to warmer waters. I saw the whals by binoculars and I went with my auntie and my dad, [he] let me use the binoculars.*

In this report, there are several identifiable clusters of statements—about physical features of the whale, having babies, and migration. Other information, particularly the statement "No other animal is bigger than a whale," seems to have strayed from its cluster. The piece is an impressive extension of the writing that Beau did during the first part of the year. And his writing does seem to develop along the path that I outlined in the previous section.

## BEYOND STRUCTURE

While this analysis has focused on the structure of children's writing, it is important to acknowledge that good informational writing is not merely well structured. The rhetorician James Kinneavy (1972) has identified "surprise value" as one of the principal features of informative writing. As readers, we expect informative writing to tell us something new. This new information may contradict other information that we have heard or read, it may amuse us, or it may shock us. Consider, for example, the following notation for January 15, Martin Luther King, Jr.'s Birthday, on a calendar:

*Dr. Charles Richard Drew, an expert in the preservation of blood plasma, is asked to organize World War II blood bank programs for both the United States and Great Britain. He also supervises the American Red Cross blood donor program. But because of the existing segregation laws, Drew, who is black, is barred from donating his own blood.*

Chances are that we will remember this notation because the revelation of the last sentence is so disturbing.

Unfortunately, many of the expository paragraphs to which students are exposed in their skill work lack precisely this surprise value. They may test out at the appropriate reading level, but their very blandness makes them difficult to remember. For example, this paragraph comes from one of the best-selling reading series:

*Fruits, vegetables, and grain are all food grown in soil. Fruits and vegetables can be eaten cooked or raw. Grains are usually ground into flour and used in making bread. All are good sources of vitamins. Grains are also a good source of protein. (Skillpack: Ride the Sunrise, Level 12, 1985, p. 45)*

Do fourth graders, for whom this passage is intended, really need to be told that fruits and vegetables are food? Does any child who has ever eaten an apple need to be told that fruits can be eaten raw? It should also be noted that the paragraph is structured very much like Beau's report on whales. It is a collection of information in three clusters—where the food grows; how it is eaten; what food value it has—that could be rearranged without any damage to overall sense. As one fourth grader astutely observed, "I bet they write these things just so they can ask us questions about them."

One of the challenges of teaching exposition is to help students understand the surprise value of their information. Lucy Calkins (1983) recounts a very useful method for helping students assess surprise value. A group of fourth graders, after doing the initial reading on their separate topics, each had to teach their classmates what they had learned. Birger, who had chosen squirrels, reported to the class that squirrels' bodies "click" when they are too cold. The class was fascinated and asked, "Why do they click?" Birger explained that the click helps raise the body temperature of the squirrel. The response to his new and unexpected information on the click taught Birger about surprise value. His listeners were far more interested in the click than they were in learning that squirrels are usually brown or gray and that they live in trees.

Another important issue in informational writing is the use (or misuse) of written sources. When students begin to write reports based on information from books, they face the temptation of plagiarism: The sources provide the information so well that any change in the language seems like a degradation. I have found that the text often holds such sway that students have trouble breaking away from it. The apparent sophistication of their reports reflects the texts they use and not the analysis they have done. The sources use the student rather than the student using the sources.

The teacher's task is to create situations where students must transform the information in the sources. The typical report assignment makes this transformation difficult because the student is asked to create a text very similar to the sources; the student report is a junior version of an encyclopedia entry. This being the case, students are reluctant to diverge much from the source, since it is the model that they have been told to emulate.

There are several ways to facilitate the transformation of information:

1. Change the audience. Children who read encyclopedia-type sources could be asked to rework this information into a book for very young children.
2. Change the form. Children could be asked to use information drawn from factual sources in stories (see Wilde, 1988), pamphlets, or scripts for radio broadcasts (which could be recorded on a tape recorder).
3. Change the purpose. Students could use information that they've gathered to persuade people of a point of view. For example, in the following piece, the writer uses her new knowledge of killer whales to argue that they should not be kept in captivity:

   *One awful thing to think about is—what is it like to be in captivity? You see the Orca jump and perform for thousands of people only because someone signaled him to do it. But have you ever seen the killer whale when he's not performing. He's slowly swimming around, not able to use his sonar and get the different and interesting sounds of home, but only able to get the same sharp and boring vibrations of the cement tank. But not only is his sound world gone—his beautiful dorsal fin is now flabby and drooped with no beauty anymore. In his tank he doesn't get enough exercise to keep it high and erect like an Orca in the wild.*

   *Next time you see a marine animal perform for lots of people ask yourself, "Would you give up the free glistening waters of home for this?" (Chittenden, 1982, 49–50)*

   Peggy, the author of this piece, clearly knows a great deal about killer whales, particularly about the importance of sound to their navigation. But, rather than simply reporting this information, she has *used* it, transformed it for her own purpose—which is to persuade us that these whales suffer from their captivity.
4. Change the nature of the source. If students must gain much of their information from interviews, the very act of taking notes is an act of transformation—turning speech into

writing. Susan Benedict (1985) provides a good description of this process among second graders.

5. Have students explain what they have learned without looking at their notes. Calkins (1983) reports on this procedure in a fourth-grade class. After extensive library research, students had to study their notes and then put them away and write what they had learned.

In "The Analytic Language of John Wilkins" (1953), South American writer Jorge Louis Borges calls our attention to a (fictional) Chinese encyclopedia, entitled "The Celestial Emporium of Benevolent Knowledge":

*On these pages it is written that animals are divided into (a) those that belong to the emperor, (b) embalmed ones, (c) those that are trained, (d) suckling pigs, (e) mermaids, (f) fabulous ones, (g) stray dogs, (h) those not included in this classification, (i) those that tremble as they are mad, (j) innumerable ones, (k) those drawn with a fine camel's hair brush, (l) others, (m) those that have not broken a vase, (n) those that resemble flies from a distance. (103)*

Borges clearly is poking fun at attempts to catalog the world's contents. But pretentious as this passion for inventory might be, it is one that begins early—when the two-year-old embarks on the interminable game of "whazat?" By identifying the incremental moves that children make from "whazat" toward mature expository prose, we will be better able to assist this development. And, by naming the forms that children use, we will begin to possess a vocabulary to discuss their progress. In this learning process, we are really no different from the children we describe: We, too, must begin by labelling.

# 4
# Archimedes' dream

This chapter is about children and the language of influence. And it begins at bedtime—not in those idyllic moments when our children are comfortably in our arms following the bedtime story, but in the more chaotic times before and after, with the rich array of delaying tactics that children employ to prolong the day. Children show themselves to be master rhetoricians in the home, borrowing patterns of argument from their parents and using them to conquer.

The following story illustrates what might be called the rhetoric of bedtime. Sarah, age three, was tucked in bed at the usual time, 8:15. Just as my wife and I settled down in the living room, Sarah appeared at the top of the stairs. She needed a glass of water, which we got for her. After that, she appeared at the top of the stairs at about ten-minute intervals, with a different problem each time. Her pajamas itched. Her room was too dark. She'd forgotten to kiss us good night. She had forgotten to kiss the dog good night. Each time there was a reason for her appearance; she never said that she simply didn't want to go to sleep. After solving each so-called problem, we sent her back to her room, telling her, a little more sternly each time, that it was way past her bedtime. At 9:30, she appeared again.

"Sarah, go back to bed."

"But Mommy, I can't."

"Why can't you?"

Then, very earnestly, "I've got a question."

"Well, all right, come down and ask your question."

Sarah made her way down the stairs and walked slowly up to her mother.

"Well," Beth asked, "What's your question?"

Sarah paused, obviously thinking fast, and then said, "How you doin'?"

Obviously this is the story of two parents conned by a three-year-old. But why were they conned? First, the child understands the exception rule: The household runs on sets of rules that are to some degree negotiable; when two systems of rules conflict, negotiation determines which system prevails. Bedtime rules specify times for teeth brushing, bedtime reading, and lights out. But other sets of rules can be called on to suspend these bedtime rules temporarily—the child can appeal to the physical-discomfort rule (being thirsty, too hot, too cold, itchy, and so on), which takes precedence. The appeal is to a hierarchy of values in which one system overrules another.

But the final "I've got a question" ploy is even more subtle. I believe that Sarah used this opening successfully because of the conversation rule. Parents often are reluctant to cut off conversation initiated by their children, particularly when children pose a question. If the parent answers the question, the child may ask a second and third one. And Sarah understood, I believe, that the alternative—refusing to entertain a question—violated the norms of conversation. And even a refusal to answer would continue the conversation, prompting the question, "Why can't I ask you a question?"

The following bedtime exchange between Abby (at age five) and her mother is another example of the conversation rule. Abby is in her room, and it is lights-out time.

BETH: Abby, when I come in your room, there's no more talk.
ABBY: But, Mom, can I tell you just one more thing?
BETH: OK, what? [*Abby tells.*]
[*A few minutes later*]
ABBY: Mom?
BETH: Quiet, Abby, no talk or I'll leave.
ABBY: But, Mom, it's OK because it's what were talking about before.

The parent clearly is unwilling to impose silence at the price of refusing to hear information. Abby also exploits the vagueness of the ground rules by claiming that her continued conversation is consistent with Beth's allowing her to "tell [her] just one more thing."

Language stories like these suggest that young children—even before they enter school—can be very adept at argument, particularly in the use of what Stephen Toulmin (1969) calls "warrants." According to Toulmin, the most basic argument, "*a* because of *b*," rests on a warrant that allows us to connect *a* and *b*. If Sarah says "I should have a candy bar because Andy had one," the validity of her claim rests on our willingness to accept the warrant stating that, if one child gets a treat, they all should. If, instead, she makes the statement, "Give me a candy bar because I want one," she asks us to accept the warrant that whatever she wants she should get—an unlikely prospect.

This all may seem like straightforward logic, but Toulmin wants to distinguish argument from logic—indeed, he wants to prove that a good argument is not one that adheres to some universal standard of logic but one that is accepted as persuasive by a particular community. "I should have a candy bar because Andy had one" is no more logical than "Give me a candy bar because I want one," but the first is built on a warrant that is generally accepted in our family and the second is not.

Surprisingly, there has been very little research on the types of arguments that children have with adults. I say "surprisingly" because, in these exchanges, children demonstrate their understanding of the warrants that can be used to influence adults. Such arguments show children moving—at a very early age—beyond the egocentric "I want it because I want it" to reasoning that reveals an awareness of family norms. We can also see in them the seeds of deliberative abilities that, one day, will (or can) be used in school discussions and school writing.

One difficulty in studying family arguments is that, unlike bedtime reading, they do not occur at specified times but unpredictably, at any time during the day. My wife and I tried to write down exchanges that occurred during a two-week period. These transcriptions are not verbatim, but they do reflect the nature of the warrants used by the two younger children in our family, Abby (age five years, ten months) and Andrew (three years, three months). I'll report on five exchanges.

*Exchange 1.* I am heating water for my morning coffee, and Andrew asks me to make him some scrambled eggs.

TOM: I'll cook you scrambled eggs after I have my coffee.
ANDREW: You can cook when you gettin' you coffee.

In this exchange, I am trying to put off cooking Andrew's breakfast by claiming that I can do only one thing at a time. Andrew responds by denying the inevitability of this one-thing-at-a-time argument. No doubt, he is already aware that this type of argument—promising to attend to a request after I finish something—is perceived by his older sister as a delaying tactic. It is one that she turns back on her parents at bedtime, and she uses it in the next exchange.

*Exchange 2.* Abby is sitting in an armchair reading a catalog, even though her mother has told her a number of times to clean up her room, a task that she always does very reluctantly.

BETH: Abby, com'on. It's time to clean up.
ABBY [*continuing to read her catalog*]: Mom, you know what Katie's idea is? Once you start something, you have to finish it.

There are at least two tactics at work here. There is the "conversation rule," which Beth must break by refusing to respond to a question if she is to get immediate action on her request. More tellingly, Abby is able to justify continuing to read the catalog by citing a principle that both Beth and I use when it is to our advantage. The next move for the parent is difficult. There is the possibility of a pure power move—"Just do it, don't argue." Or the parent can show that the class of action in which the child is engaged is not covered by the norm that she is citing (that is, it refers only to jobs). Soon the angels begin dancing on the heads of pins.

*Exchange 3.* Andrew's two sisters are playing in Sarah's room, and Andrew, just in from outside, wants to jump on Sarah's bed.

ANDREW: I going to jump on Sarah bed.
BETH: No, you can't.
ANDREW: I going to take my boots off.
BETH: You can't jump on Sarah's bed. You can only jump on the bed upstairs.
ANDREW: I going to *sit* on Sarah bed.

To explain this exchange, some information on house rules is needed. Children *are* allowed to bounce on the upstairs bed if their shoes are off, but they can't bounce on Sarah's bed at all. What's interesting is the way that Andrew anticipates the objection that he believes Beth will make—"you can't bounce on the bed with your boots on"—by saying that he will take off his boots. This "disarming" move might also be viewed as additional evidence that young children are not as egocentric as is frequently claimed. Andrew's argument is not egocentric but sociocentric; he grounds his request on a family norm, not solely on a personal wish.

*Exchange 4.* Andrew and Abby are both seated in the big armchair in the living room, and Andrew is screaming that Abigail took his book. Since Abigail has the book, it appears that Andrew's complaint is justified.

TOM: Who had it first?
ABBY: Andy, but I brought it down first. I had it on the sofa and I brought it over here.

This is one of many wrangles that Abby and Andy have over access to common property (particularly the new armchair). In this case, the book in question is indeed Andrew's and, technically, not common property, although Abby's argument tries to place it in that category. Her argument revolves around the ambiguity of the "first" in my question. In more explicit terms, her argument would go like this: If, by "first," you mean immediately previous to my reading it, then the answer is Andy. But a more reasonable definition of "first" would be who brought it down to the living room first and who read it first in the living room. According to this new definition of "first," I had it first and am therefore entitled to read it—even if that means taking it from Andy.

*Exchange 5.* In this exchange, I am in the dining room, and Abby is yelling at me from the living room.

BETH: Abby, get off your bum and go talk to Daddy.
ABBY: But Sarah yells from her bed.
SARAH: But that's when I wasn't awake yet.

Here, we have one of the many appeals to precedent that all three of the children consistently make. Abby's justification is that we have established a precedent for yelling from room to room because we have allowed Sarah to do this. Sarah counters by redefining the precedent—she only does this when she is waking up.

In these arguments from precedent, our children are at their most jurisprudential, and disputes are frequently complex. A key factor is, of course, age; the younger child in the dispute will use the precedent argument to gain parity with an older sibling. The older sibling will use precedent to maintain ascendancy.

Abby might argue that, if Sarah has a sleepover, she should have one; Sarah would respond that, if Abby has one, she should have five. But age is a factor only in certain types of disputes, usually those involving privileges; in others, those involving presents or the provision of candy, all of the children have equal rights. Problems arise when decisions do not fit neatly into one of these categories—for example, is it "fair" for Abby to be taken to the movies as often as Sarah? Is going to a movie a present or a privilege?

Finally, there is the question of what constitutes a precedent. One morning when I was in charge of breakfast, Sarah asked me if she could have a Pepsi with her breakfast. At the time, I was in the middle of a *Boston Globe* story on the Celtics, and I said that she could. Bad judgment, certainly, but did this establish a precedent? Sarah would like to claim that it did, but both my wife and I would claim that it was a special case that had no bearing on future requests. As children begin to spend more time outside the home, they begin to cite other precedents, the privileges of other children their own age. Sarah, for example, argued for pierced ears simply by listing all of the girls in her class who had them. Our response—until we gave in—was that this line of argument was not valid because it doesn't matter what other people do.

I do not mean to suggest that our household works as a parliamentary democracy or that this description of arguments is representative of other families, and I especially do not propose that our system is ideal. I do believe, though, that households, and particularly those with more than one child, are complex places. Some sets of rules hold for all children; some differ according to the child's age. Indeed, some forms of argument may be permissible for boys and not for girls. And, as children grow older, these rules are subject to almost continual amendment, continual discussion, in a continual attempt to come up with something "fair." From my experience, children learn to win some of these negotiations at an alarmingly early age.

## REGULATIVE WRITING

The early persuasive writing that children do obviously is not as elaborated as the family arguments quoted above, but children soon come to understand that certain types of written language hold power that oral language lacks. For example, to write one's name on a school notebook is to lay claim to it; the written name defines ownership in a way that oral language cannot. An octagonal sign declaring "Stop" causes us to bring our multi-ton cars to a stop. The child learns early that signing names to documents (for example, endorsing checks) is legally significant.

Part of the power of written language comes from the separation of the writer from the text. A human being can engage in dialogue; a written text cannot. As Plato said in *The Phaedrus*, when you "ask written texts what they mean, they simply return the same answer over and over again" (1973, 97). Plato saw this as a limitation of writing (although, paradoxically, his objection is written), but writing plainly gains authority *because* it returns the same answer over and over again. If we are motioned to stop by a policeman, we can ask him why. But the stop sign just says "Stop."

One of the most elegant demonstrations of the power that language gains by being separated from its creator occurred in the movie *The Wizard of Oz*. The wizard, for most of the movie, is only heard, a powerful, confident voice. But, at one point, while the voice is resounding, Dorothy's dog, Toto, pulls back a screen, revealing a short, fat man, who is producing the voice through a trick of amplification. The wizard, realizing that he is discovered, tries one last ploy, saying, "Pay no attention to that man speaking into the microphone." Written language, too, might be seen as a trick of amplification; it gains power by being separated from the human author. It says the same thing day and night—far more assured that the fallible human who wrote it.

In *The Development of Writing Abilities, 11–18* (1975), James Britton and his associates make a useful distinction between "regulative" discourse and "persuasive" discourse. Regulative discourse is defined as "language which lays down a course of action to be followed, makes demands, and issues instruction where compliance is assumed"; persuasive discourse is "writing which attempts to influence action, behaviour or attitude in cases where compliance cannot be assumed" (218). Not surprisingly, Britton and his colleagues found little regulative writing in the schoolwork of the eleven- to eighteen-year-olds they studied. Young children, however, are attracted to regulative writing, particularly insofar as it helps them to secure rights to their property. Regulative writing might be viewed as a preliminary form of persuasive writing.

Aside from writing their names on possessions, children often use writing to assert control over space—usually, their rooms. After a bedtime dispute, Abigail placed the following sign on her door:

*DADKTGOiNMiROHM*

*Dad can't go in my room.*

I asked her whether that meant that I couldn't tuck her in at night. She didn't say anything but added "NOK" to the sign. The next day, after another argument, she crossed out the "NOK." On another keep-out sign, she listed the people who could come in her room. This limited-admission policy was also evident in a sign that Sarah's friends once made for a yet-to-be-constructed clubhouse: "Old Boys 2$ 50c," a price designed to keep the unwanted group out.

At other times, Sarah used regulative language to lay claim not to territory, but to her rights. I had returned after a week-long trip, and it was past Sarah's bedtime. She had placed a sign on the door to the house:

*Go up to my room and bring the present*

In this case, she accurately determined that she was in a position to assume compliance and so did not have to use the requesting language that she used in situations where compliance was not assured.

Some signs, however, combine the regulative and the persuasive; for example, "Slow—Children at Play." Even the standard railroad-crossing sign might be viewed as an admonition to be careful indicated by the shape of the sign accompanied by a reason (the symbol of the tracks on the sign). On one of her keep-out signs, Sarah (at age nine) added "I'll turn out the lights myself" to counter the only possible objection that she could imagine. Paul Bissex's keep-out sign, quoted in Chapter 1, is another example of regulative language shifting to persuasive language, for he offers a reason—"GNYS AT WRK"—to justify his command "DO NAT DSTRB" (see Bissex, 1980).

All of these examples of regulative writing have occurred in or around the home; there are school applications, however. One first-grade teacher encouraged her students, early in the year, to make signs to hang on the classroom walls. One student wrote:

*Stop and walk. Keep running outside.*

The teacher speculated that creating these signs helped students become more comfortable with school rules.

When they write rules and keep-out signs, children are indicating authority in a fairly overt way. But there are other forms where the authority of the writer is not displayed so directly. In some cases, the child uses what John Searle (1970) would call an indirect speech act. If I say to my wife, "Are you through with the paper?" I am not really asking a question, I am requesting that she pass the paper over to me if she is done. Regulative language, then, may not take the form of a command but may still assert rights. One day, Maggie, a kindergarten student, taped a sign to the playdough table:

*IHIVANT HAD A TR IN PAD*

*I haven't had a turn in playdough.*

Her statement is not simply informative: Through an indirect speech act, she is laying claim to her turn.

Other messages are backed by the authority of the writer. For example, I frequently leave a note for my wife if I am going out. The messages are very simple—when I expect to be back and, sometimes, where I've gone. Yet these notes presuppose that I have the right to go out without asking permission or giving an explanation. Without being aware of it, I am asserting certain prerogatives, assuming compliance with my decision to go out. The authority implicit in these notes became apparent to me only when Sarah began to write them. One day, I came home from work and found a note in Sarah's handwriting taped to the door:

*I Wel Be Back at 5:00*

When she got back at 5:00, I asked her if her mother had said that she could go out, and Sarah said no. Her note shows not only that she had developed the encoding skills necessary to compose it but that she understands the presumed authority of the writer of such notes.

Other documents take on the power of the institutions that issue them. I remember that, as a child, I was afraid of losing (or even bending) my report card on the way home. The arbitrary, unexplained grades and checks that it contained made it all the more authoritative, far *solider* that anything that might be said at a teacher-student conference, which seemed unmysterious and bland by comparison. Sarah frequently would imitate grade reports and the certificates of accomplishment passed out in her gymnastics class:

*Jenesdes ov the Wek [Gymnast of the week]*
*Dae*
*Name*
*Kep Yaor Had pu [Keep your head up]*
*You have bin Asin to LaVl Toe [You have been assigned to level 2]*

In some of her letters to her friends, she would take on the role of teacher, evaluating their work:

*Dear Carey*

*I like the numbers that you or Tammy wrote. I like your printing. I have a plan. You write or give this message to Tammy. She did very well on her whole name. You did only your first name but you did OK. I am having a raffle at my house.*

In the last sentence, she shifts from her "teacher" role to her "friend" role.

These examples suggest that children naturally attend to and appropriate the regulative language around them. And this is hardly surprising, for they, like us, swim in it. But, because we have been swimming longer, we fail to notice how pervasive it is.

## REGULATION TO RHETORIC

In order to make requests, children need to determine when they can expect automatic compliance and when they cannot. We do not expect very young children to do this—everything that they say can sound like a command. But many parents begin to enforce a distinction when their children are about three years old, which leads to dialogues like this:

CHILD: Give me a glass of milk.
PARENT: Now, is that the way you're supposed to ask?
CHILD: Can I have a glass of milk?
PARENT: That's better.

These exchanges teach children that compliance is contingent upon the use of the proper request form.

From the time Sarah began writing, she was able to determine which situations required request forms and which, like the note to me after the trip, did not. In the fall of her first-grade year, I visited a private school where children did a great deal of writing. After the trip, I described the school to Sarah, and she wrote to the teacher, Judy Egan:

*Dear Judy*

*My Daddy told me about your class's spelling. I would like it if you would write a letter to me. My name's Sarah.*

A month later, Sarah, now calling herself "Sally," made a similar request to Kelly, a third grader:

*Dear Kelly*

*Soon will you write a letter to each other.*

*Love Sally Newkirk*

Both letters are considerably different in tone from the letter that she wrote to her friends grading them on their handwriting. In the letter to Judy, she appropriately uses a conditional—"would like"—and a subjective—"would write." In the letter to Kelly she signals her request appropriately with "will."

I contend that the request is a bridge to persuasive writing because requests often cannot rely on requesting language alone—they must also include reasons why the request should be granted. In her most extensive request, written to her friend Carey, Sarah took another step on that bridge. A fire at Sarah's school had required all of the children to be bussed to a school in another part of town. Sarah wrote the letter because Carey had been sitting with some other children.

*Please can you sit with Sarah Newkirk on the bus. Deep down in side we are the same. We are close friends. I hope you will accept my suggestion. Please, oh, please can you sit [with me].*

Here, Sarah does more than ask Carey to sit with her; she gives two reasons to strengthen her request—they are friends, and "deep down inside [they] are the same." Present in this request-plus-reasons form is, I believe, the basic argument structure.

The next example illustrates a student modifying language that is regulative (and inappropriate), revising it into a proper request. Greg, a first grader, was angry at children from an adjacent classroom who had been throwing paper under his classroom door and disrupting class. Greg first asked if he could go over to the offending classroom and tell the guilty students to stop. His teacher told him that he could not interrupt the other class but could send a note. He agreed. His first version:

*You are hereby ordered to stop throwing stuff under the door.*

When his teacher read the note, she asked Greg whether he thought that it would persuade the students to stop. After rereading what he had written, he decided that it wouldn't and produced a second version:

*Dear Miss ———*

*Would you please stop your kids from throwing thing under the door.*

While Greg recognized that this version was an improvement

over the first, he used deletions and insertions to make one more version:

*Dear Miss ———*

*Would you please ask your students to stop throwing things under the door. They are bothering us.*

In this final version, Greg softened his request even more (the teacher is to *ask* her students to stop and not simply to tell them to stop). And, significantly, he added a reason for his request.

Children attempt other forms of persuasion when they apologize for misdeeds or make excuses. The standard apology contains three components: an admission of improper behavior; an expression of regret for this behavior; and a request for forgiveness. To these might be added a fourth component—a promise not to misbehave again. The three basic elements were present in a letter that Sarah, at five years, two months, wrote to Beth after getting into her sewing materials, which were strictly off-limits:

*Dear Mom*

*I'm sorry for getting into your stuff. Don't be mad. I love Beth*

This letter is reminiscent of the apology quoted in Chapter 1 ("Tim, I love you. You are a good father. I am sorry that I said, 'go home'"). In both, much of the force of argument lies in the expression of regret.

The excuse similarly acknowledges a transgression of rules but also cites contributing reasons that, presumably, will be recognized as valid. A late excuse, also quoted in Chapter 1, is an example:

*I [am] here now. [I had to do] things for mom. And the clock went off on [the] wrong time. [That's] why I am late.*

*Signed Shawn*

Shawn acknowledged that he had been late but tried to convince the teacher that this was due to circumstances beyond his control. We see a similar structure in another popular genre, the letter to the tooth fairy explaining the loss of a tooth. Addie, a second grader, wrote the following letter above a drawing of a tooth dripping blood:

*Dear tooth farry my too fell out*
*But i can't find it.*
*thee only thing i know is that grammy was here. And she had my tooth and when she left we could not find it*

*From adrienne kathleen rule*

This is a more legalistic letter. Addie states that there is an adult witness who might verify, and is probably responsible for, the loss. In one of her tooth-fairy letters, Sarah simply asked the tooth fairy to look in her mouth to verify the loss (see Figure 4–1).

The "for sale" signs that accompany the various capitalistic enterprises children launch provide another example of a move toward persuasive language. Taylor (1983) describes in some detail a sign developed by the children that she was studying. A group of eight-year-olds had decided to sell ice water on a hot summer day. Their sign read:

*ice water*
*One dime each glass*

A twelve-year-old, Kate, seeing that they weren't getting any customers, revised the sign to read:

*ice cold water*
*3 for 25*
*VERY GOOD FOR YOU* *DOESN'T ROT TEETH LIKE LEMONADE*

When this version still attracted no customers, Kate went home and brought back a pitcher of lemonade. One of the eight-year-olds turned over the sign, and Kate wrote:

*ICE COLD LEMONADE*
*10c*

FIGURE 4–1 *Sarah's letter to the tooth fairy*

Some adults, passing the stand, now bought some lemonade. As one customer walked away, the younger children gathered around the sign, giggling. They were changing the sign to read:

*ICE COLD LEMONADE*
*5c*

After this final change, the children lost interest in selling lemonade. Taylor concludes that the process of marketing the product interested them far more than the actual selling.

The same could be said for most of Sarah's signs (and, for that matter, most of her early writing). It was making them that she enjoyed, particularly when she could do so beside her mother. Her lemonade sign, "Just for 10c and if you a tad more," was never used. Neither was the sign for a cheerleading exhibition:

| | |
|---|---|
| *Cheleten* | *Cheerleading* |
| *11Pm Entremesun 2PM* | *11PM Intermission 2PM* |
| *ThaA's fun in The ara* | *There's fun in the air* |

These signs normally are not thought of as school writing, but, in Ellen Blackburn Karelitz's first-grade class, children invented a genre of advertisement writing. Several children had built towers with cusinare rods. Karelitz asked them to count the rods and determine the "cost" of their towers. When they were done, they posted the price, and she suggested that they write an advertisement that might sell the towers. The children acted out the commercial for the class and answered questions about the merchandise. This incident started a miniboom in advertisement writing. One girl, who rarely wrote stories, cut out a large photograph of a flower, mounted it, and around it wrote:

*This flower is good because it grows ten times faster than the [ordinary] flower.*

Another child sold a city—containing eighty washing machines, twenty dryers, and two thousand parks—for $200,000,308.99. Another example (Figure 4–2) shows an insect that resembles Gonzo of the Muppetts. The text:

*If you don't buy me I will have a temper tantrum. He chases cockroaches away. He is twice the size of a cockroach.*
*At Bradlee's*
*Buy it.*

These children have been exposed to so much advertising that they easily appropriate the persuasive techniques of copywriting.

FIGURE 4–2 *"Buy Me" note*

According to the model developed by Britton and his associates to analyze writing, persuasive and regulative writing belong to the general category of "transactional" writing, the language used to get things done. Transactional writing is believed to develop out of speechlike expressive writing that is "relatively undifferentiated" (Rosen and Rosen, 1973, 95). Yet the samples I have included in this section are striking in their differentiation; children seem to be able to differentiate the request from the demand, the apology from the excuse, and they are clearly capable of understanding the kinds of language and reasoning used in advertisements. In the next section, I will examine ways in which these initial forms of persuasion are developed into longer arguments.

## THE LITANY

As might be expected, when children try to write arguments longer than the assertion-plus-reason couplet, they employ an old friend—the list. Philip, a kindergartner, was familiar with the itemized bills that his father sent out. He used one of his father's bill forms to itemize complaints about his mother—and to charge her for her misdeeds (Figure 4–3). In one third-grade

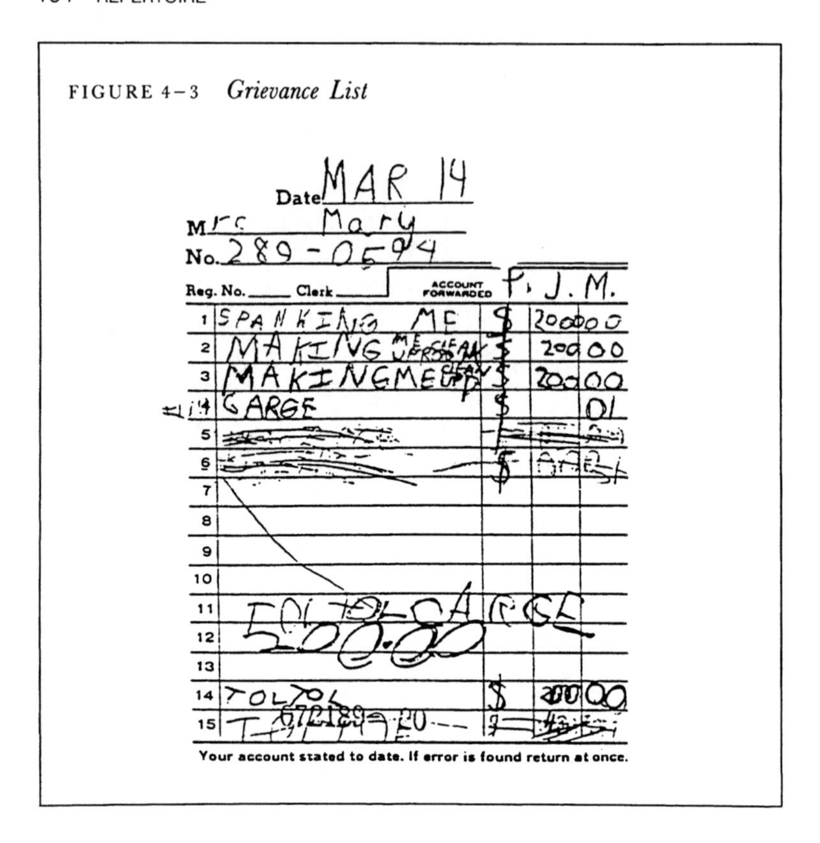

Date MAR 14
Mrs Mary
No. 289-0594
Reg. No. ___ Clerk ___ ACCOUNT FORWARDED P. J. M.
1 SPANKING ME $ 2000 00
2 MAKING ME CLEAN $ 200 00
3 MAKING ME CLEAN UP $ 200 00
4 GARGE $ 01
11 TOLTOL GARGE
12 500.00
14 TOLTOL $ 200 00
Your account stated to date. If error is found return at once.

FIGURE 4–3 *Grievance List*

classroom, the boys began writing lists of reasons for their likes and dislikes, accompanied by lists of ways to enforce these preferences. There were, for example, "25 Ways to terrorize your sister or brother's room during a Slumber Party," "80 ways to Torture a Dream Baby," "Why I Hate Girl Cabbage Patch Kids and Like Boys," and "10 Bad things About MY Brother," which begins:

1. *He always wakes me up early on Saturday and Sunday morning when I was trying to sleep.*
2. *He takes my things that he says are his even if he knows there mine.*
3. *He always gets things his own way accept for several things.*
4. *He uses things of mine when I tell him not two*
5. *He never lets me look at his toys and never shares them.*

One of the most elaborated of these pieces was the heartfelt "My Stupid Sister":

*My stupid sister is clumsy. Yesterday she busted the channel-changer and it's stick on nick. because of my sister we can't watch TV for a month.*

*My sister tried to jump rope in the house. She has broken; 3 glasses, 2 light bulbs, and my dad's glasses. She feeds the cat 10 times a day (wich is pretty stupid because our cat is begining to look like fat albert). Another bad thing about my sister is that she loves to eat and when she can't find her favorite food she yells LOUD! and if she doesn't get it in the next 10 seconds she cries and if that doesn't work she gives up. My sister also lies any time she can She has lied about liking dinner 749 times. She also lies about eating her lunch (I know this because when she comes home she is starving). My sister is also a hot shot she shows off all the time (and every time she does it I feel dumb).*

This carefully nursed grievance is expressed through a complex argument that cites specific evidence to support general complaints. The layers of this argument:

Top-Level Assertion: My sister is stupid
- First midlevel assertion: She is clumsy.
  - Evidence: She broke the channel changer.
  - Evidence: She jumped rope in the house and broke a number of things.
- Second midlevel assertion (implied): She acts foolishly with the cat.
  - Evidence: She feeds it too much, and it is getting fat.
- Third midlevel assertion (implied): She's a bad eater.
  - Evidence: She cries if she doesn't get her favorite food.
- Fourth midlevel assertion: She's a liar.
  - Evidence: She's lied about liking dinner.
  - Evidence: She's lied about eating her lunch.
    - Evidence: When she comes home from school, she's starving.
- Fifth midlevel assertion: She's a hot shot.
  - Evidence: She shows off all the time.

In pieces like this one, nourished by family arguments, the writer shows skill at the embedding expected in the academic essay.

Not all reason lists are this negative, however. One of the most frequent uses of this form seems to be the letter of appreciation to an adult, usually the mother. Taylor (1983, 35) cites the following example from Bonnie, age seven years, seven months:

*Dear Mommie*

*I really love you. Yes I do. You care for me. And I know why you have to tell me to have gum only every other day I know it all. It is for my own good. So I don't get cavities you are the mother I want for ever and ever.*

*Love Bonnie*

*xxxx* *000000000000000*
*xxxx* *000000000000000*
*xxxx*
*I love you*

Even in this short letter, the argument moves from general to specific—from a statement of affection, to a reason ("You care for me"), to evidence for the reason (an instance of the mother's care). We see the same pattern in the following letter from a second grader to her mother:

*Dear Mom,*

*I want to thank you for a lot of things. For instance my Cabbage Patch kid, my set of Laura Ingalls Wilder books. And driving me to school and thank you for buying my clothes and all the other things you do for me. I forgot to say thank you for bringing me to the pool. Because I know you do not like going there.*

*Siserley Jessie*

Note how the "for instance" indicates a shift from the general to the more specific.

Children can also develop their arguments in written dialogues with partners. Jana Staton (1980, 1981) has pioneered the use of dialogue journals in the middle grades, and Nancie Atwell (1987) has extended the technique in the letter writing that she has done with eighth graders. In the early grades, written dialogues allow students to draw on their oral proficiency to build more extensive arguments than they could achieve solo. I stumbled on this technique one afternoon when Sarah, age five years, two months, was agitating to go into her room to retrieve her ballet equipment while her sister was still asleep. I told her that she had to wait, and she gave me a dark look. I started the written dialogue:

TOM: Are you angry with me?
SARAH: Yes.
TOM: Why?
SARAH: Cose you wut lat me go too get my lee a trd [leotard] and sose and tiye [tights] and lag womrs.
TOM: I will let you go up in 10 minutes.
SARAH: I will go rite now.
TOM: But you will wake up Abby.
SARAH: I don't care if I wake Abby up.
TOM: But isn't that mean?

SARAH: I don't care if that's mean.
TOM: But don't you love your sister?
SARAH: Yor tinkins in onu thr prrt of the Bran I am not tinkin abot LOVE Abby I WOT MY LEE A TRRD [Your thinking's in another part of the brain. I'm not thinking about "love Abby." *I want my leotard.*]

I switched hemispheres and let her go up.

Both the reason list and the dialogue are generative strategies; they can help young writers discover the range of reasons that they might use to support a claim. Children may need to push this generation to excess before they begin to select the most effective reasons. It is fine that, in one of the "Why I Hate" books, a child says that he hates Cabbage Patch Dolls because they are stupid or that a third grader arguing for pierced ears claims that eight is the right age for them because seven is too young and nine is a little old. As Moffett (1968) put it, the bush must become rank before it is pruned. Graves (1983), too, has noted that a stage of accumulation precedes one of selection. As students become more self-critical, they could be asked to determine which reasons are stronger and why. They could also be asked to consider evidence opposing their positions.

## THE POSSIBILITY OF PERSUASION

Children do not learn the language of persuasion by filling in blanks or by writing the standard letters that many workbooks require. They learn it from experience, by being in situations where they consider options and then make and explain choices, where argument is not simply one more form to learn. Argument, as the politicians remind us regularly, is the heritage and responsibility of a free people. When we speak directly about language, we are also speaking indirectly about power.

In most schools, however, students are almost completely disenfranchised. The most extensive—and distressing—of the recent studies of education was done by John Goodlad and reported in *A Place Called School* (1984). I quote what I consider to be the most disturbing finding in this book:

*Students in the classes we observed made scarcely any decisions about their learning, even though many perceived themselves as doing so. Nearly 100% of the elementary classes were almost completely teacher-dominated with respect to seating, grouping, content, materials, use of space, time utilization, and learning activities. A similar situation prevailed in 90% of the junior high schools and 80% of the senior high schools, and the increase in student decision-making was only in one or two areas, usually somewhat removed from the learning activity, and more in the arts, physical education, and vocational education than in the academic subjects. . . .*

*Clearly, the bulk of the teacher talk was instructing in the sense of telling. Barely 5% of the instructional time was designed to create students' anticipation of needing to respond. Not even one percent required some kind of open response involving reasoning or perhaps an opinion from students. (229)*

Goodlad concludes that "if teachers in the talking mode and students in the listening mode are what we want, rest assured that we have it" (229). Reports such as this illustrate the utter futility of the panaceas suggested by some school reformers. Lengthening the school day, increasing the school year, intensifying testing programs are not likely to improve the situation. Without profound changes in the ways that classes are run, more time will only mean more passivity.

But, as Donald Graves has shown so powerfully, it is possible to offer children choices *within orderly classes*, although the order that he advocates is more the order of the newsroom than that of the assembly line. He describes this ideal order well in *Writing: Teachers and Children at Work* (1983). I also recommend Lucy Calkins's *The Art of Teaching Writing* (1986), Nancie Atwell's *In the Middle* (1987), and Jane Hansen's *When Writers Read* (1987). These educators demonstrate beyond reasonable doubt that we need not be locked in to the restricted patterns that Goodlad describes. And, when students are allowed to choose, they can be called upon to discuss possibilities, to weigh options, to defend, to compare. A range of discourse becomes possible—indeed, necessary.

If writing itself is choosing—placing one selected word after another—it, too, is an act of power. In one first-grade classroom, this power became apparent when a child was composing a story about an intergalactic war. The earth was under attack, in grave danger, at the point when the writer had a group conference. He read aloud what he had written and asked for questions. After a pause, a student asked, "Will the earth survive?" The writer said, "Hmmmm," and thought it over. For several seconds, he mulled over the fate of the planet. He held that power in his hands. It was his decision.

Not only must classrooms be revised if persuasive writing is to flourish, we also need to rethink current models of language use, particularly those claiming that "transactional" writing differs fundamentally from "poetic" writing. In one well-known formulation, James Britton (1970) identifies transactional discourse (where we act as "participant") as "language to get things done," whereas poetic discourse (where we act as "spectator") is defined as the "language of being and becoming." Divisions like these appeal to those of us with backgrounds in literature, for Britton's formulation clearly favors the kind of discourse in which we specialize: Persuasive and informational writing may have functional importance, but it is poetic language—the story, anecdote, poem, novel—that allows us to become fully integrated human beings. As "spectators," we can step back from the ongoing activity in our lives, reflect upon that activity, and give it shape; and, by giving it shape, we revise what Britton calls our "world representation."

Britton's explication of the spectator role is both powerful and useful, but he does not explain satisfactorily why spectatorship is linked to poetic discourse. The child who writes a list of his or her favorite sports teams becomes a spectator of this knowledge. The very act of writing is a withdrawal from the ongoing activity of the world. And, while we write, we can alternate between immersion and contemplation; there is a self that creates and one that contemplates. What you are reading is hardly poetic discourse, but, as I write it, and particularly as I read what I have written, I become a spectator of my emerging understanding of children's persuasive language. What was a welter of notes and dogeared pages two weeks ago now has patterns, categories—a shape. Spectatorship seems to be a condition that all writing—not simply the writing of poetic discourse—makes possible.

This participant-spectator distinction also contains a bias against action. Indeed, the learning in the title of Britton's book has little to do with learning to change the conditions of one's life, of using language to influence. Rather, it is learning in the spectator role, through the contemplative reconstruction of a unified "world representation." The language of action (or transaction) may provide grist for this contemplative mill, but Britton denies it equal standing with the language that constructs and reconstructs our world representation.

In this chapter, I have attempted to demonstrate that persuasive language is also the language of "being and becoming," for we learn who we are, in part, by learning how we can "disturb the universe." We use persuasive language not simply to get things done, but to establish our social identities—to find out where we stand, where we can push, what we can change, what we must accept.

I remember an unseasonably cold summer day when Sarah held her "Homemade Garaj Sall." She had set up a table at the end of our driveway, put rocks on her "sall" items—hastily drawn cards, each with its own stapled envelope—and she waited. She sat behind the table, hunched over, hands in coat pockets, waiting for the world to come to her. Our quiet street was absolutely empty. And still she waited.

She was dreaming Archimedes' dream, dreaming that, with written language as her lever, she might be able to move the world.

# 5
# "Me, personaly am a feminist": A child's letters

One gray January Sunday during her kindergarten year, I was reading Sarah one of her favorite books, *There's a Party at Mona's Tonight*. When I had finished, Sarah noted that the crocodile in the story had no name, and we decided to write Harry Allard to ask him why. A couple of weeks later, Sarah received Allard's reply:

*Dear Sarah,*

*Thank you for your lovely letter.*

*You know, to tell you the truth, Sarah, Jimmy Marshall and I forgot to give names to the crocodile and to the dog and to the chicken and to the cat in* There's a Party at Mona's Tonight. *Maybe you could help us out. I think Mary would be a good name for the chicken, don't you? And Homer for the dog. But you must help me find good names for them all.*

*I work in Salem, Mass., and I live in Charlestown, Mass. So we are really not very far away from each other. I think that is nice.*

*I am going to send your letter to James Marshall. He lives part of the time in New York City and part of the time in his house in the country in Connecticut.*

*Do you have any pets? I have two bulldogs and five alley cats. The dogs' names are Mona and Olga; the cats' names are Peter, Phyllis, Earl, Boris, and*

*Charlestown. Charlestown is the youngest . . . and the toughest. I found him in the streets of Charlestown, so that is how he got his name.*

*Thanking you again for your letter, Sarah, I remain,*

*Your friend,*
*Harry Allard*

We kept this generous letter in Sarah's scrapbook, rereading it to her when we leafed through her collection. And ten months later, during a surge of letter writing, Sarah wrote her reply:

*Dear Harry Allard*

*I like your books like* The Stupids Die. *I know a good or OK name for the alligator, Jeremy. Do send it to James Marshall.*

In this same period, she wrote a second letter:

*Dear Harry Allard*

*I like your books. I want you to write a new book about the Stupids. I think it should be called* The Stupids Get to Go.
[p. 2] *By the way I can write Supr-Calle-fraj-lestic-XE Be ale A Dosh US*

These letters were among the 160 that she wrote up to age seven years, four months, when I stopped collecting. Some were simple cards wishing Merry Christmas or Happy Valentine's Day; others were longer, such as the fan letter to Michael Jackson that I quoted earlier or her letter to "lawmakers," arguing that television should have people signing for the aid of deaf viewers. In all, she wrote to fifty-one different people or groups in the following categories:

- Family and extended family 48 letters
- Friends 48
- Teachers 15
- Friends of her parents 9
- Tooth Fairy and Santa Claus 5
- Herself 5
- Public figures 4
- Neighbors 2
- General or unknown recipient 24

Most of these letters were written from October to December 1983, not coincidentally, one of the most eventful periods in her life. She was adjusting to first grade, her best friend had a new baby sister, her mother was expecting a child in January, her school burned down and she had to take a bus to the school on the nearby air-force base. And there was the seasonal excitement of the Christmas season. Moreover, Sarah's own writing fluency had increased, so letter writing had become easier, not only in terms of spelling, but in her mastery of the conventions.

Virtually all studies of literacy in the home document the attraction of letter writing for young children, but it is useful to ask what journalists call a "dumb question"—Why letters? What do children find appealing about the writing of letters? Here are some possible answers.

*Availability of models.* In 1922, Emily Post wrote the following lament in the fourteenth edition of *Etiquette*:

*The art of letter writing in the present day is shrinking until the letter threatens to become a telegram, a telephone message, a post card. (491)*

Although she noted that letters between young men and young women were flourishing "like unpulled weeds in a garden where weeds were formerly never allowed to grow" (491), according to Mrs. Post, scarcely 10 percent of the mail consisted of personal letters.

We hear a similar complaint today—that the telephone has taken over the function of the personal letter. Still, children see letters of some kind every day. They bring announcements home to their parents, bring in letters after absences, watch parents groan over bills around the first of the month. Even junk mail can have a fascination for children, particularly those sweepstakes letters declaring million-dollar winners. (Jerome Harste suggests passing junk mail on to young children, saying, "Here, this is for you.") And if the telephone has replaced much personal letter writing, many of us try to send something on holidays and birthdays, when some written communication—even if only a signed card—is expected.

*Letters and gift giving.* Because letter writing tends to occur around holidays and birthdays, it is closely related to giving and receiving gifts. The letter itself, if decorated with hearts or stickers, becomes a small gift. A number of Sarah's letters to relatives are to thank them for Christmas or birthday gifts, a ritual exchange—letter for gift—that is certainly a good bargain in a child's eyes.

*The flexibility of the letter.* While much writing needs to have a single purpose, the letter-writer can shift purposes: it is perfectly appropriate to shift from thanking the recipient to asking questions or providing information. The "By the way" in the second Allard letter is an instance, one of many, where Sarah shifts from the initial intent of the letter, offering advice, to a secondary intent, telling about her accomplishments. In another letter, written as a birthday card, she adds on a knock-knock joke:

*Happy Birthday Momy*
*to the niceest mom in the world*
*hope your birthday is as happy as can be and happy wishes all year Love*
*Knok knowk*
*how's thear*
*Carrie Carrie how*
*Carrie me bake to vergena*

(AGE SIX YEARS, SIX MONTHS)

In other letters, she attaches unrelated ideas or information with a "P.S." and, sometimes, a "P.P.S."

You will recall that, in Chapter 3, I suggested that our culture offers children *intermediate forms*, manageable ways of handling various communication situations. The list is an intermediate form that allows children to communicate information; similarly, the card is an intermediate form that allows even very young children to say thank you or to offer congratulations—it may require no more than a signature. Sarah's second piece of writing, done at age four, was such a card. Under the concept of intermediate forms, children's writing no longer is viewed as flawed adult writing. This is appropriate, it seems to me, since a key characteristic of children when they write is their expectation of success: They pick tasks that can be done successfully or modify them so that success is possible. Letter or card writing can be done—successfully—at almost any level of complexity. It is a game that anyone can play.

*Maintaining friendship.* One of the language functions defined by Michael Halliday in *Learning How to Mean* (1975) is the "interactional function": We use language to open, maintain, and redefine our relationships with others. I suspect that an underlying intent of even our newsiest letters is simply to maintain contact, to say "I'm thinking about you." We often forget the actual content of good conversations; what remains is the comfortable feeling of intimacy and companionship.

Two major studies of letter writing in the earlier grades (Karelitz, 1988; Greene, 1985) discovered that children regularly wrote letters to confirm, renegotiate, or repair friendships. (Karelitz quotes a twenty-five-note exchange between two first graders, beginning with amicable plans for a sleepover, shifting to complaints about teasing with promises made and promises broken, and ending happily with plans for an afternoon get-together.) Many of Sarah's letters fall into this category. Almost the youngest and very nearly the smallest student in her first grade, sometimes feeling herself to be on the margins of the friendship groups, she used letters to consolidate her position.

Sarah's letters resemble closely those quoted by Karelitz and Greene, but with one major and curious exception: Sarah rarely sent her letters. She would write them and then put them aside, drop them, lose them. I would collect them from under chairs and among old newspapers. The fact that her letters were not received by anyone did not seem to bother Sarah or diminish her interest in writing them.

I found this indifference puzzling until I read Denny Taylor's (1983) account of children making a sign advertising first an ice-water, then a lemonade sale (described in the last chapter). These children were interested primarily in making the sign; once it was complete, they lost interest. This example, in turn, reminded me of the forts my best friend and I built as children—we rarely *used* a fort to have any battles; building it was what counted. Once it was done, we went on to something else.

What interested Sarah in letter writing was not the prospect of receiving a response at some future point but, I am convinced, the sense of closeness she felt in *writing* the letters. So this chapter is built on a paradox: Sarah chose one of the most interpersonal types of discourse, explored its conventions, showing her awareness of audience, intention, and the "grammars" of various letter types—and rarely bothered to send them.

## THE THANK-YOU LETTER

One of Sarah's first extended letters (and one that *was* sent) was written to friends of ours, Jane and Tom Hansen, after a Thanksgiving meal at their house. It was written in her third month of kindergarten and shows both her exploration of invented spelling and her use of a dot system, almost identical to that described by Bissex (1980), to separate words.

*DER.JEN.AT.TOM*

*I LOVED.TO.B.AT.U.HM.FES.RF.JAS.FVEE*

*I LOVE TO PLA.UT.OLE*

*LOVE SARAH N*

*Dear Jane and Tom*

*I loved to be at your home for Thanksgiving.*
*I love(d) to play with Olie [their dog].*
*Love Sarah N*

(AGE FIVE YEARS, TWO MONTHS)

It is possible to see in this first thank-you letter what might be called a "letter grammar." Just as the subject precedes the verb in a typical declarative sentence, there is an appropriate order for the thank-you letter: a general statement of thanks ("I loved to be at your home for Thanksgiving") followed by a more specific example of the good time ("I love to play with Olie"). In Chapter 3 I defined such two-unit combinations as couplets, although most of the couplets in that chapter were identification-plus-attribute couplets ("This is my knife. My knife is sharp"). Both types of couplets are important initial expository units in which there is movement from general to specific.

Sarah's thank-you letters became more complex (and more frequent) in the first grade. In fact, she became so familiar with the general-to-specific pattern that she created form letters, where all she needed to do was fill in blanks:

*Dear Nan and Pop*

*Thank you for the* ________________________________.
*I really liked* ____________________ *too, and*

________________________________________.

*Sarah Newkirk*

(AGE SIX YEARS, THREE MONTHS)

A second form letter was even more explicitly general to specific:

*Dear Santa Claus*

*Thank you for the presents I really enjoyed them. Thank you so much for the* ____________________ *and* ____________________. *I really liked* ____________________ *best of all.*

*Sincerely,*
*Sarah Newkirk*

(AGE SIX YEARS, THREE MONTHS)

Many of her thank-you letters during that Christmas season followed this form:

*dear ukle bob*

*thak you for the tip a writer and the care bare modele I like snoopy's gift thak brin [Brian, her cousin] you sneke devl.*

*love sarah joyanne newkirk*

(AGE SIX YEARS, THREE MONTHS)

*Dear easter bunny*
*I like your gifts. your coclate bunny it was good*
*by by*
*Sarah N*

(AGE SIX YEARS, SIX MONTHS)

This pattern was open enough for her to use it in a letter of thanks to a long-term substitute teacher that she had in first grade:

*Mrs. Sanahan*

*you were a good subatute I liked you and all the fun things you did with us match [math] reading spelling Phonics everthing I [love] you I feel sad to leve you by by I have to be going*

*Sertainly*
*Sarah Newkirk*

(AGE SIX YEARS, NINE MONTHS)

This letter seems to follow the Santa Claus version of the form: There is a general assertion (she was a good substitute), a general reason (all the fun things she did), and then a specification of those "fun things" (math, reading, spelling, phonics).

The form thank-you letters offer plans for what might be called single-purpose letters. Yet, while a number of Sarah's letters were restricted to the single purpose of thanking, many expanded to include a second purpose—that of sharing information about herself. The second Allard letter is clearly double purpose: It offers a suggestion for a new Stupids book and also informs Allard that she can spell the longest word that she knows.

At least two additional structural problems occur when one writes a double-purpose letter. First, one must distinguish between the ostensible purpose of the letter (to thank, congratulate, give advice) and the casual purpose (to chat, gossip, bring the recipient up to date). In conversation, we often begin with the casual and then get down to business (and, in the Midwest, where I grew up, this can take a while); with letters, the reverse often holds—the ostensible purpose comes first.

Along with determining the order of the purposes, one must usually incorporate some kind of transition or pivot between the two. In the second Allard letter, Sarah writes, "By the way," almost as if there had been a lull in the conversation, and she felt that she could shift topics. I do not mean to suggest that all of her double-purpose letters contain explicit transitions. Some additions come in postscripts, and, occasionally, she makes a shift without any transition at all, as in this thank-you letter, written after her sixth birthday:

*Dear ant Pat, uncle Bob, Mike Brian*

*Thank you with all my heart for the cabbage patch kid. I might change the name I am on level 9 Mystery Sneaker highest in my class I got a rock carrier from Nan and Pop*

(AGE SIX YEARS, ONE MONTH)

But in the letter she wrote two months later, she frequently feels a need to signal the shift of topics. The Michael Jackson letter quoted in Chapter 1 is a good example:

*Dear Michale Jackson*

*I love yoru songs aspesple your abum thriller. I like to hear you won 8 gramy awards you should feel very proud of yousealf. Congratulation Michale Jacson and again congratulation. I hope I become a famos Ballarena and I can sing bake round music some day. I want to be a famos Girl.*

*Love*
*Sarah Newkirk*

We recognize the opening sentence as the familiar opening—a statement of thanks or praise followed by a specific example. The shift comes after the word "congratulation." There is no explicit transition, but Sarah continues the theme of the first part of her letter, saying, in effect, "you, Michael Jackson, are now famous and I, Sarah, want to become famous too."

In a thank-you letter to her Uncle Bob, she deftly shifts from thanking him to saying something about her Christmas. Note how the "it" referent changes between the third and fourth sentences:

*Dear ukle Bob*

*[1] Thak you for the tip-a-writer [2] it is very good [3] I brae [brought] it up to ukle Bill's hoes [house] for the rel Christmise [4] it is going to be fan [5] it is tomoro [6] I can't Blev it! [7] thaks Snope*

*Love*
*Sarah Newkirk*

The opening is a variant of the form letter—a statement of thanks plus a comment on the gift. In the next sentence, she begins to shift toward speaking about herself. The "it" of this sentence is the typewriter, but, in the next sentence, "it" is the "real Christmas" that she will have at her Uncle Bill's, her topic for the rest of the letter.

Sarah attempted a third transition strategy in a thank-you letter to Jane Kearns, a teacher in the summer program that I direct:

*Dear jan Kerins*

*Thank you for the lovely gifs. The Gift rmiss [reminds] me of Care Bares I Relly like them esbeshle Love-a-lot and Cheer Bar. Bithday BAre had a Good idae the most in potoh [important] word in happy birthday was happy Becus he knows it is very inpoton [important] to be happy.*

(AGE SIX YEARS, THREE MONTHS)

In this letter, "reminds" is the pivot, indicating a mental association between the gift and one of Sarah's interests, Care Bears. It is one more device that allows her to shift the agenda in a letter of thanks.

It is useful to compare the way Sarah pivots her letters with the strategy of another first grader, Andrea, in this letter of thanks to her uncle:

*Dear Uncle Phil*

*Thanks so much For telling me tha name of that song that you whare trying to tech me. Gess what? I have lerned it. I know it better by heart. I am having a Recitl. I am playing that song at the recitl you sure have a big house. I wish you cald come to my recitl. I thought Buster and the baby kittens in the BArn whre cute. I miss you.*

*Love Andrea*

Here, too, the opening offer of thanks shifts to the personal information—the pivot is "Guess what?" But Andrea ties her personal information to the song that her uncle taught her: She knows the song by heart; she will play it at her recital; she wishes her uncle could come to the recital where she will be playing this song. Even when Andrea moves away from the theme of the song to talk about the kittens, she continues to explore common ground.

This examination of thank-you letters suggests three developmental principles:

- The argument that children begin writing by reproducing speech or by writing expressive discourse outside discourse conventions (Britton et al., 1975) underestimates children's awareness of what semioticians call "signifying structures." Similarly, the notion that children focus their attention on the conventions of spelling before they consider issues of organization (Bereiter, 1980) underestimates children's ability to work on multiple fronts at the same time. Sarah began to write letters by observing the conventions of the thank-you letter. The Thanksgiving letter, written at a time when spelling was still difficult, is recognizable as a thank-you letter. Its components—the general statement of thanks followed by a specific instance—are both appropriate and in the expected order.

- Children's writing contains what might be called a bias toward order. In Chapter 3, we saw that children tend almost invariably to make connections in their writing. Even the early lists, which might seem like random collections of attributes, are often more closely ordered than they appear, and soon children are connecting these elements explicitly. In the same way, Sarah tried a number of ways to connect the two parts of her letters, which became more complex by elaborating (and not abandoning) the form she used in her first letter. Even fourteen months after the Thanksgiving letter, she still began with a general statement of thanks followed by a particular instance. But, in her more extended thank-you letters, this couplet constitutes the opening step of the letter, which is followed by a bridge to her own personal agenda.
- The structures used in Sarah's thank-you letters—particularly the shift from general to specific—are basic to almost all expository writing. With some modifications, her Santa Claus form letter could achieve a number of expository purposes.

## KEEPING IN TOUCH

Most of Sarah's letters were more casual than the thank-you letters quoted above, and, as I have mentioned, most were written during a period bounded by two major events in her life—the fire that destroyed most of her school and the birth of her baby brother. Having to take a bus to her new school precipitated one of her few self-pitying letters (Figure 5–1). The picture shows her school on fire, and a sad face—Sarah's—looking out of a window. Although the window appears to be in the school, it is more likely the window of the school bus that she must now ride every day. The letter reads:

*Dera Mis Mills*

*I am going to go on a Bus I dot wot to go on a bus.*

*Love*
*Sarah*

(AGE SIX YEARS, TWO MONTHS)

Dera Mis Mills
I am going to
go on a Bus
I
dot
wot
to
go
on a
Bus
Love
Sarah

FIGURE 5–1 *Sarah's letter*

One of the problems with riding on the bus was getting to sit with the right friend. At first, her best friend, Carey, was sitting with someone else, prompting this letter, which I quoted earlier as an example of deeply felt persuasion:

*Please can you sit with Sarah Newkirk on the bus. Deep down in side we are the same. We are close friends. I hope you will accept my suggestion. Please, oh, please can you sit [with me].*

(AGE SIX YEARS, TWO MONTHS)

While most of her letters are considerably more upbeat than this, their intent is similar—to establish and celebrate closeness. The purposes of individual letters, however, vary widely. Sarah uses letters to congratulate, console, inform, boast, plead, request, inquire, suggest, invite, thank, gossip, play, apologize—and, in many cases, she combines purposes in a single letter, as in this one to her first-grade teacher, who had to miss much of the year because of back problems:

*Dear Mrs. Mills*

*My Ucele Broke his wist. I hope you'll be back next year to tech the kindergarters. I [picture of heart] you Mrs. Mills. I am sary you couled see us too much. This year was fun by by I am on level 5*

*Sertainly*
*Sarah Newkirk*

*I am in a contest*
*I am still the best*

(AGE SIX YEARS, NINE MONTHS)

Sarah begins with information about her uncle, shifts to an expression of concern and sympathy for her teacher, and ends with news about herself, particularly her current reading level and standing in her class.

Sarah's letters cannot be classified neatly by function; it is undoubtedly the multifunctional nature of the letter that appeals to her (and to all of us). But the following rough sorting gives some sense of her range of purposes.

*Requests*

Some of Sarah's earliest letters were essentially requests for letters or for visits. Midway through her kindergarten year, she wrote to a girl whom she had met at Thanksgiving dinner:

*Dear Kelly*

*I have missed you. If you ever come to visit my address is 133 Thornton Portsmouth Love Sarah*

(AGE FIVE YEARS, FOUR MONTHS)

About three months later, as I mentioned in the previous chapter, she wrote to Judy Egan, the head teacher in an innovative private primary school that I had just visited:

*Dear Judy*

*My Daddy told me about your class's spelling. I would like it if you would write a letter to me. My name's Sarah*

(AGE FIVE YEARS, SEVEN MONTHS)

In another letter of request, this time to a friend with whom she had just argued, Sarah uses similar phrasing:

*Dear Tammy*

*I would like it if we could get alon together*
*Love Sarah PS*

*Can we like each other*

*Love*
*Sarah*

(AGE SIX YEARS, TWO MONTHS)

The syntax of these requests is complex; in all three, there is the statement of request and the action request. And, in each letter, "if" is the pivot.

- If you ever come to visit my address is 133 Thornton
- I would like it if you would write a letter to me.
- I would like it if we could get alon together.

Interestingly, these constructions appear in some of her earliest letters. This leads to a chicken-and-egg question. Does Sarah's verbal ability allow her to attempt the request form or does the nature of the request push her into this syntactic thicket? While I cannot sort out this cause and effect, I do think that simply beginning with "I would like it" puts the child in the position of naming a requested object or in action. If, as in the case of these letters, an action is desired, the child must attach an "if" clause to the request statement.

This is an indirect argument for a diversity of writing and letter forms in the classroom. Would a child attempt this syntactic form in a story or in an attribute list? It is unlikely.

Letters requesting information challenge children to formulate questions. Sarah wrote a series of letters to her friend Carey after the birth of Carey's sister, Amy. These letters were almost entirely questions:

*Dear Carey*

*How Dose it fel to Be a Big Sistr how is you mothr Don't you fel prod how is justis [Justin, her brother] abat this*

(AGE SIX YEARS, THREE MONTHS)

In another set of letters, Sarah wrote to her former kindergarten teacher concerning a rumor that she was pregnant. First, Sarah put the question directly:

*Dear Mrs. Spinny*

*I herd you were premnat. is it ture?*
*no*

———————

*yes*

(AGE SIX YEARS, THREE MONTHS)

And a little later:

*Dear Mrs Sipinny*

*ancew*

*I like yoru big dresses what sixe are your* __________. *I'm*
*6, 7, 8.*
*Hi! see ys soon*
*Allways*
*Sarah N.*

(UNDATED, FIRST GRADE)

Jennifer Greene (1985) reports a similar use of check-off boxes in her study of letter writing in an elementary school, where girls would check yes or no to indicate whether they liked a particular book. Both Sarah and these girls are probably adapting a form from their workbooks for their own purposes.

*Play*

Playfulness is a sign of mastery. Last week, my younger daughter learned to ride a twenty-inch bike, and no sooner did she feel confident riding it, than she began to play with that competence. "Watch this," she said, and then, for a split second, rode the bike using only one hand. The same thing occurs with language competence; once comfortable with a routine, we begin to play. Adults satirize, exaggerating routines to comic proportions; children may change the words of a song or nursery rhyme in a faintly seditious way ("My eyes have seen the glory of the burning of the school"). Very young children play with their knowledge of the world—a three-year-old can burst into hysterics after suggesting that the dog can answer the telephone.

One indication that Sarah was confident with the letter form was her willingness to play with it. She would write letters to herself, transforming herself from an "I" to a "you" or a "she." She wrote one such letter from her mother to herself on a night that her mother was out for a meeting:

*Dear Sarah N*

*I will miss You tonite now. 8 1983*
*I had fun with you and ABBy today I hope you take Yors ppla [apple] jushe [juice] tonite*
*I Love You*

*Love Beth*

(AGE SIX YEARS TWO MONTHS)

In the same month, she wrote a letter to herself from Abby:

*Dear Sarah*

*I cole you Sarah I like you I will nevr forget You You are a [heart picture]*

*Love Abby*

(AGE SIX YEARS, TWO MONTHS)

Her most complex letter of this type was written by Sarah to Sarah. It is playful in two ways: She tried to catalog the "silly" language that I use when I talk to the two girls ("jube jube girls," "groovie," "delicious and nutritious") and the tossing games we play on the bed ("pancake," where they are flipped, and "dribble," where they are bounced). But she was also playing linguistically, using the third person to distance both me and, interestingly, herself, to whom she referred as "his older daughter." The result is a letter that might have been written about Sarah, Abby, and me to someone outside the family:

*Dear Sarah N*

*Tom likes his jube jube girls. Jube-jube girls are groovie He likes to play Dribble AND pancake. His girls are delicious and nutritious. His older daughter can write SUpr-Clal Fraj Lestek XE BE AL A dosh US*

*Love*
*Sarah*

(AGE SIX YEARS, TWO MONTHS)

Sarah also seems to role-play in some of her letters. She tries out voices that she has heard, particularly the voices of teachers. We hear an echo of such a voice in the letter to Michael Jackson when she tells him he "should be very proud." One of her most teacherly letters, quoted in Chapter 4, was written to her best friend Carey:

*Dear Carey*

*I like the numbers that you or Tammy wrote. I like your printing. I have a plan. You write or give this message to Tammy. She did very well on her whole name. You did only your first name but you did OK. I am having a raffle at my house.*

(AGE SIX YEARS, TWO MONTHS)

She also tried this more adult voice in the announcement she wrote for her seventh birthday party. The arrangements for this party were complicated—children would have to come from the air-force base to her house—so the announcement had to include some explanation:

*A bithday party*
*treser hunts pinata pin the hert on the ranbow*

*parents are welcomed to participate in treser hunts pinata*

*hi: a bithdae party will be held*
*for: Name Sarah Newkirk*
*Time: 2:00 to 4:00*
*Place: 133 Thornton Street*
*Phone 431—8098*
*P.S. if your Mom and Dad both go to work you can come on bus 516 with me. Tell your Mom and Dad not to go trou all the fuss*

Sarah did not use language like "parents are welcomed to participate in treser hunts" in her normal conversation, but it is the kind of "invitation language" that she had read before: She used parents' language to invite parents. The last reminder about the bus also seems to be the motherly kind of advice that she hears regularly. She was playing adult in this invitation.

It may be too much to claim that these letters show that, from an early age, Sarah could take on the perspective of someone other than herself when she wrote. It is probably more accurate to observe that, because she had access to letters from parents and notes from teachers, she could use these familiar voices. I feel that researchers are too ready to assume that the failure of children to negotiate audience relationships is due to cognitive deficiency. The common explanation, derived from Piaget's claims about egocentrism, is that children lack the mental development to see the world from any perspective but their own. This traditional view assumes that writing for a particular audience requires a mental transposition; in fact, as I have tried to argue in this book, it depends more on an intuitive understanding of the language that audience usually reads. It is for this reason that we can often write for an audience without constantly imagining how that audience is reacting.

### *Contact*

Many of the letters already quoted indicate a major theme in Sarah's correspondence—her desire to maintain contact with her friends. Her letters are full of pledges of friendship and requests for letters. In one of her longest letters, written to a friend who had moved from the area, Sarah virtually reintegrated the girl back into the school.

*Dere Kim*

*This is what your pictures came out like. I miss you. My address is 133 Thornton*

*and city Portsmouth*
*and state NH*
*and name Sarah Newkirk*

*What is yours*
*Write Back*
*Your a good friend*

*I can write the word Snowman*
*I wish you were in my class*
*I like Your pictures*
*You would be in Carey's Class*
*Miss Deleros's Class*

*wriet me back soon*
*I wish You Didn't move I wish you were here*

(AGE SIX YEARS, ONE MONTH)

In September of her first-grade year, her soulmate Eric moved to South Carolina. This prompted a series of twelve letters, the last written in November, which attempted to keep the connection alive. The first was written right after he left:

*Good by Eric*
*Hope you come back in 6 months to see the little BABY*
*The scribbling is my sister's.*
*Griil Boy [Eric is supposed to check his prediction]*

(AGE FIVE YEARS, ELEVEN MONTHS)

This is also the first instance I can find of Sarah using a check-off box. Three weeks later:

*I am sorry I can't invite you to my birthday*
*I miss you I look for a letter every Day*

(AGE SIX YEARS)

And later, as in the letter to Kim, she told Eric which class he would have been in if he hadn't moved:

*Dear ERIC*

*You would be in my Class. Her name is Mrs Mills and Mrs Ward*

(AGE SIX YEARS, ONE MONTH)

In other letters, she kept him informed about her new boyfriends.

Many of Sarah's letters to her friends seem to be almost

interchangeable with the letters quoted in the most extensive study of children's letters ever conducted, carried out by Jennifer Greene (1985) in a predominantly bilingual elementary school located in an East Los Angeles suburb. While Greene found that students wrote on a wide range of topics, friendships seemed to be the central theme of most. Note, for example, the similarity between one of Sarah's letters and a typical letter from Greene's study in both of which is an affirmation of friendship followed by a "did?" question:

*Dear Tammy*

*I like you now. Do you like me? Did you know they found a time capsule in New Franklin School. Hows Tiffy [her sister] doing. Meanwhile I bet you like that baby. I get to watch the olympics on TV. How are you doing. Three more months of school.*

(AGE SIX YEARS, TEN MONTHS)

*Dear Patricia*

*I'm glad you are still hear. Because I like you alot. And I don't whant you to go because you are my Friend and I like you very much and I don't whant you to go. did you see Mary Poppins on Sunday night because it came on at 8:00 and it was funny I made some dogs and the pretty whants are you and me.*

*Love Lizzy (234)*

(FOURTH GRADER)

Greene's research provides welcome evidence that letters of this type have broad appeal for young writers.

*Advice*

During first grade, Sarah was always concocting some plan. There were clubs that never met, talent shows that were never presented. She bombarded her friends with ideas for things to do. Like the children described by Denny Taylor (1983), she seemed to enjoy the planning most. In a number of her letters, she offers advice or suggestions. In a letter written to Carey after the bussing began, she asks her to "aspd my asadshun"—"accept my suggestion." In the letter evaluating Carey's writing, she writes that she "has a plan."

She also had advice for adults. To the organizer of the lawn fete held at the end of her first-grade year, Sarah wrote:

*Dear Mrs Penition,*

*I have an idea for you all you need is a ball and a coupal children someone throws it [and] has to cach it befor the other peson caches you*

In second grade, she became interested in Helen Keller and began to see herself as something of a champion for the rights of the handicapped. This prompted a letter to "lawmakers":

*Dear Lawmakers*

*Think learning regular. Then think blind and deaf and blind-deaf learning. I am a reader of Helen Keller and She did not have many shows that were not hard on teachers eyes. Then I want to provide t.v. with Sing [sign] speakrs and get more books to get printed for the blind and deaf blind*

*Love Sarah Newkirk*

Helen Keller was heroic for Sarah because she overcame handicaps but also because she was a woman. In fact, Sarah's interest in women's rights was the subject of another letter, this one written to the television show "You Can't Do That on Television" after we had threatened to limit watching time because she was only seeing reruns:

*Dear You can't do that on Television*

*I would suggest you make some new shows because my [Dad] is saying I don't have to see it any more. I would suggest you make a show on well feminists and women right's fighters*

*Me, personaly am a feminist*

*Sincerely*
*Sarah*

By the time she wrote this, her interest in letter writing was waning. She was back in her rebuilt school, she was involved with gymnastics, her best friend Carey was in her second-grade class, and she spent much of her spare time reading. When she did write letters, they were sent without being read by snooping parents. This pattern has continued into the fourth grade, broken only by one letter, written as part of a school assignment. Each class member had to write a letter to a person from history that he or she admired. Sarah chose Susan B. Anthony, another feminist:

*Dear Susan B. Anthony*

*I admire you because you dared to stand out for your rights. When you were on trial for wanting to vote, you told the judge how it was your right to vote. It was unfair for the judge to make a script before he heard the argument of the lawyers.*

*Women have come a long way. I wear tight-fitting pants to school. I ride a bicycle in the summer, spring, and fall. There are women governors and my town has a woman mayor.*

*How does it feel to be on a silver dollar? How did it feel to have people make fun of you everyday?*

*Sincerely*
*Sarah Joanne Newkirk*
(AGE NINE YEARS, FIVE MONTHS)

I'm sure that many of her classmates thought that this assignment—writing to someone who would never receive the letter—was artificial. But Sarah, of course, had been doing this all along.

# IN THE CLASSROOM

# 6
# Questions, comments, and stories

In the second grade, I made a useful discovery about talk, one that kept me out of trouble. In that grade, for the first time, we sat in rows, and most of our time was spent on silent seat work—endless addition and subtraction (with the cumbersome proofs). I also remember the teacher setting up lines and lines of imitation clocks from which we would read and then record the time. It wasn't so much the work as the expectation of silence that got to me. I can remember a physical sensation of *having to talk*, as compelling as having to sneeze or go to the bathroom.

When the need could no longer be ignored (which happened frequently), I discovered that I could hunch over, so that the teacher couldn't see me, and talk to Emily Siverling, who sat in front of me. The beauty of this tactic was that Emily was more likely to get in trouble than I because she was visible. If she turned to listen, the teacher would notice her, and, if she laughed, she would be the one breaking the silence. So, with apologies to Emily, thirty-two years after the crime, I begin this chapter on talk.

"Talk" has had mixed press. In Bartlett's *Familiar Quotations* (1968), talk is more belittled than praised. It is often compared unfavorably with action, as in the Biblical proverb:

*In all labor there is profit: but the talk of the lips tendeth only to penury. (24)*

Or in Goethe's maxim:

*Create artist! Do not talk. (479)*

Talk also suffers in comparison to knowledge:

*Speech was given to the ordinary sort of men whereby to communicate their mind; but to wise men thereby to conceal it.*

(ROBERT SOUTH, QUOTED IN BARTLETT, 376)

The Jacobean playwright, Ben Jonson, makes a similar distinction:

*Talking and eloquence are not the same: to speak, and to speak well, are two things. A fool may talk, but a wise man speaks. (304)*

Quotations like these are barely balanced by more companionable ones like this one from Lewis Carroll's poem "The Walrus and the Carpenter":

*"O Oysters, come and walk with us!"*
*The Walrus did beseech.*
*"A pleasant walk, a pleasant talk,*
*Along the briny beach. . . ." (745)*

So, while talk may be "pleasant," it can keep us from the more serious business of thought and action. "Actions speak louder than words." "Talk's cheap."

Schools are ambivalent at best about the importance of talk. While "speaking" is considered to be one of the "language arts," it usually exists at the periphery of the curriculum, with the central attention going to teaching students to read and write. This bias toward literacy (and away from what Andrew Wilkinson called "oracy") is not hard to fathom. Speaking seems like a biological endowment, like breathing, mastered without being taught by all children who are not biologically impaired. Talk fills the air before class starts, and, for the teacher, achieving silence seems like a greater challenge than initiating conversation. School boards and parents are more likely to be impressed with reading-score gains than they are by reports of conversational virtuosity.

Even those teachers who value talk must feel as though they are chasing the wind when they seek to monitor the oral abilities of children. Oral language vanishes on creation, yet it is everywhere; attending to it is like attending to water as one swims.

Furthermore, what should one look for in the oral language of young children? If one is looking for growth in conversational ability, how does one identify it? And are there connections (as one might expect) between children's talk and children's literacy?

These are, of course, enormous questions, addressed in such major works as Britton's *Language and Learning* (1970), Moffett's *Teaching the Universe of Discourse* (1968), Barnes's *From Communication to Curriculum* (1976), Heath's *Ways with Words* (1983), and Gordon Wells's *The Meaning Makers* (1986). These questions also take us into the area of cultural variations in the use of oral language. As long as we view talk as a natural endowment, children who participate actively in classroom conversations seem more endowed, and the quiet ones less endowed. But, as the title of Heath's book reminds us, children with different backgrounds possess different "ways with words." Many school practices that are routine to white middle-class children—for example, being asked questions by an adult who knows the answer—are mystifying to children who are not used to the routine.

To complicate matters further, certain oral routines promote literate modes of thought. For example, much early talk about books involves asking the child to name an object and then to state one of its attributes. From a pure communication standpoint, this naming is hardly necessary—the parent knows whether a picture shows a tree without being told. Similarly, Sarah Michaels (1981) has reported that many teachers expect children to begin show-and-tell sessions by naming the object that they intend to show. A child would be expected to say "I brought this shell," even though classmates can already see what the child has brought. It would be just as reasonable to say "I brought this" and point to the shell. By requiring the specific label (as opposed to "this" followed by a gesture), the teacher encourages the child to use a linguistic specificity that will prepare him or her for creating texts that are explicit enough for a reader.

In this chapter, I will lay out a basic argument for the relationship of talk to writing, focusing on what I consider to be the most powerful—Vygotsky's theory of the zone of proximal development. Then I will describe a kindergarten and a first-grade class where students shared their writing daily with the entire class. In this second section, I will try to show that the more orthodox notions of the writing process that view talk as prewriting need to be reconsidered. Writing can just as easily—and profitably—be viewed as pretalk.

## WRITING AND TALKING

The work of Lev Vygotsky is, in many ways, a curious foundation upon which to build a theory of instruction. Trained as a literary critic (the first in his list of works is on *Hamlet*), Vygotsky later switched to the study of physically defective and mentally retarded children. Between 1925 and his death in 1934 at the age of thirty-eight, he worked at the intersection of three areas of study—psychology, defectology, and mental abnormality—and, in addition, undertook medical training in his later years. His work was unavailable in English until almost thirty years after his death, and the work most directly related to instruction, collected in *Mind in Society*, was not published until 1978.

Vygotsky's influence is even more curious because he was a Marxist, producing his major work during Stalin's regime, although it is not certain that he would have survived the purges that began soon after 1934. But it may be Vygotsky's mastery of dialectical thinking (an adaptation of Marx's dialectical materialism) that gives his work such explanatory power. Vygotsky viewed development as a dialectical interaction of biology and culture. He insisted that, to understand the higher mental functions, one had to understand the neurological dimensions of thought (a project continued by Vygotsky's brilliant student, A. R. Luria), although biology alone could not account for mental growth.

Vygotsky drew on and extended Engels' concept of "tool" to explore how humans internalize their culture. According to Engels, we are transformed by the tools that our culture teaches us to use, and these tools can, in turn, be used to transform the culture:

> *The specialization of the hand—this implies the* tool, *and the tool implies specific human activity, the transforming reaction of man on nature. . . . (quoted in Vygotsky, 1978, 7)*

Think of the relationship of a tennis player to the racket. During the very first lessons, the racket feels external, something that the self acts on; in Martin Buber's terms, the relationship is one of I to it. But, as the player practices, there is a process of incorporation: The racket becomes part of the self. Even our language suggests this internalization—we say "I hit the ball," when, really, we moved a racket, which hit the ball.

Vygotsky's bold extension of Engels was to consider language (and other sign systems like numbers) as a cultural tool that we internalize and use to act upon our environment. According to Silvia Scribner and Michael Cole:

*Like tool systems, sign systems (language, writing, numbers) are created by societies over the course of human history and change with the form of society and the level of its cultural development. Vygotsky believed that the internalization of culturally produced sign systems brings about behavioral transformations and forms the bridge between early and later forms of individual development. (Vygotsky, 1978, 7)*

Vygotsky's concept of language as a cultural tool has been so influential because it avoids the anomalies of the dominant universal models of development. For one thing, it accounts for cultural differences in cognition. Different cultures offer up different tools—different ways of conversing, different ways of reading, different "ways with words"— which members of these cultures then internalize. If we view all humans as progressing through universal, invariable stages, a divergence from this norm is classified easily as a deficit. By contrast, Vygotsky allows us to take a foxlike view of development.

A second contribution of Vygotsky's concept of development is the role of education that it suggests. A major problem with Piaget's work was discovering what it meant for education, a difficulty that Vygotsky pinpointed:

*[Binet and others] especially feared premature instruction, the teaching of a subject before the child was ready for it. All effort was concentrated on finding the lower threshold of learning ability, the age at which a particular kind of learning first became possible.*

*Because this approach is based on the premise that learning trails behind development, that development always outruns learning, it precludes the notion that learning may play a role in the course of development or maturation of those functions activated in the course of learning. Development or maturation is viewed as a precondition of learning but never the result of it. To summarize this position: Learning forms a superstructure over development leaving the latter essentially unaltered. (80)*

Essentially, Vygotsky turned this position on its head.

If development involves the progressive internalization and integration of "cultural tools," then instruction (both formal and informal) can lead development. This is the case, according to Vygotsky, because

*every function in the child's cultural development appears twice: first, on the social level, and later, on the individual level; first,* between *people (*interpsychological*), and then* inside *the child (*intrapsychological*). . . . All higher human functions originate as actual relationships between human individuals. (57)*

This distinction prepares the way for Vygotsky's powerful concept of the "zone of proximal development." Characteristically, he works toward this concept by critiquing traditional means of instruction where learning is matched to the development levels already achieved—where instruction follows development. He then makes the disarmingly simple observation that "what children can do with the assistance of others might be in a sense even more indicative of their mental development than what they can do alone" (85).

Vygotsky defines the "zone of proximal development" as the "distance between the actual developmental level as determined by independent problem solving and the level of potential development as determined through problem-solving under adult guidance or in collaboration with more capable peers" (86). This collaborative instruction, these social, interpersonal interchanges that occur in the zone of proximal development, ultimately are internalized as part of the child's independent cognitive competence.

Vygotsky's discussion of this zone is maddeningly brief, leaving numerous questions. How, for example, does an educator determine what this zone is? At times, Vygotsky refers to stages and levels, as if everyone is moving on a predetermined track, yet his use of such terms seems curiously at odds with his theory of language as a cultural tool, with different cultures and subcultures internalizing different tools. Secondly, what kinds of interaction best lead the child from *potential* to *actual* development? Finally, there is the problem of relating child development to the learning of school subjects (Moffett's great question, as well), which Vygotsky identifies but does not address:

> *Each school subject has its own specific relationship to the course of child development, a relation that varies as the child goes from one stage to another. This leads us directly to a reexamination of the problem of formal discipline, that is, to the significance of each particular subject from the viewpoint of overall mental discipline. (91)*

This observation closes the chapter on the interaction between learning and development, reminding us how much work Vygotsky leaves us to do.

Despite the tantalizing brevity of Vygotsky's explanation, it does offer a good starting point for examining the role of talk in development. If what he calls the "higher psychological processes" originate in "relationships between individuals," then conversation or dialogue is surely at the heart of the learning process—we incorporate (literally, "take into the body") social patterns of communication into our individual thought processes. Vygotsky's major work, posthumously titled *Mind in Society*, might have been called just as accurately *Society in Mind*.

## SCAFFOLDING

James Miller, a researcher in cognition and language, once noted that there were two dominant theories of language acquisition, one, the behaviorist stimulus-response model, that was impossible, and the other, proposing a language acquisition device, that was miraculous (referred to in Bruner, 1983). Jerome Bruner, examining mother-child talk, has theorized that caretakers provide a "support system" for the young child. The child's talk with the caretaker is not imitation, as the behaviorist model suggests; rather, the parent, acting in Bruner's words as an "agent of the culture," does more than provide input for the child's language acquisition device.

One type of support that the parent provides is *scaffolding*. In talk with children, caretakers often help them assemble a story or a request by asking questions or offering prompts. A request, for example, has several components: the child needs to indicate the person whose help is requested, the action or sequence of action requested, and the place where this action will occur. To put all of these pieces together in advance is very difficult for a young child. In the following transcript, drawn from Bruner (1983), Richard (at twenty-two months) is trying to get his mother to get up, go to the cupboard, and get something out of it (it's not clear whether Richard knows that the telephone is in the cupboard until he sees it):

RICHARD: mummy, mummy
MOTHER [*remains seated*]: What?
RICHARD: muh, mummy mummy come [*points briefly to the cupboard*] [*section omitted*]
RICHARD [*steps up to cupboard, one door of which is open and the other bolted shut. Throughout the following, Richard alternates between looking at mother and looking into cupboard, touching the closed door, or putting hand inside the open half*]: up, up, up
MOTHER: Up the cupboard?
RICHARD: cupboard
MOTHER: What do you mean, "Up cupboard"?
RICHARD: up cupboard; up cupboard, up cupboard, up
MOTHER: Do you want me to get up?
RICHARD: get up [*Mother and observer laugh.*] cupboard; cupboard; cupboard up, cupboard up, cupboard up, cupboard up
MOTHER [*gets up and joins Richard beside cupboard*]: I can't pick the cupboard up! [*Opens cupboard and talks softly to Richard.*]
RICHARD [*stands squirming, looking down. Looks into cupboard, spies a toy telephone*]: telephone
MOTHER: How about these two telephones? You get out the

telephone and make a telephone call. [*Starts to walk away; cupboard door swings shut again.*]

RICHARD: mummy [*goes to mother, pulls her by the hand toward the cupboard*] mummy get out telephone [*tries to reopen cupboard, then watches mother*].

MOTHER [*props open door]*: There you are! You get the telephone out then.

RICHARD [*reaches into cupboard*]: plates out [*excited*].

MOTHER: Mm?

RICHARD: plates out

MOTHER: Plates out!

RICHARD [*extracts plates from cupboard, carries them back to sofa, looking up to mother and smiling.*] (110–11)

In this dialogue, the mother provides guided assistance to Richard as he assembles his request. First, Richard indicates that he wants *something* from his mother. The "What?" from the mother prompts him to indicate where he wants her to go. Her question, "Do you want me to get up?" prompts him to indicate an intermediate action. Once at the cupboard, Richard identifies what he wants from the cupboard—the telephone. And, significantly, near the end of the exchange, Richard assembles a complete requesting statement, "mummy get out telephone."

A number of researchers (Applebee and Langer, 1983; Cazden, 1982; Graves, 1983; Sowers, 1985a, 1988) have adapted this scaffolding model, initially used to describe language development in very young children, to describe school instruction. Susan Sowers has modified the guidelines for scaffolding in tutoring situations (Wood, Bruner, and Ross, 1976; Ratner and Bruner, 1978) for application in the writing conference. The person doing the scaffolding helps the writer to focus attention on critical features of the text; the conference has a predictable structure; the roles are reversible (that is, once the child is familiar with the patterns, he or she can assume the role of questioner); and the tasks are "amenable to having the constituents varied" (the role of the "scaffolder" can change as the child gains competence) (Sowers, 1985a, 321–23).

We can see a number of these principles at work in the following transcript of a conference conducted in one of the classrooms from which Sowers drew her data. The student, a first grader named Donna, is just finishing her writing and begins her conference by explaining that the scratches around her neck in the picture that she had drawn were supposed to be her skates. After Donna reads the piece, the teacher paraphrases it:

TEACHER [*turning the pages as she summarizes*]: You're talking about when you went ice skating. You said you put on warm clothes like a warm sweater and a warm pair of pants. And then you walked to the ice skating pond and then you fell a lot. And then you started to ice skate good. And you skated a lot and then you went home.
DONNA: Is that a good story?
TEACHER: What do you think?
DONNA: Yes. It tells about what I did when I went ice skating yesterday. I think that's good to know what I did when I went ice skating yesterday.
TEACHER: Is there anything else you did when you went ice skating?
[*Interruption.*]
DONNA: You know, I think this story does make a little sense and tells what I did when I ice skated.
TEACHER: You think it what?
DONNA: I think it tells a little sense and tells what I did when I went ice skating. [*Pause.*] I did fall a lot.
TEACHER: How did you feel when you fell?
DONNA: Cold. My sore toe was getting sorer every minute.
TEACHER: Why was it getting sore?
DONNA: Because I kept falling on my sore toe and that hurt—a lot.
TEACHER: You said you fell down a lot and then all of sudden you said you were skating good. How did you feel. . .
DONNA: Because I was very happy when I started to skate good.
[*Interruption.*]
TEACHER: Donna, if you think about this story and the story you wrote about the fantastic whale—remember that story—which do you think is better?
DONNA: This one because I think it makes more sense. It tells you what I do when I go ice skating. And this one's true and the other one isn't—"The Fantastic Whale."
TEACHER: Is there anything else you'd like to add to this story?
DONNA: I think it's just right the way it is.
TEACHER [*accepting Donna's decision*]: You like it just the way it is.

(Newkirk, 1988, 156–57)

This conference follows a pattern familiar to Donna: first, the teacher paraphrases the piece, an operation that Sowers calls "reflecting." then there is the request for additional information, and, near the end of the conference, the teacher asks for the student's evaluation of the piece and a decision about whether it should be changed. Donna is so familiar with the types of questions that she reverses roles and asks the teacher, "Is this a good story?" a question that the teacher normally asks her. The atmosphere is casual, and there is no hint of criticism when Donna decides not to make any additions. The entire exchange seems to take place at the edge of Donna's competence, at or near her zone of proximal development. She will expand her text orally ("in collaboration"), but she is not yet ready to do so independently.

But scaffolding, like any model or metaphor, limits at the same time that it explains. To begin with, scaffolding is developed around exchanges between people of unequal abilities (a parent and a child, a tutor and a pupil). Conversations among peers, which do not fall into the master-apprectice classification, may be quite different. Secondly, there are inherent problems with the metaphor itself—a scaffold is constructed around a building that is under construction, to give it support until it can stand on its own (D. Searle, 1984). If the teacher or caretaker is the scaffolder, then the child is the building, being erected to specifications over which he or she has no say. It may seem that I am stretching a point here, but the emphasis on predictability, or "offering [students] a structure in which utterances can be inserted" (Sowers 1985a, 322), can (and, in my experience, often does) lead to rigid, formulaic discussions—the antithesis of conversation. As one first-grade teacher noted, "It's not predictability I want, it's unpredictability."

A third objection is similar to one that I made in Chapter 2. In that chapter I argued that treating drawing as rehearsal for writing devalues drawing, transforming it from a valid and important medium of expression into a form of prewriting. Drawing is often treated as a crutch—and a crutch is a scaffold too—that will disappear once the child no longer needs it to visualize a subject to be written about. In other words, drawing is swallowed up by the competent mind. Similarly, if talk is viewed as a scaffold for writing, it becomes a means and not an end. Like good medicine, we know it has been effective when we no longer need it.

A useful mental exercise is to turn this viewpoint upside down. What happens if we view writing as a part of the talk process? What if writing is pretalk? What if conversations about writing did not follow predictable text-based routines but were allowed to proceed more serendipitously, as good conversation does, often moving away from the child's draft altogether? In the next section, we will look at some group discussions among kindergartners and first graders that seem to break out of the scaffolding pattern.

A fourth reservation about the scaffolding model concerns its reliance upon questioning as the primary form of elicitation. For many children, this questioning is familiar—for example, Richard, the child in the dialogue quoted earlier, will have responded to tens of thousands of questions by the time he enters school and so will recognize them as helpful prompts to extend his language. But this may not be as universal as researchers like Bruner (1983) have suggested. Susan Philips (1972) found that children at the Warm Springs Indian Reservation in central Oregon were not comfortable when asked questions and that "learning by making public mistakes" (381) was not a congenial way for them to learn. Sarah Michaels (1981) has found that some black children perceive teacher prompts and questions as interruptions. Heath (1983), in her study of a black community in the Piedmont, near the border between North and South Carolina, found that children there did not learn to speak by answering questions. She writes:

*Children [in Trackton] do not expect adults to ask them questions, for, in Trackton, children are not seen as information-givers or question-answerers. This is especially true of questions for which adults already have an answer. Since adults do not always consider children appropriate conversational partners to the exclusion of other people who are around, they do not construct questions especially for children, nor do they give the young an opportunity to show off their knowledge about the world. (103)*

As one woman in her study commented:

*Ain't no use me tellin' 'im: Learn dis, learn dat, what dis? what dat? He just gotta learn, gotta know; he see one thing one place one time, he see sump'n like it again, maybe it be the same, maybe it won't. (105)*

These children learn how to participate in discussion by attending to the words of their elders, often imitating part of the conversation or oral routine and adding variations to the imitation later. For boys, in particular, learning to converse means learning to take the stage, to perform.

Thus, cross-cultural work suggests that an interrogative scaffolding approach may be both unfamiliar and unappealing to some students, who may favor a performatory approach. In conversations about writing, these students may want to break away from discussing the text through questions and answers so that they can take their own turn, tell their own story, give their own performance. And, as the transcripts in the next section will demonstrate, many decidedly middle-class children push beyond the scaffolding structure so that they can, as the Hawaiians say, "talk story."

## DEBBIE'S "QUESTION"

It was sharing time in Florence Damon's morning kindergarten class at Mast Way Elementary School in Lee, New Hampshire. As always, the children had spent most of the morning at different task areas in the room, one of which was the writing table. For most of the year, sharing time had involved having the children sit in a circle on a large rug in one corner of the classroom, after which Florence would invite a child to read a part of the piece of writing that he or she had been working on. She would ask a question or make a comment and move on to the next child, until everyone had had a turn. By the final quarter of the school year, when a research assistant and I began to tape these group shares, this procedure was becoming difficult to complete—the children were writing more and, understandably, wanted to share "the whole thing."

In late April, Florence changed the procedure, limiting each sharing to three children, who would sign up in advance. The children would sit in "the author's chair" (Graves and Hansen, 1983), an adult chair so big that their feet seemed to dangle a foot above the floor. A child would read and then ask for questions or comments from the classmates in the circle. (By this time, most of the children understood from Florence's modelling that questions asked for more information, while comments generally identified something that was liked.)

It is Marc's turn to share, and he reads a piece about his visit to Sea World and about swimming there—presumably at his motel near the park. After he finishes, he picks among the raised hands:

MEGAN: I liked your story.
MARC: Thanks.
JOSH: Why did they let you swim there?
MARC: 'Cause, 'cause, 'cause we wanted to swim there.
AARON: Why did you want to go to Sea World?
MARC: 'Cause I like it there.
AARON: How did you know why Sea World was there?

MARC: We saw where the baby Shamu babies were born when we went there.
[*Unidentified*]: I saw a baby Shamu when I sent to Sea World.
KRISTY: My grammy went to Sea World and she saw baby Shamu and she taped it.
CHRIS: I went to Disney World and I saw Candu, Shamu, and baby Shamu.
BRIAN: What was your favorite thing at Sea World?
MARC: The killer whale.
ERIN: Did you like it at Sea World?
MARC: Yeah.
DEBBIE: Once I went to Disney World with my parents and my brother and, um, we were trying to catch Space Mountain, and it was about twelve midnight or something, and we were the last people on, and they closed the chain, right when Mom was right there, and she said, "Wait, hold it, I'm his wife," and he, this guy, let Mom in and we all got on it. And while we were running we only had about eight minutes and we passed mom's parents looking, and we were like "Oh my God," cause they live in, um, where's David moving?
MRS. DAMON: David, Connecticut?
DAVID: No. I'm moving to Rhode Island.
DEBBIE: My grandparents are from Rhode Island, and we're like, "Why are, why are our grandparents here right now?" We were wondering.
DAVID: Did you see any jellyfish?
MARC: Yeah.

The most obvious shift in this discussion comes when Debbie enters it. Up to that point, Marc holds the floor, even though his answers seem like those of the reluctant witness. Marc, his experiences at Sea World, and his account of those experiences are the initial focus of the talk. Even the brief comments of Kristy and Chris do not take the attention away from Marc. But Debbie's story does; Debbie speaks for as long as Marc did; she treats his story as a turn, not as the obligatory focus of all conversation. When she comes to a gap in her memory, she asks for help without relinquishing the floor.

Debbie's entry into the discussion poses a dilemma for the teacher: Should she be allowed to move attention from Marc to herself? The answer is no if the purpose of a group share is to help the writer by making evaluative comments and asking questions—as the scaffolding model suggests—since Debbie clearly is diverting the commentary from Marc's writing. But, if the group share is viewed as a discussion, *initiated* by the writing, Debbie is participating, and participating well.

For one thing, Debbie's comment is "topical." Erving Goffman (1976) describes this feature of conversation:

*There is the question of topicality: Often the subject matter must be adhered to, or a proper bridge provided to another. There is the question of "reach" and the etiquette concerning it: Just as an addressed recipient can—whether encouraged to or not—respond to something smaller or larger than the speaker's statement, or to only one aspect of it, or even to non-linguistic elements of the situation, so, too, a statement can be addressed to something more than the immediately expected response. (291)*

Debbie's story, which seems like a non sequitur on first reading the transcript, follows logically on several shifts that have already occurred in the talk, particularly on Chris's statement, "I went to Disney World and I saw Candu, Shamu, and baby Shamu." Chris himself maintained the theme, initiated by Marc, of killer whales and tourist parks, introducing Disney World as the place where he saw the whales. Debbie then picks up on the topic Chris introduced—Disney World—to tell her story about Space Mountain.

Debbie also shows herself to be a good storyteller. In her narration of about a hundred words, she recounts one major crisis—the mother not being allowed to join the family—and one coincidence—suddenly seeing her grandparents. She interjects dialogue to heighten interest, and, though her turn is long, she is able to hold her listeners' attention. Her skill is twofold: By building on Chris's comment, she is able to situate her story so that it does not seem gratuitous, and she is able to tell it effectively. She understands both the grammar of the conversation and the grammar of the story.

## FINDING THE EGGS

Most of the transcripts that we made were of share sessions in Pat McLure's first-grade classroom. Unlike the kindergartners, who sometimes had to be reminded to sit in the author's chair or would raise their hands and then forget their questions, the children in Pat's class were veterans. Group discussions traditionally had taken place in her classroom, but, until fairly recently, these had been show-and-tell sessions. Writing now replaced the rocks and dolls that the children used to bring in, but the pattern of sharing was similar.

Pat starts off her first-graders' day with writing. As soon

as the coats are hung on the pegs outside the door, children pull out their writing folders, pick a seat, and get to work. On most days, Pat is engaged in a conference within five minutes of the official start of school at 8:40. She can begin so quickly because the children are responsible for most of the class's routine jobs: A fifth grader comes in and takes care of lunch money, and a member of the class is in charge of the "job can," a coffee can with hooks on the side on which name tags are hung. Among these routine jobs is signing up two people for group share, which begins after the writing period, at 9:10, and runs to 9:30. The child in charge of group share picks up a clipboard, checks a sheet at the back to see who has not yet been asked to share (when everyone in the class has been asked, the person with this job puts in a new sheet), and walks around the class asking people if they want to share. Once two people have signed up, the clipboard is placed in the corner of the classroom where shares take place.

At 9:10, without any announcement from the teacher or any alarm going off, students head toward the share corner, where they form a tight circle. The first child to share takes the author's chair, a yellow cane rocker with bright cushions. When the group is seated and quiet, the child begins to read a passage from a book, a piece of writing done by a classmate, or, most frequently, something that he or she has written.

On April 23, Misa shared her account of hunting Easter eggs. After reading, she called on class members who wanted to enter the discussion. I will quote both the text that Misa read and the discussion that followed. When reading this transcript, consider the issue of topicality, the way that students successfully bridge from Misa's story to their own:

MISA [*reading and showing accompanying pictures*]: "My uncle is named John and my aunt is named Karen. I woke up. I jumped on them. I went downstairs. I saw a cat. It was very little. I am looking for the Easter eggs. The hardest place is the refrigerator. My uncle looked in the fridge. He said, 'Oh.' He made me go over to the fridge. It was there. I took it out. The end."

KATE: I think it was a nice story.

REBECCA: Where are some of the places that the Easter bunny hid the eggs?

MISA: One was in the fridge, one in my sister's baby bouncer.

JAIME: Baby bouncer?

MISA: That's where you put your baby; it's called a "Jolly Jumper."

MARTIN: If you put an egg in there, the egg would bounce.
MISA: No, it wouldn't. And, um, he hided it on the shelf, and in the flower pot [*laughs from everyone*], 'cause it, it didn't really show 'cause the flowers were all pink and the egg was pink. And, um, in my aunt's and uncle's and my shoes and my sister's shoes.
ANDREA: My brother found one in one of his shoes.
MISA: And...
MARTIN: Why, did he step in his shoe? And crush it?
MISA: I can't remember all of it; that's all the ones I remember.
KATE: You got practice on Easter because whenever we came over... [*she gets too quiet—something about hiding eggs*].
MISA: Oh, yeah. I, we, hided the eggs for my uncle to find, and I hided them in the hardest place. The last one he found, well, um, see there's a counter, there's two counters, but it's not close together, there's like this little tiny crack, and I, um, I put it in there and he couldn't even find it until I gave him a clue.
KATE: I thought it was fun to do.
MARTIN: Um, did you know something? I, um, I got this box, it was my basket, and, um, um, um, there were two eggs, they were over at the side and when I turned up to the door where we let our cats in, guess what was there? An Easter egg. Right under the TV. And my brother, when he was a little kid, guess where his basket, we only found my sister's, my mother's and my father's, but guess where his basket was? My mother said and my father said, it was in the, um, in the pots or something. It was a good hiding place.
BILLY: Um, I think that's, um, nice because I, the Easter Bunny took a bowl, I couldn't hear him, at my mother's house, he took it, he put it in the sink, with no water in the sink, he put the egg inside of it, and then he tipped the bowl over, and when I looked, there were all the eggs, right there under the bowl. Then Mom said the paper's all wet and the sink was wet. And if Easter Bunny could take a towel and wipe it off instead of just putting the wet paper just there too.
EMILY: Um, my mom, my dad hided one of our Easter eggs for our Easter hunt in the, um, wood, in somewhere and we had this little, little place in our house, and hid a little Easter egg up there so no one could see it so my sister ran over and took the Easter egg out because she finally found it.
JEFFREY: Um, on Easter, I was looking around for eggs, then after we were done, after we came home from Easter, we, um, from Easter church, um, I found more and my brother was

just down there eating, and I found about ten more pieces of candy, and then, I had, um, about, first I didn't see all the candy, I had, um, I had, um, thirty-six hundred pieces of candy. I did.

MISA: I only had thirty-six.

SEAN: Last Easter, I had an Easter hunt for my Easter basket, and I got up about 6:30, I went downstairs, I saw this note on the TV [*Martin says, "Oh, no.*]" I'm like, "What's that?" and I go upstairs, back in bed, come downstairs about five minutes later, I read the note, I go to the kitchen because the note says to go to the stove. There's a note there that says, "Go to the microwave." I go to the microwave, it says, "Open the microwave door," I go into the living room, I'm like [*Jaime says, "Scared?"*]. Five minutes later I go into the other, I go into the kitchen. I open the microwave door, and there's a ring toss and my Easter Basket. [*Some laughs.*]

ADAM: Um, Um, on the last, on the last Easter, on the last Easter, when I woke up, it was Sunday, well, ah, what I did was I jumped up on my bed, jumped down, and I walked over to Zachary's [*his brother*], and jumped on his bed, and he said, "Mommy," he thought it was a monster and, um, then he was scared [*inaudible*]. And Zachary only got four eggs 'cause he didn't know the correct spots, he only looked in mine and Zachary's shoes. And, um, I got, um, seven of them, and, um, I looked downstairs, and in the den, and all over the place. I even found one in Mommy's hand upstairs. She was hiding one.

AMANDA: I had an Easter egg hunt, we hid the eggs all over, in the flowers and everything, and, and my mom [*inaudible*].

HANNAH: I like your illustrations, and, um, I like the cover of the book, how you put the lines on it. And I like the color of the book. And, um, I like all the pictures. And it's funny when you jumped on your, um, uncle and aunt when they were sleeping.

MISA: I always do that. In the evening I say "I'm going to wake up at 1:00 and jump on you." But I really wake up at five.

HANNAH: And, um, whenever it's Easter or Christmas, I go up to my mom and I yell and scream "Time to wake up" and I start jumping on them.

These exchanges took approximately ten minutes, and involved thirteen class members, well over half the class. *The teacher said nothing.*

In analyzing this discussion, I do not mean to suggest that the children consciously plotted their strategies for participation. Yet, if we are to value talk such as this, we need to be clear about the communicative skills of the class members. One of their most obvious skills is their ability to work within the themes that Misa had established in her piece of writing—waking up others on holiday mornings and finding well-hidden Easter eggs. Even ten minutes after Misa had finished reading, Hannah's comment, the last of the discussion, continued the theme that Misa had originated. While staying within Misa's themes, the participants worked variations on them: Jeffrey talked about looking for Easter candy; Sean explained how he looked for his Easter basket; Adam reported on waking up his brother.

The spontaneity of the discussion also obscures the complexity of what the children were attempting when they told their stories. One problem was describing where a difficult-to-find egg was hidden, something that Misa did quite well:

*. . . he hided it on the shelf, and in the flower pot, 'cause it, it didn't really show 'cause the flowers were all pink and the egg was pink. . . .*

*I hided them [the eggs] in the hardest place. The last one he found, well, um, see there's a counter, there's two counters, but it's not close together, there's like this little tiny crack, and I, um, I put it in there . . .*

The children who followed Misa's lead struggled to do what she did, to describe an obscure hiding spot. Martin tried:

*. . . but guess where his [my little brother's] basket was? My mother said and my father said, it was in the, um, in the pots or something. It was a good hiding place.*

Billy tried to describe a hiding spot under a bowl, but his description was diverted by an explanation of drying the bowl (or the egg). And here is Emily's attempt:

*. . . my dad hided one of our Easter eggs for our Easter hunt in the, um, wood, in somewhere and we had this little, little place in our house, and hid a little Easter egg up there . . .*

In exchanges like these, the first description can become a model that others approximate—Martin even borrowed Misa's flower-pot hiding place. I imagine that, just as there is a zone of proximal development where the child can, in collaboration, demonstrate competence (the group clearly helped Misa with her description), there is territory just at the edge of that zone. It is possible that Martin, even with the aid of questions, could not have been more specific; Misa's description may have provided a model just out of his reach. In fact, she may have given him a glimpse of his own future.

Sean may have done the same thing when he told his story about finding the ring toss game. His story came a few turns after Martin's, which also included his account of finding an Easter egg:

*...when I turned up to the door where we let our cats in, guess what was there? An Easter egg.*

More than any of the other stories, Sean's uses such short episodes to build tension:

1. I got up at 6:30.
2. I went downstairs.
3. I saw a note on the TV.
4. I think, "What's that?"
5. I go back upstairs.
6. I come back downstairs about five minutes later.
7. I read the note.
8. I go to the kitchen because the note says to go to the stove.
9. I go to the microwave because the next note says, "Go to the microwave."
10. There's a note there that says, "Open the microwave door."
11. I go to the living room because I'm scared.
12. Five minutes later, I go into the kitchen.
13. I open the microwave.
14. There's a game of Ring Toss and my Easter basket.

Martin followed Sean's story closely, interjecting "Oh, no," when Sean mentioned the first note. Ralph Waldo Emerson said that one's reach must exceed one's grasp; I would wager that Martin was reaching to tell stories like this one.

All of the stories told in this share session were, if not absolutely true, at least plausible. Jeffrey may have come the closest to crossing the line when he claimed to have found 3,600 pieces of candy (although first graders use numbers in a fairly creative way). But this class evolved a fairly complex rule concerning veracity (and, as far as I could tell, the teacher did not enforce or even endorse it): It is permissible in written fiction to claim that you have done things that you have not actually done but impermissible to do so in a group share. A child who had written a story about flying a jet and crash-landing near the Pyramids could share this story but would be required to identify it as "not real" if asked, and no one could respond with a fictional story about when he or she (in this classroom, it would have been a "he") crash-landed.

This issue of distinguishing the true from the imaginary recurred in a number of sessions, and, according to Pat, one of the first questions asked in a share session in September was "Is that true?" In one of the sessions that we recorded, it was the dominant theme.

Rebecca, a leader among the girls, has written about a "Blood Rock," which she found in a local cemetery. In sharing time, she explains that, according to legends, "they smashed Indians' heads on it." Throughout the session, Rebecca maintains a tentativeness about what she had seen. Cheryl asks her if it is a "fairy tale," and Rebecca replies:

*I don't know if it is a fairy tale, but it's true, I think. But my Nana or my granpa don't know if it's true.*

Rebecca describes the rock as having some "orangey stuff" on it. "We don't know if it's blood or just rust or something on it." Jaime suggests that the rock may be a grave, and, characteristically, Rebecca replies, "I don't know, it may be a grave. My Nan thinks that they might be at the grave of Indians."

Midway through the share, Brad tells his story:

*Once I went to India and I saw an Indian and an Indian head, and somehow its skin was under it and all the skin was still on, then, um, I cracked it open, and there was only one piece of muscle under it like, and I cracked it some more and I saw the skull, and I saw all the squished-up blood vessels.*

His attempt to tell a more "disgusting" story than Rebecca's draws some "ooohs" from classmates, but Rebecca's comment is quiet but firm: "Don't tell me that again." Brad has crossed the line, and Rebecca informs him of that fact. The only even mildly critical responses that I heard involved the violation of this veracity rule.

This rule was also in effect during the group shares when a fiction piece was read, particularly if it was far removed from the experiences of class members. It was possible to respond to stories like Misa's on the Easter egg hunt by telling one's own story, but how could someone respond to a jet-plane-at-the-Pyramids story without telling what my mother would call a "story." I found the shares on fiction stories less interesting for this reason—they lacked the associative storytelling that occurred when real-life events were the focus of the share. But some boys in the class did find a way around this dilemma:

Beginning with "I'm going to write a story...," they would relate the fictions that would be in that story (although they rarely went on to write these imagined stories). For example, here's Jaime's response to Jeffrey's "volcano story":

JAIME: Maybe in my volcano story that I write, I take a jet, and, um, it's my jet, and you, me, Jeffrey, Richard, Brian, and Justin and Adam and Martin and Jimmy, we all go. We all go through the air in a jet, and it's a crowded jet, and it's a crowded jet and we are going through the air 100 miles per hour.
BRAD: More than that, 500 miles per hour.
SEAN: 5,000 miles per hour.
BRAD: The jet will fall out of the air going 100 miles per hour.
JAIME: And we land right on top of a volcano that hadn't erupted and we climbed up, and, um, it started to erupt when we got to the top and you [Sean] said, "Uh oh."
SEAN: I know, "Uh oh, spaghettios."
JAIME: No, and then we roll right on down the hill...and then, well, Justin staying in the jet and, well, the rest of us, besides Justin, are going to the top of the volcano, um, one of us accidentally falls in, but you threw a rope down, and I grab it, and then you pull me up and then we run to the jet because the volcano's erupting. And then, and then I say, "Prepare for takeoff." And you take off. And we land back in, and I forgot the way back so we landed in your yard.

Jaime was followed by Brian, who began, "I'm going to make a story where it's me...." It seems that, in this exchange, the group of boys who specialized in adventure stories had found a way of building fiction stories without violating the veracity rule. They cast their fictions in the future tense as projects that they are going to attempt. It is highly unlikely that Jaime will ever find himself in an exploding volcano, but it is at least possible that he could write a story in which he does.

Up to this point, the focus has been on the longer contributions to the discussion, yet not everyone made extended comments. Some students seemed to make formulaic comments, sometimes the same one for almost every piece of writing. A child might ask, for example, "What's your favorite picture?" or make the comment, "I liked your story," as Megan in Florence Damon's kindergarten class did for almost every piece. In one first-grade class, a child insisted on complimenting every writer on his or her picture—even when there was no picture. During my interview with Pat McLure, she commented on these questions:

*I really do think that some of them need the security of the patterned questions for a while before they'll try others. I don't think we can outlaw them. I think it's important that everybody in the group—anybody—can get into the discussion on any given day. That has a lot to do with the sense of community that you build up. You have a few of these predictable comments and someone will kind of repeat them and then all of a sudden they'll be more comfortable with telling their own story. We have conversation starters. You go to a cocktail party and you're mingling with people and there are certain things you say: "Hi," "How are you?" "How've you been lately?" "Did you have a good winter?" There are certain things you can talk about that are safe, easy starters for you.*

One of Pat's roles is to model questions and responses that go beyond the formulaic. Most of her questions are about specific information that relates to the piece of writing, and her comments show how to be specific when praising the writing. "Sometimes I'll say what my favorite picture was and then give a specific. And, hopefully, somebody will pick up on the idea that's there's a little more to it than a patterned response." The way that Hannah comments on Misa's group share is a good example of a student following the teacher's model:

*I like your illustrations, and, um, I like the cover of the book, how you put the lines on it. And I like the color of the book. . . . And it's funny when you jumped on your, um, uncle and aunt when they were sleeping.*

Hannah's comment also shifts the discussion back to Misa, which is another role that Pat plays. She wants the discussion to fulfill two potentially conflicting purposes—to provide an opportunity for the author to receive responses and questions, as well as an opportunity for the class to discuss topics raised in the writing. If discussion shifts too completely away from the author, Pat will often bring it back with a question. Pat also makes a record of each share session in a notebook with a section for each student. When taking notes, she does not try to analyze a discussion (that will come later, when she uses her records to speak with parents and write progress reports). Rather, she tries to record the discussion as faithfully as she can.

This analysis has stressed the skills that individuals gain by participating in groups like the one that forms in Pat McLure's classroom at 9:10. The more closely we look at transcripts of share sessions like Misa's, the more complicated they appear, and the more impressive the contributions of the participants. The children know how to enter a discussion by building on established themes; they show linguistic skill in their descriptions and narratives, critical skill in their ability to be specific about their reactions, and social skill in their ability to live by communal standards of veracity. But, if we stop our analysis here, we may be missing the most fundamental reason why group discussions are important. It is not because they foster individual competence as social patterns of exchange are internalized, but because they create communities. And it is profound belief in the potential of groups that came through clearly in my interview with Pat. She expressed some frustration that she didn't have time for share groups in other subjects:

*I really think you could have group shares for just about everything. I mean if students work with the computer and they figure directions for the LOGO turtle to go one way or the other or they've made a design. If they could share with all of us what they did, it would make it that much more valuable for everyone. We could all be part of it.*

This desire to be part of the achievements of others, to partake in them, is not something that we transcend as we become more comfortable with literacy. It is not a scaffolding that can be removed once these social processes become internalized, particularly in the case of writing. Mina Shaughnessy (1977), speaking of older basic-writing students, notes that:

*The spoken language, looping back and forth between speakers, offering chances for groping and backing up and even hiding, leaving room for the language of hands and faces, of pitch and pauses, is generous and inviting. Next to this rich orchestration, writing is but a line that moves haltingly along the page. . . . (7)*

Clearly, for young writers, writing is the richer for existing in a generous sea of talk.

The same may be true for the more experienced writer. There is a residual loneliness in reading and writing. Richard Rodriguez has written movingly in *Hunger of Memory* (1981) of having to leave the family room and the warmth of talk there, to study alone in his room. Walter Ong (1981) has spoken of the paradox of the writer, who, seeking to reach thousands or tens of thousands of readers, must close the door and work alone. We all pay tribute to talk when we take every possible opportunity to find our groups, to talk endlessly, as writers do, about our work, to arrange readings, to beckon to the oysters:

*"O Oysters, come and walk with us!"*
*The Walrus did beseech.*
*"A pleasant walk, a pleasant talk,*
*Along the briny beach. . . ."*

# 7
# One teacher, one classroom: A conversation with Kathy Matthews

Deerfield, New Hampshire, lies thirty miles inland, where the topography changes from the flat coastal plains to gentle hills. Still untouched by the frantic development of the seacoast, farms and woodlands have not been turned into housing tracts. Deerfield is best known for its fair in September, where people come to admire handmade quilts, watch ox pulls, and get a flavor of the nineteenth century.

The George B. White School in Deerfield evokes a traditional New England home. A sprawling building, originally a small elementary-junior-high school, it has had two new additions in the last twenty years. Now, portable classrooms—a more recent New England tradition—extend from one side of the building. There are plans for a new school. To reach the main office from the front of the building, one must go down a set of steps, walk through the small gym-cafeteria where first graders might be practicing hopping, up a series of steps along a corridor of classrooms, and then down another series of steps into the most recent addition.

Kathy Matthews teaches second grade in the front (old) part of the building. Even though the school is no longer small, her classroom seems cut off. Only the very occasional announcement over the loudspeaker interferes with the impression of a one-room schoolhouse, an atmosphere that she tries to foster. Near the center of her classroom, at the edge of the carpeted area for group sharing, is an old school desk, made by Sears Roebuck in the mid-nineteenth century. On the desk, Kathy has carefully placed a quill pen in a glass inkwell, a basket made of sweet grass filled with beeswax balls, an 1879 McGuffey Reader, and an 1838 edition of *The North American Arithmetic for Young Learners,* which begins by asking children to practice counting: "See this flock of blackbirds: they are lighted upon the bars of a gate, and are all singing together. Find how many there are on each separate bar." An inviting introduction, I thought, to the study of arithmetic.

I spoke with Kathy in her kitchen of her home, which was built about 1730. The centerpiece of this kitchen is an immense cast-iron stove with gleaming nickel-plated trim and a copper water tank. The stove crouched on the floor, short legs slightly bowed, its feet the size of lion paws. As we sat at the kitchen table, a large tabby cat rubbed against Kathy's boot until she picked it up and began stroking it.

"There's a part of me that is rooted very much in another century and would like, in my twentieth-century classroom, to create the kind of atmosphere that we're rapidly losing in America, and that is the atmosphere of the one-room schoolhouse were it's a real family learning together. I know that I may be glamorizing it, but I had an experience in a two-room schoolhouse in my first two years of school, and that is an important part of me. I went from there to a really large school, and that was the beginning of getting lost in education.

"My fondest memories come from those two rooms. I had five kids in my first grade. I can't remember many details, but I remember really sensory things—the smell of the room, and the feel of sitting near the window and the sun coming through, the smell of the wax crayons, the sound of the room next door, the muffled sound. And the other things, having to go across the street to the dairy to get the milk. And very fond memories of the teacher, who was very sensitive and caring. It was very traditional, I'm sure. I was reading Dick and Jane. At the same time, her attention helped instill life long interests—an enjoyment of reading and an appreciation of visual things.

"What I try to do with kids is to create that sense that we're all at different levels of learning and being, but we're all a family working together—the sense I had as a child in that school. So the desk is sort of a link for me between my own past and my interests plus what I want to generate for kids. It's symbolic, I guess. And we spend a lot of time looking at the way life used to be. The desk is something real. They can sit in it, or I can sit in it and talk about what it would have been like 130 years ago."

This chapter will focus on the uses of writing in Kathy Matthews's classroom, and, for the most part, I will let her do the explaining. But it is about more than writing; it is about curriculum and ways of thinking about curriculum. Too often, a curriculum is conceived as a management plan, imposed from the top and implemented by classroom teachers—the teacher acts as a technician. For Kathy and, I believe, for most teachers, decisions about how and what to teach are rooted in personal philosophies about teaching, which are, in turn, often rooted in our own experiences as learners. Our philosophies may be only disguised autobiographies; we try to re-create for students the best of our own educational pasts. So what follows is not a description of techniques to be plugged into a writing program; Kathy's approach to writing is hardly a program at all, in the traditional sense. Her daily decisions about writing have long roots, both in her own experiences, positive and negative, as a learner and writer and in her sense of history.

"I grew up believing that I could not write, that I was never going to be a writer. I was told by teachers again and again that I couldn't do the job in that area. I was totally paranoid about sharing writing with other people. Getting involved in PROJECT WRITE [a local writing project that drew on Donald Graves's work in Atkinson, New Hampshire] was a terrifying decision for me. I discovered through working with Judy Egan [a teacher in PROJECT WRITE] and reading William Zinsser [*On Writing Well*, 1980] that there really was a process to writing and that the error had not been in me but in the way I had been taught, in that I had never been given time to work my own way through my process. It had to be done picture perfect the first time. Don Murray helped me, too. I could identify with the process of self-discovery that he described. He gave voice to things that I didn't know I had before, that I had my own process for doing things. So I began to trust that."

The growth of this awareness that she had her own process of learning paralleled the evolution in her teaching of writing. She originally adopted the conference/workshop model developed by Donald Graves and his associates at Atkinson, New Hampshire (where Kathy taught for four years).

"I was feeling a lot of satisfaction on one level but some

dissatisfaction at another level because it wasn't quite me. I felt like I was wearing someone else's clothes. As I began to gain more confidence in myself, or began to get past the initial period that I think everyone goes through—'Am I really doing the right thing?' 'Am I really doing this the way it's supposed to be done?'—I realized that there wasn't a right way to do it. And, once I could let go and stop worrying about the framework and really start paying attention to the kids, it was the kids who led me because I started to watch what they were doing."

Kathy's initial writing-process model, with which she became uncomfortable, focused on the writing done in a set block of time during the day and, at least in the first descriptions of the approach, stressed personal-experience writing. She still has a writing block, during which children can write on topics of their choice, usually autobiographical and personal experiences, although she does not push them in that direction. During this block, Kathy meets individually with students for conferences, and she does most of her direct teaching of writing skills at this time (although these are reinforced throughout the day). She focuses more on revision during this time block than she does during other parts of the day. And each writing block ends with a group sharing, with the writer taking the "author's chair" (Graves and Hansen, 1983), reading the piece aloud, and then asking for questions and comments.

Important as it was for her students, Kathy felt that a single block of writing time wasn't enough. There were valuable writing experiences that the students were *choosing* not to have. And not all students excelled at story writing, although this seemed to be the thing to do at writing time. She needed to find a way to extend the range of possibilities and began to look at ways to do so outside of writing time. Most importantly, she felt that the writing itself was disconnected from learning in the other subject areas.

"What I need to stress to you is that I'm not coming to the class as a writer. I'm coming as a writer, a reader, a mathematician, a scientist, an artist. I have to have expertise in all these areas to have a fully functioning, integrated curriculum—because that's the most important thing of all, for children to see that learning is not segmented into all these pigeonholes called curricular areas. I think of it like weaving. The strands of the curriculum are like the threads of the warp with their different colors and textures. Each separate yet, taken together, acting as one. The writing is the weft that is woven in and out, over and under and around the warp to create the fabric, the tapestry, of learning. For me, the writing holds everything together—and pulls it together into something taut and recognizable. It's not a separate curriculum."

The bedrock of Kathy's curriculum is the relationship that she establishes with her students at the beginning of the year. When I visited her classroom in November, she warned me that she could only do what she did because of a "foundation of trust" that had been laid earlier.

"I think it starts before school begins, when I go out and visit all the kids in their homes to introduce myself to them and to get to know them in a more secure setting. That's where I begin to lay that foundation of trust and to let them know how I'm going to approach things. And then we begin talking from the very first day of school about how we're going to be a very close 'community,' using that term. We're going to work together. There're going to be problems, there're going to be thrills, there're going to be all of these things. But there're going to be responsibilities, and one of the responsibilities is to respect each other.

"I have to lay that groundwork immediately so that kids know they can take risks and no one is going to ridicule them. That I'm not going to let someone laugh at their writing, and I'm not going to laugh at it. I take their work seriously. I don't think I'm an adult looking at kids' writing and saying, 'Isn't that cute.' But I try very much to establish a writer-to-writer dialogue with kids. They begin to trust what I'm going to do. And that keeps building and building, by my not trying to take over their process, by my not trying to tell them this is the way I want you to do it, but by giving them support and reinforcement—gradually, the trust becomes self-fulfilling. They assimilate it into their whole approach to the classroom.

"It's interesting because, this year, I've had four children who came from very traditional schools in other places, one girl, in particular, came from Florida. She had a difficult time adjusting to my classroom. I was giving her a completely different message than her previous teachers had given her. They had told her that she could only write words that she could spell, could only write what they had written on the board, and that she had to copy that story or poem or whatever it was. Or they would give her a story starter. And she came into this classroom where this crazy lady with curly hair is telling her that she can write on anything she wants—"Don't worry about the spelling, don't worry about the handwriting"—and she was paralyzed. But, after a few days, when she saw that no one was ridiculed, that we were really supporting each other with a sense of enjoyment, she loosened up."

Kathy speaks of the "foundation of trust" primarily in terms of promoting risk taking by her students. Yet it frees her as well; if students are willing to experiment without fear of failure or ridicule, they will participate more readily in any new initiatives that Kathy might suggest. In the previous school year, for example, as part of the class's study of the Deerfield community, Kathy reenacted a bit of Deerfield history. Deerfield was part of Nottingham, seven miles distant, until the mid-1800s.

"To understand why two communities would separate and because we were wanting to focus on what school was like for children, we took a seven-mile horse-drawn ride over the back roads to the old Nottingham Square Schoolhouse. And we spent the day living this moment in 1835 history. It was an incredible experience to have all the kids dressed up and for me to dress up like an old schoolmarm. They had to bring their lunches and lunch baskets, and they had to bring food typical of the time."

Kathy's writing lesson that day stressed good handwriting. "Neatness," she reminded her students, "is essential to good education." Letters should be formed with "a fluid motion." To reinforce this message, she used an old Shaker practice of placing a mint candy on each child's writing hand. "If it stays on," she said, "you may keep it. If it falls off, I will take it back."

Kathy's metaphor of the "curriculum as tapestry" is persuasive, but, to me, it seems too static. As she commented later in the interview, "the design of the warp and weft are ever changing with each class of children, with each new experience in the day." It is Kathy's ability to improvise that has always made her classroom a fascinating place to visit. Each activity seems to have its own history or story. When I visited her classroom in November, the focus was on the barn dance as a traditional community celebration. I asked her how that came about.

"The beginning of that was really part of our discussion about how communities celebrate and how, in the past, celebrations in a rural community like Deerfield were closely linked to the earth and the seasons. The culmination of the harvest season was a dance, a significant celebration. Coincidentally, we were reading *The Little House in the Big Woods* [by Laura Ingalls Wilder]. There was a big barn dance, a big celebration, in that. But it really went back to last year, when children's authors Bill Martin and John Archambault came to our school. They recited *Barn Dance!* for the kids before it had been published. It came out before Christmas last year, and I bought the book for the kids for Christmas, and the very first time I read it, the natural rhythm of the book caused the children to get up and start dancing at just the right moment, and, when the dancing part of the book was done, they stopped. It was one of the most incredible things that could ever happen—that kids would spontaneously do that.

"This year we read *Barn Dance!* again, and we were talking about the harvest season as we were reading *The Little House in the Big Woods* again—and it just kind of came together. I guess I got the idea one day when I said to one of the teachers that I'd like to have a barn dance, and she said, 'You can use my barn.' And it just grew from there. That meant we had to bring in a folk musician and a folk-dancing teacher who taught the kids basic folk-dancing steps. And, from there, all the language and vocabulary that the kids developed was incredibly exciting—just their awareness of folk music. These kids had never had any kind of understanding of the language involved in folk music, and they went into hysterics when we talked about "My baby done me wrong, my baby done me dirty."

"One of the best things happened when we went to see *The Nutcracker* in Boston. In the party scene, the children were doing the same dance that these children learned to dance. And I had never realized that before. They were doing the Lady's Chain and the Promenade—and the children's faces just lit up like, 'My god, we know this, we know what this is about.'

"And I think so much of what Don Holdaway has helped me learn about literacy learning is that providing experiences for children enriches language and that language enriches experience. It's become a part of my thinking about how critical it is to elaborate and extend experiences in many directions because it does become a wonderful cycle—the circle that keeps coming around."

After the barn dance, the children wrote about it in their daybooks (journals), and Kathy herself wrote about it in her monthly newsletter to parents (which she shared with her students in draft form), quoting from *Barn Dance!* and from the students' journal entries:

OCTOBER–NOVEMBER NOTES

*"He tiptoes through the kitchen. . . an' he tiptoed up the stairs. . . as quiet as a feather. . . on a breath of air. . . he hummed a little do-si-do. . . an' flopped himself in bed. . . with wonders of the barn dance. . . dancin' in his head."*

*The music of the fiddle and the mandolin has faded into memory. Firewood and snow shovels clutter the floor where young feet danced in rhythmic patterns. Two weeks have passed, yet "the wonders of the barn dance" still dance in our heads. It was a magical night—a time when strangers and friends were brought together by the ancient bond of music and dance.*

The circle keeps coming around.

## THE JOBS OF THE CLASSROOM

Just as Kathy attempts to connect past and present, she tries to connect the life of the classroom with adult professions and the literacy involved in those professions. In her October-November newsletter, Kathy explained her concept of "authenticity" to parents:

*Learning for authentic purposes is central to my philosophy of teaching. I don't isolate the curriculum into chunks or pieces, nor do I put the children through pages of empty exercises. Rather I strive to help the child see how everything is fused together. I want them to understand that what and how they learn has meaning and purpose: we read and write, compute information, investigate questions to make sense of the world, to become functioning members of our society, to know what it is to be human. And I want them to know that all learning is interconnected.*

*We don't write, for example, to learn the mechanics of spelling, handwriting, grammar, punctuation. Instead, like adults in their world, the children write to communicate with others through stories, plays, lists, letters, notes, advertising, journals, news, etc., etc.*

*Sometimes I'm the one who carefully constructs the authentic experience; other times examples spring spontaneously from the children and I gently guide them in the direction of curriculum goals. But always their learning experiences have purpose and dignity.*

"Authentic," for Kathy, means corresponding to the purposes for which adult societies use language; in effect, she tries to efface the differences between school and community. While preparation is part of her goal, it is not the kind of preparation that is justified with the argument responsible for so many sins in education—the "even-though-you-don't-like-this-you-need-it-later-on," education-as-sour-medicine approach.

More central to Kathy's philosophy is the belief that children *enjoy* purposeful work and are motivated to achieve the sense of power and dignity—of competence—that comes from accomplishing adultlike tasks. The four-year-old delights in helping to wash the car. Much of children's fantasy—preparing make-believe meals, making a clubhouse out of chairs and blankets—attempts to duplicate the purposeful activities of those who are older. Even witches cook.

Kathy has assigned classroom jobs to her students for a number of years, but only recently has she connected writing to many of these jobs. For example, she asked the students to write "job descriptions":

*The News Reporter: The news reporter should watch the news and write the news every day on the newspaper.*

*He or she should write the date on the top of the newspaper.*

KATIE

*The Mathematician: The mathematician has to do a graph every morning.*

*The mathematician has to keep the math area clean. He or she puts things away if they aren't in the right place.*

JASON

*The Meteorologist: Every day, the meteorologist writes the temperature, the precipitation, the air movement, the sky conditions, the forecast, and the outlook.*

*The meteorologist writes about the moon, too.*

SHANE

*The Horticulturalist: The horticulturalist has to water the plants in the class. The horticulturalist has to spray them and take care of them and not give them a whole lot of water.*

*He or she has to try not to break the plant. Dead leaves and flowers have to be picked off.*

*The horticulturalist has to feed the plants, too.*

(AUTHOR UNKNOWN)

Among the other jobs are artist, scientist, architect, sanitation worker, naturalist, and postal clerk. These official titles are used when talking about the work in the classroom, one of the many purposeful ways in which Kathy introduces new vocabulary.

The writing associated with the jobs actually begins as soon as children enter the classroom. The mathematician picks up a clipboard with a sheet of paper containing a survey question; within the next twenty minutes, the mathematician has to ask every class member the question, record the answer, and write a statement summarizing the results. One difficulty with this job is keeping track of who has been surveyed, so that no one is left out. One student, Debbie, decided that she needed another student to help her, and so, with Kathy's encouragement, she wrote two "Help Wanted" signs, which she posted on the classroom walls. One read:

*Help*
*Wanted for the Mathematician*
*I Need Help on Checking if I had*
*Not missed any one*
*for more information*
*Go to*
*Debbie*

Often the surveys ask for information about the class members (How long have you lived in Deerfield? What's your favorite part of Thanksgiving dinner?). But one survey dealt with an unsolved crime. Someone (something?) had dug up the bulbs that the class had planted in front of the school. Jason, the mathematician for the day, determined "that people are most unlikely, and a dog is most likely, and something else is in between."

In these surveys, a variety of language activities are fused: The mathematician must read the survey form, interview every member of the class, and summarize the results in writing. The student gets arithmetic practice by adding up the responses in each category, totalling the sums, and seeing if the final total equals the number of students in the class.

This combination of reading, writing, and arithmetic is also built into the word problems that students write, which are duplicated for the class to solve during math time later in the morning. Many of these problems use the names of people in the class:

*Once Jenny, Crystal, and Amy went to get their pictures taken. Chad brought 22 boys. How many children are there?*

MELISSA AND CRYSTAL

And some are small narratives:

*Once upon a time long ago a little girl named Ann was having a birthday party. Ann was a good little girl. She only had five people come. They all went to breakfast together. Everyone got one egg and two pieces of bacon. How many pieces of food all together.*

KATIE

*There were 10 planes. Launch was at five p.m. They started at three p.m. It took them one hour to go to base. One ship blew up. BANG! Three ships ran out of gas and blew up. Two ships crashed. How many were left?*

AARON

Aaron's problem poses an additional challenge, requiring students to distinguish between relevant and irrelevant information.

The class assembles at 8:20 to hear reports from various job holders. Most of the children sit on a rug, while a couple of students sit on the bench of the old desk. Kathy sits in a Boston rocker (circa 1820) by an easel. The meteorologist has filled out the weather report on an oversized piece of lined paper on which Kathy had written the categories of information to be gathered. Kathy reads what the meteorologist—in this case, Amy—has written:

WEATHER REPORT

*Date: 11/17/87*
*Time: 7:55*
*Temperature: Cool*
*Precipitation: Dry*
*Sky Cover: Foggy*
*Air Movement: Slightly breezy*

*Today's Forecast: it is supposed to be warm and sunny*

*Extended Outlook: it is supposed to be warm the rest of the week with chances of showers*

*The moon is: waning*

The class updates the report. Kathy asks them to look outside to see if there is still a breeze. The trees are motionless, so she crosses out "Slightly breezy" and writes "Still." The children also notice that the street is now wet after a light rain, so "Damp" is substituted for "Dry." Again, vocabulary work, reading, and writing are fused in one activity.

Next comes the news, which, like the weather report, is written on oversized paper (approximately twenty-three by eighteen inches). Amber, the reporter for the day, has written:

*Today is tuesday .n.o.v. 17, 1987 11/17/87*
*.n.o.v. 17 .n.o.v. 17*

*Today's news: Amber's dog looked like she did a jumping jack and she did and her name is mia.*

At the beginning of the year, Kathy had written all the news, but she has begun to hand that job over and hopes that the news increasingly will be written by the reporter. Kathy and the class read in unison what Amber has written, and Kathy compliments her on using the third person (the children naturally want to use "I"). She then writes out "November 17, 1987," explaining that she would like the news reporter to use the full date. On another day, she might have provided a very brief skills lesson, perhaps on using one period for abbreviations or a capital letter for "Tuesday."

Children then raise their hands and tell their news. When it's Kelly's turn, she tells a fairly detailed story about her parents hiding birthday presents and her strategy for snooping. Kathy asks, "What's the news you want me to write down?" and Kelly dictates, "Kelly was snooping for birthday presents when her mom wasn't home last night." Within ten minutes, the paper is full, and Kathy and the class read it in unison:

*Amber's dog looked like she did a jumping jack and she did and her name is Mia. Tom Newkirk came back to visit. A raccoon was walking in front of Jenny H.'s house. Kelly was snooping for birthday presents when her mom wasn't home last night. Miles is leader today. Chad's mother is going to make up some math problems for him to do. Jenny D. and her mom saw three gray squirrels in her yard. Melissa's dog knocked her over this morning. Katie's glad it's art today because she's working on a present for her sister.*

It's the class biologist's turn now. Miles goes to his desk, returns with a fern in a plastic bag, and reads what he has written about it:

*This is something I picked off a stone wall. There is a little animal. I think it is a little caterpillar.*

Miles passes around the fern, and the children wonder aloud whether the caterpillar will turn into a butterfly and how long that would take. After the sharing session, Miles will place his display, with his explanation, in the biology area of the class.

Melissa, the class naturalist, comes forward with a bird's nest that she has found. She, too, has a written explanation:

*I found the birds nest behind my wood pile. It used to be in a tree but a bird came and ate the little birds. I was getting my ball when I found the nest on the ground.*

The children crowd in to look at the nest. Kathy asks them to think about why the nest fell out of the tree, and they speculate on that. Then Melissa, like Miles, takes her exhibit to the appropriate display area. The morning share ends with an explanation of the arithmetic work to be done in the next time block and a reminder from Kathy that some of the work areas could be neater.

## MAIL

During the morning, students interrupt their work occasionally to write notes, which they fold and place in a cardboard mailbox. Like most of the writing activities in Kathy's class, the mail system evolved over a period of years. "Learning to write letters is part of the second-grade curriculum—we have a very open curriculum. It's my responsibility to know the content of the curriculum, but then I'm free to interpret it in any way I want to. So it's in my mind that, at some point in the year, we're going to deal with letter writing. And it just came about spontaneously because, for years and years, I've had this discussion with kids about the problem of interrupting me in conferences and how to resolve that. What I did years ago was to try to get them to come to the conclusion that they should write me notes if there was an emergency. I've done that successfully every year—to plant the seeds for them to come up with the ideas." Kathy smiles, "I call this 'creative guidance.'"

"This year's kids wanted to take it even farther. They wanted to write notes to each other. And that evolved into this incredible discussion about the mechanics for that, and one thing led to another, and it evolved into a genuine post office. Here was a community of kids talking about a particular need that the community has—the need to write to each other. And they realized that fulfilling that need required certain responsibilities and a lot of logistics. They created the office of postal clerk. And they're not done with it yet. They really want a legitimate post office, so one of the things I'm going to have to do over vacation is rearrange the classroom because they are still insistent that they need individual mailboxes. And they need a postal office where they can sell stamps. So we're getting into economics and money—which is timely because we deal with that in the second-grade curriculum."

So just what is the curriculum in this classroom? And who decides it—the teacher, the students, the school? The answer, as this description of the postal system suggests, is very complicated. Recent critics of the writing process, such as George Hillocks in *Research on Written Composition* (1986), have described the "natural process approach" as being almost entirely student directed, with the teacher playing a supporting but not a directing role. Even in careful descriptions like Kathy's, certain expressions suggest that the students do the leading and she does the following. The idea of the postal system, she claims, came from the kids. It came about "spontaneously," and "one thing led to another." Language like this seems to corroborate the criticism that whole-language education or the writing-process approach is laissez-faire. But Kathy's descriptions also contain a countervailing language. She speaks of "planting seeds," of framing the discussion on interruptions so that students at least would see the possibility of writing notes. She speaks in the interview of her "overwhelming responsibility" to be an effective model and of the power that gives her. Her influence is strong in virtually every area of the class—not only what and how students learn, but how they behave toward each other at lunch and recess. It is her class.

So the language of freedom is juxtaposed with the language of authority. Part of the challenge of explaining the writing-process/whole-language approach is the difficulty of reducing it to an assertion, for, in dialectical fashion, each assertion calls up a contradicting assertion, an antithesis, that is also true. A few years ago, Neil Postman debated ending his book, *Teaching as a Conserving Activity* (1979), with "and vice versa." This "vice versa" complicates any statement about the locus of responsibility in the writing classroom. Kathy can say that an activity comes from the kids and then go on to explain how the activity has a long history in her own teaching—and, paradoxically, both statements are true. The children actively chose to establish the post office, yet the choice reflected their understanding and acceptance of the set of values and priorities promoted by the teacher.

Kathy's original reason for encouraging note writing was at least partly pragmatic—to avoid interruptions in conferences—but the need for students to write to each other is not as obvious; they can move around the classroom and talk together. But letters became another, more formalized and adult, way of making connections. Deborah, for example, sent a note with a picture of a rainbow to Mr. Sweet, the principal, who wrote back:

*Dear Deborah,*

*Thank you for the beautiful picture of a rainbow. I have put it up on my wall in my office.*

*You are a very good artist. Thank you again.*

*Sincerely,*
*Mr. Sweet*

The formalized graciousness in this reply would be difficult to duplicate in conversation. An apology can also sound more formal and dignified if it is written, as in the following letter that Crystal wrote to Debbie:

*Dear Debbie:*

*I like you a lot. I am sorry that I made a mistake and gave you [the letter for] Debbie M. I hope you forgive me. I am really sorry very sorry.*

*Love Crystal*

Letters also appeal because they can serve so many functions. Katie wrote to Amber to set up a meeting at recess:

*Dear Amber*

*I have to see you urgently at first recess and it's urgent.*

*Love Katie Smith*

In letters, the writer can also shift topics with ease, from boy talk (in second grade?) to reading habits:

*Dear Jen Someone wrote me a note it said, "I love you. You are cute." Who could of wrote that. I wish it was Rich. I am reading Little house on the prairie. My mom thinks I can read good.*

Aaron made three shifts in this letter to Katie, beginning with a serious compliment before moving on:

*I like your very sensible answers and questions. Now a joke for you Q. Why did the turtle cross the road. A. to get to the I will tell you at the count of three. One two three look at the back of the page. Now a Shel Silverstein poem*
*THE SADDEST THING I ever did see*
*Was a woodpecker pecking at a plastic tree he looked at me and then says he, "Things ain't as sweet as they used to be*

*[back of the page] to get to the Shell Station*

When Amy was asked to pick her favorite letter, it was a story that Kelly had sent her, in which they both were characters:

*Dear Amy once upon a time two little girls were walking to school [and they] saw a big wolf and they ran as fast as they could and Kelly slipped and Amy ran back to help Kelly then the wolf got so tired that his tongue hung out and then me and Amy saw the school the teacher said, "You girls look so beautiful." The two girls sighed. The End.*

Some students used the letters to complain. Deborah complained to Crystal about being youngest in the class:

*Dear Crystal:*

*I don't appreciate people who are mean sometimes. It's hard being 7 when you are the youngest. I want to be 8 but I have to wait for next year.*

One of subtlest letters was written by Katie on her word processor. She printed up copies for all the members of the class, adding each name by hand:

*Dear*

*I really think that Mrs Matthews has been trying hard to get us to clean up after ourselves. I don't want to push you around, but I think we should try to do that, as a favor to her.*

*PS do not show Mrs Matthews this note because I want it to be a surprise for her.*

Note the rhetorical skill of this writer, who wants to persuade without coercion. In the amazing sentence "I don't want to push you around, but I think we should try to do that, as a favor to her" the writer couches her request in a very complex construction in order not to appear bossy.

Not all of the letters were serious or even welcome. Students received pictures that made no sense, hastily drawn mazes, and "I like you, do you like me?" letters. Typically, Kathy and the group discussed this issue, and the group began to describe such letters as "junk mail."

### END-OF-THE-DAY BOOKS

At the end of the day, a half hour before the bell, Kathy announces that children should get out their daybooks and write. Suddenly, the classroom is quiet, almost calm. "I started daybooks several years ago when I was trying to pull us all together at the end of the day instead of it being frantic and all frayed. At the same time, I was visiting a friend, and she was using daybooks, so I borrowed her term and began using the same format. I consider it the best part of my day, because, when it is working well, it shows me the kids doing reflective thinking. They do writing that is different from other kinds of writing they do. It's also a time when I model my writing, too, so it's instructional because they can see that I can focus on one thing and expand it fully."

One girl, Kelly, profited from Kathy's model of descriptive writing. In much of Kathy's daybook writing, she tries to capture a mood through focused description, as in this September entry:

*The woods are warm in the patches of sunlight yet cool in the shade. The breeze was fresh and clean and carried the toasty sense of autumn that I love so much. Dry leaves skittered across dry needles of hemlock and pine, but the ground was cool and moist beneath the trees. Here and there bright splashes of color showed against the background of grey bark and brown—deep orange of spotted newt, scarlet red of partridge berries, pink-flushed white mushrooms poking shyly through the ground.*

Kelly's early entries were simple inventories, such as the following:

*September 9 1987 Today we did a story we are studying butterflies today we have gym we have information books we have lots of fun. the end*

Kelly wanted to know how Kathy "did it," how she was able to create such a visual picture, and they had a talk about details. This conversation led to an extraordinary transformation in Kelly's writing. Here is her daybook entry for September 30, just three weeks after the entry just quoted:

*The rain [is] drizzling. I hear the people whisper, kids rushing to get to their classes rushing from door to door trying to find their classes I love to hear rain fall I love to splash in puddles when you come back you have to take off your socks [they] are soaking wet they're black from soaking up the mud they're disgusting. It's black as night when mom puts my socks in the wash.*

Kathy's writing served, in Vygotsky's terms, as a "zone of proximal development," a model that could help children like Kelly see where their writing could go. For example, in her entries, Kathy regularly will reflect on what she is describing, and this prepared the way for one of Kelly's attempts at reflection:

*Have you ever thought about a new century like the year 2004 that you might be a mother or a father it seems so strange but [in] the year 2004 imagine how strange to look back at 1988 Just think how free you will be when you're a grownup but think how sad it would be because you would have to look back at your second grade and you can't go back to second grade and plus you might have moved away from your best friends.*

"I read the daybooks at least once a week, and, if I see that a child has gotten into a rut, I will say to the person 'It looks like this is happening to you and what can we do about it?' to help redirect them. Or I might try to do something different with my own writing."

After about ten minutes of writing time, the class again meets on the rug, and each child reads his or her entry. There are no responses, questions, or discussions after each reading, just listening. "I struggle with that. Sometimes, I want there to be a lot of time for them to respond because, if someone says something sensitive, I don't like just leaving it in the air. But I've pulled back from that temptation. Just because they are not talking doesn't mean they are not savoring it or thinking about it. Sometimes, you can just pull it into your own system, just do with it what you will and let that be very private. Again, that's where my own evolution is important. I've broken away from the writer's workshop/conferencing model where that's the only way you respond to somebody's writing. It shouldn't be the case. There are just as many ways to respond as there are to write. Having the mathematician do a graph and getting kids to respond to that is entirely different from the way they would respond to someone's narrative piece, and that would differ from a response to newspaper writing. It creates something different for the audience each time, too."

We had speaking for an hour and a half, and, though it was only midafternoon, the December sun had already begun to set, and the kitchen was getting cooler. Kathy moved the space heater closer to the kitchen table and searched for a way to sum up what she had been saying. After a pause, she said, "I approach writing through a philosophy of learning, but it's more than that—it's really a life philosophy. That all learning is a process. The symbol of the circle has profound meaning for me in a personal as well as a professional way. The circle is ongoing. There are no sharp edges to delineate a beginning and an end. Many times, the image of the circle is stretched out into a spiral—isn't it Bruner who talks about spiral learning? I see that happening in my personal life as well as my teaching—you come around again with a new perspective, with new insights, but the same philosophy. It's not a matter of 'doing writing process' that I can stuff into an already stuffed curriculum. It's a matter of a philosophy about learning, and the writing process is an aspect of it."

Kathy offered to give me a tour of her house before I left. The kitchen where we had been talking was a nineteenth-century addition to the original house. The main room of the house, the keeping room, is set with worn floorboards a foot wide and runs the width of the house. Built into one wall is a huge working hearth with a beehive oven. The windows, which I hadn't noticed at first, are as old as the house. I asked if she and her husband were doing renovations, and Kathy took me to the small entranceway and showed me several exposed beams, set 250 years ago during the decade when George Washington was born. "We're doing mostly structural work," she explained. "It doesn't show, but it's vital."

# PROCESS AND EXPERIENCE

# 8 Roots of the writing process

A true story.

One morning, at three o'clock, the phone rang. I remember an almost instantaneous feeling of panic: Someone has died—my parents, my brother—why else a call at this hour? My wife answered the phone and came back to tell me that it was the University of New Hampshire's campus police and I was to call them at my own office number.

I called my number, and someone from the campus police answered. He introduced himself in that wooden way of policemen and explained the reason for the call. "Professor Newkirk, I'm in your office, and it appears to have been ransacked. The light was on when I came by. The door was open. The file drawers are open, and there is paper strewn on your desk and the floor. The curious thing is that the typewriter is still here and your tape recorder is still on your desk. Nothing seems stolen." There was a pause. "I don't mean to be facetious," he finally said, "but could you have left it this way?" I sighed, admitted that I probably had, and asked him to lock the door.

This has become one of the emblematic stories that people tell about me to explain who I am ("Newkirk, yes, did you hear about the time he got the call from the police . . ."). I tell it now because I may leave this, the last chapter, in similar chaos. I should now be wrapping things up, perhaps summarizing the themes of the book, putting the file drawers in order, turning out the light. Instead, I will try to go beyond the more specific focus of this book—the range of young children's writing—to define the writing-process approach. The classrooms described in the previous two chapters are "writing-process" classrooms, but what does that mean?

In fact, the term "writing process" (also called "process writing"—too close to "processed writing" for my taste) is used so widely to describe so many different approaches to writing that, often, it is not clear what it means. This is probably inevitable. Educational terms, like radioactive elements, begin to decay immediately and have a very short half-life. Supple concepts rigidify. We hear debates about the virtues of the three-step Graves versus the five-step Graves. We see publishers' attempts to provide the ultimate guides to grammar instruction, spelling lists, and the (usually "step-by-step") writing process.

Beyond this, however, there is a still more basic need to explore the roots of the writing process. For one thing, discussions of the writing process have been ahistorical. One could think that no one had ever had these thoughts about writing before Janet Emig's case study of twelfth graders, which was published in 1971. Most glaring is the almost complete absence of references to John Dewey. Also ignored are the Romantics—Rousseau, Wordsworth, Coleridge, Emerson—whose insights (and excesses) still color the debates on writing. Too often, this complex body of work is described dismissively with the same epithet that labels the movement—"romantic," meaning naive, impractical, unworthy of serious attention.

An historical explanation will make it clear that anyone advocating a child-centered approach to writing instruction must face some very difficult questions. For example, what authority does the teacher possess? To what extent does the child choose his or her own path of development? To what degree are these paths directed by school and, indirectly, community? There are also questions relating to the very idea of "process." If we describe the intent of the curriculum as teaching processes, are we saying that content is largely irrelevant, since these processes can be applied to any content? How do we respond to charges such as those made by E. D. Hirsch (1984) that we are guilty of "formalism," defining a curriculum in terms of skills or processes without relation to content? Put another way, if one of the tenets of the writing process is that students should almost always choose their own topics, are we not saying that there cannot or should not be any common content to be learned?

These questions are not simply theoretical; they are practical as well. Suppose first-grade students continue to choose to write space stories that are imitations of TV cartoons. Should teachers, at some point, try to promote kinds of writing that they feel are more challenging, less stereotyped? To what extent would this interfere with the children's sense of "ownership"? Would it be an infringement? And if teachers do try to redirect children's efforts, how can they explain (if only to themselves) that one type of writing is more valuable? What scale of values are they applying?

I will examine the writing-process approach by analyzing key assumptions that seem to underlie it. These assumptions are often encoded in what the British critic Raymond Williams (1976) calls "key-words" and what Richard Weaver (1953) calls "god terms." These terms are often "incipient propositions" or "terms to which the very highest respect is paid":

*By "god term," we mean that expression about which all the other expressions are ranked as subordinate. . . . Its force imparts to the others their lesser degree of force and fixes the scale by which degrees of comparison are understood. (Weaver, 1953, 212)*

A god term will also point to its opposite, which becomes an ultimate rebuke. If "science" is treated as a god term, "tradition" might qualify as a term of rebuke. If "fact" is a god term (it was one of Weaver's candidates in 1953), "opinion," "speculation," and "belief" are its foes.

Before looking at the god terms of the writing-process approach, it is important to note two implications of Weaver's argument. First, god terms frequently come to be "uncontested"; that is, they do not need to be justified or even defined carefully. Their simple evocation is often powerful enough to carry the day; they offer the possibility of persuading without arguing. Second, the use of god terms and "devil terms" leads to a kind of binary thinking. The choice is either-or: "Nature" is *opposed* to "culture"; "authority" is *opposed* to "autonomy"; "society" is *opposed* to the "individual;" "aesthetic" is *opposed* to "utilitarian." By contrast, a dialectical approach tends to see these terms as existing in a creative tension. One does not rule out the other; each is dependent on the other for its vitality. Without this tension, we drift toward rigid, dogmatic positions that deal with human complexity only by ignoring it.

## PROCESS

The dominant term used by proponents of the writing-process approach is, of course, "process." It meets Weaver's requirements well, because it calls up its opposite term of rebuke, "product." In an important article, Donald Murray ([1972] 1982) urged teachers to teach writing "as a process, not a product." In this and subsequent publications, Murray and others argued that students do not learn to write simply by studying finished products or being told to create such products. At about the same time, Francis Christensen (1967) quipped that we don't teach students to write, we expect them to write.

This shift in emphasis produced a number of improvements in instruction: writing conferences, attention to prewriting techniques, peer-response groups, and others. It also initiated a trend away from group-comparison experimental approaches in writing research toward approaches that focused more carefully on what writers did as they wrote. I do not question the value of these changes. My question is different: Does the concept of "process" furnish an adequate philosophical basis for a writing approach? The answer, I believe, is no.

One problem is the polarization of "process" and "product." These terms are not, I would argue, alternatives. If we view students as entering a literate community—joining the club—it is through reading that they come to grasp the rules under which that community operates. While texts do not necessarily explain their own production, they do show the learner how things are done. Virtually every example of student work in this book illustrates this borrowing or appropriating of models offered up to the child. Murray (1980, 3) has written that we cannot infer the process from the product, "a pig from a sausage." My guess is that we do this all the time.

An adequate theory of writing must reject this polarity. Michael Polanyi's (1958) distinction between "focal" and "subsidiary" awareness provides a more satisfactory way of relating "process" and "product." He illustrates this distinction by describing the way that we direct our attention when we pound in a nail:

> *When we use a hammer to drive in a nail, we attend to both nail and hammer*, but in a different way. *We watch the effect of the strokes on the nail and try to wield the hammer so as to hit the nail most effectively. When we bring down the hammer, we do not feel that its*

*handle has struck our palm but that its head has struck the nail. Yet in a sense we are certainly alert to the feelings in our palm and the fingers that hold the hammer. They guide us in handling it effectively. . . . The difference may be stated by saying that the latter (the feelings in our palm) are not, like the nail, objects of our attention, but instruments of it. . . . I have a* subsidiary awareness *of the feeling in the palm of my hand which is merged into a* focal awareness *of my driving in the nail. (55)*

Polanyi makes two other important points about these types of awareness. First, when we shift our attention to the instrumentalities for completing an action, we become clumsy and self-conscious. If we concentrate on our hand, we're likely to miss the nail entirely. And, because we cannot really concentrate on our instruments, many skills are, in Polanyi's terms, "unspecifiable" or "tacit."

But what does this distinction have to do with the process of writing? When we write, our focus is on meaning—what we want to say. Right now, I am trying to connect Polanyi's concepts to the process/product distinction, and I'm thinking of little else. But, as I do this, I am also guided, tacitly, by my subsidiary awareness of the conventions for this kind of chapter and by models drawn from my reading. While I may not be thinking of specific models, I undoubtedly rely on them at almost every turn. Furthermore, I cannot imagine how I could put *my meaning* into written language if I did not have tacit models to guide me.

There is a strange captivity in all this. Writing, curiously, is an act of both assertion and submission, of origination and convention. We seek to write something original, yet that uniqueness is always partial—we are always borrowing, imitating. This paradox is illustrated eloquently in the following tribute to E. B. White, which appeared in the "The Talk of the Town" section of the *New Yorker*. The (unnamed) writer of the column notes how hard it was to find his style:

*I kept getting it wrong, because I thought it was incumbent upon me to sound like a writer. . . . For a long time I dressed in the styles of my time: terse and brave, like Hemingway; rough and low-down like O'Hara; sad and windy like Wolfe. I wasn't happy in these disguises, but I didn't know any better; young writers have more sense than this today. White set me straight. I'd been reading him right along, to be sure, but the qualities of "One Man's Meat" and "Quo Vadimus?" and the Comment pieces and "The Fox of Peapack" and "Here is New York" and the rest were so plain and clearly pleasurable—a glass of cool water, a breeze on the face—that they didn't feel like literature. . . . He was there to be liked and befriended but surely not to be emulated. It took me a long while to see how foolish this notion was, but when I did see it, I stopped imitating other writers (even E. B. White), and tried to be clear the way he was. (1985, 33)*

At first reading, this writer seems to be saying that White taught him not to imitate other writers but to find his own style. In fact, the tribute is more ambivalent. He leaves us with a paradox when he finishes by saying that he "tried to be clear *the way he [White] was.*" Is he still imitating White or not? The statement is both a declaration of independence and an admission of dependence. To add to the complexity, this writer, who claims not to imitate White, is writing a column for "The Talk of the Town," which White virtually invented, and, in his tribute, is clearly adopting the studied casualness of White and his successors.

There is a final irony. The writer is describing White's influence on his own writing process, yet it seems that he never met White. His only connection is with White's essays and commentaries—*products.* "Qualities" in White's writing influenced him. Means and ends—the pig and the sausage—intertwine in the act of writing. There is no choice between product and process. We must choose both and attempt to describe their complex relationship.

The writing process is also used to write about some content —we can't write writing—but how do we decide which content is more important for students to write about? Or do they make that decision? Is all content created equal? These objections are raised by advocates of "cultural literacy," most notably, E. D. Hirsch, who would surely find the writing-process approach to be a particularly glaring example of formalism. In the following passage, simply substitute "processes" for "skills":

*The notion that reading and writing are generalized skills has been an attractive theory in many countries, but especially in the United States. Formalism has served the very American ideal of practical efficiency. What could be more efficient than to learn a habitual skill that could be transferred to an indefinite number of future tasks. Another attraction has been its concord with the characteristic American ideals of diversity and pluralism. What could be more democratic and federalist than to leave the actual contents of teaching up to our diverse local school districts? (1984, 372)*

But the ultimate form of pluralism, Hirsch would surely argue, is to leave the determination of content to individual children. If virtually all the writing that children do is on self-chosen topics —if one topic is as good as any other—how can writing-process advocates avoid the charge that they regard content as irrelevant as long as children are engaged in the process?

I believe that answers can be made to this challenge, but Hirsch's basic argument is compelling. We cannot derive from the term "process" much of a clue as to what the process should be used for. The term implies nothing about the aims of writing. Philosophically speaking, the concept of process is neutral. According to Hirsch (1984), that may be one of its attractions:

*In the recent past, there has seemed to be enough truth in the idea that literacy is a transferable skill to make educational formalism a respectable theory to hold. One should add that it is also a safe theory to hold. Specialists in reading or writing or literature who adopt formalist theories need not commit themselves to any particular contents or values. They can present themselves as technicians who remain above the cultural battle. (373)*

Later in this chapter, I will try to show that Hirsch's own proposal for teaching cultural literacy is poorly supported—and would be educationally disastrous. But his criticism of formalism and his call for a less safe position, which acknowledges more explicitly the values that underlie an approach, are healthy. An approach that emphasizes the writing process has to stand for something more than *process*.

Two other terms that are often called upon to justify the writing-process approach are "choice" and "ownership," and both have the same problems as the term "process." Like "process," both have the virtue of directing attention to something that is neglected in traditional instruction. In Chapter 4, I cited Goodlad's study, *A Place Called School* (1984), which found that children made virtually no choices in their own education. Nearly 100 percent of elementary classes are dominated by the teacher in everything from seating to learning activities. Students in these classes are largely passive; they listen to the teacher for 50 percent of the school day and speak for 5 percent; only 1 percent of the day is spent on talk involving reasoning or opinions. Language instruction is dominated by basal reading and language programs where most of the work is in the form of worksheets or workbook exercises.

Goodlad, in a revealing allusion, compared his sensations during the study to those of someone watching Andy Warhol's *Haircut*, which focuses, for what seems a very long time, on the impassive face of a man getting a haircut. The tedium becomes close to unbearable. Then the man flinches and the audience bursts into applause. Goodlad found such a sameness from school to school—the focus on routine, the passivity, the lack of affect—that he felt like he was waiting for the flinch. Clearly, any call for reform must emphasize increasing the choices that students make. To think, after all, is to choose.

But "choice," like "process," is philosophically neutral. We cannot speak for long about choice without having to modify it—it is not simply choice that we're after, but wise choice or intelligent choice. Some choices are so unwise (not attending school, not writing) that we don't allow them. We have little patience for characters like Melville's Bartleby, who says, "I prefer not to." So, paradoxically, we want students to choose, but we want their choices to be consistent with our goals. The French philosopher Jean-Jacques Rousseau described this paradox in his book on education, *Emile* ([1762] 1979):

> *Let him [your pupil] always believe he is the master, and let it always be you who are. There is no subjection so perfect as that which keeps the appearance of freedom. Thus the will itself is more captive. The poor child who knows nothing, who can do nothing, who has no learning, is he not at your mercy. . . . Doubtless he ought to do only what he wants, but he ought to want only what you want him to do. (120)*

According to this argument, children should not *feel* coerced; they should engage willingly in schoolwork. But, because the teacher, in Rousseau's words, "disposes of everything which surrounds the child" (120), choices should be consistent with the aims of the educator. This, undoubtedly, is what we mean by oxymorons like "intelligent choice" or Rousseau's "well-regulated freedom."

The instant children walk into a classroom (and to choose not to would violate the law), they meet up with ideologies of literacy that limit choice. They learn that the day is divided according to different "subjects"; they learn that more time is devoted to some subjects than to others—more to reading than to art—and thereby learn the relative importance of symbol systems; they learn, in most schools, that they should work independently and that they will be judged independently. Even in writing-process classes, children learn which kind of writing gains approval, and they "choose" to meet that expectation. The seemingly neutral question "Is there any information you would like to add to this piece?" is a clear invitation to take a particular view toward written texts. From this question, children learn that:

1. The text is primarily the *words* of the text, not the words plus the picture or accompanying oral commentary.
2. The text is an object that can be judged to be complete or incomplete.
3. The text can be changed; it is not finished until the writer determines that it is.
4. The text is judged primarily in terms of "completeness" (beginning writers are rarely asked to shorten a piece).

When children are asked questions like this one, they are being asked to adopt a set of values that may be at odds with those that they already possess. I remember one first grader who had written a very brief account of her birthday party. The teacher asked a series of questions eliciting more information, ending with, "Don't you think people who read your story would like to know more about your party?" The girl thought for a bit and then said, "I got it. If they want to know more about it, I'll invite them to the next one."

There is, of course, nothing deceitful in having expectations or goals for students—would we trust a teacher who didn't? Certainly, children lack choices in the traditional classrooms described by Goodlad, but choices can only occur in environments, in social settings, where students are constrained to some degree, where the freedom is "well-regulated." The danger, as I see it, is that we may be blind to the values by which we judge choices. Or teachers may worry that they *impose* these values on children who should be free to make their own choices. I've heard teachers speak, hesitantly, about "intervening in the learning process of children" in much the same way that they might speak of sneaking into a child's room. But the authority of the writing-process teachers that I've seen is more pervasive than that; their classes reflect their values in a powerful way. Unfortunately, neutral terms like "process" and "choice" say little about these values.

The term "ownership" is usually used to defend the rights of students to determine the topics and strategies used in writing. It is used to assert the autonomy of children, their right not to be dominated by the expectations or demands of teachers or schools. Also inherent in this term can be a mandate not to "appropriate" (literally, take the property of) student texts or to deny "students' rights to their own texts" (Brannon and Knoblauch, 1982). Donald Graves worked another variant when he argued that schools perpetuate dependence, what he called a "welfare system," by always providing topics. By expecting children to choose their own topics, he continued, we will break this welfare system and create a situation where children are self-sufficient.

The language used to argue for ownership is often highly polarized. The intentions of the teacher or school are often viewed as opposing or suppressing the intentions of the student. For example, Cy Knoblauch and Lil Brannon (1984) argue:

*The teacher's agenda is the one that matters, for the responsibility for anticipating expectations lies wholly with students. To the extent that the teacher's expectations are not satisfied, authority over the writing is stolen from the writer by means of comments, oral or written, that represent the teacher's agenda, whatever the writer's intentions may initially have been. A student's job is to match an Ideal Text in the teacher's imagination which is insinuated through the teacher's commentary, not to pursue personal intentions according to the writer's developing sense of what he or she wants to say. (120)*

Note the set of polarities. The student has authority over the text; the teacher steals it. The teacher's expectations matter; the student's don't. What the student wants to say seems almost inevitably to be at odds with the teacher's agenda. The only honorable course for the teacher is to relinquish authority, becoming one voice among many responding to the student's text, because "there are no optimal responses, only more or less honest ones"(132). Honesty becomes the teacher's only permissible value.

"Ownership," "process," and "choice" are useful counterterms; they call attention to the inadequacies of traditional writing instruction. But "ownership," in particular, suggests an absolute valuation of the child's decisions—and an absolute rejection of institutional expectations. In Knoblauch and Brannon's statement, we can find echoes of earlier rejections of societal domination—by Wordsworth, Thoreau, Whitman, or Emerson in his essay, "Self-Reliance" ([1841] 1965):

*Society everywhere is in conspiracy against the manhood of everyone of its members. Society is a joint-stock company, in which the members agree, for the better securing of his bread to each stockholder, to surrender the liberty and culture of the eater. The virtue in most request is conformity. Self-reliance is its aversion.*

*Whosoever would be a man must be a non-conformist. . . . Nothing is at last sacred but the integrity of your own mind. Absolve you to yourself, and you will have suffrage of the world. (260)*

We may be stirred by Emerson's rhetoric and still be disturbed by his glorification of the self. Do we see such a glorification in educational schemes that are "child-centered" or view the goal of education as "personal growth"?

A dialectician, such as John Dewey, would argue that it is a mistake to treat either the child or the society as the fixed point of attention. In his essay, "The Child and the Curriculum" ([1902] 1956), Dewey wrote:

*But here comes the effort of thought. It is easier to see the conditions in their separateness, to insist on one at the expense of the other, to make antagonists of them, than to discover a reality to which each belongs. The easy thing to do is to seize upon something in the nature of the child, or upon something in the developed consciousness of the adult, and insist upon* that *as the key to the whole problem. When this happens a really serious practical problem—that of interaction—is transformed into an unreal, and hence insoluble, theoretic problem. Instead of seeing the educative steadily and as a whole, we see conflicting terms. We get the case of the child vs. the curriculum; of the individual nature vs. social culture. (4–5)*

Near the end of his career, after he had seen a number of "progressive" schools in action, Dewey ([1938] 1963) warned even more sharply against adopting a philosophy of reaction. His description of the debates going on at that time has a very contemporary ring:

*To imposition from above is opposed expression and cultivation of individuality; to external discipline is opposed free activity; to learning from texts and teachers, learning through experience. . . . (19)*

The danger, as Dewey saw it, was in developing principles of education "negatively," by inverting traditional emphases. By proceeding this way, the progressive movement took "its clew in practice from that which is rejected instead of from the constructive development of its own philosophy" ([1938] 1963, 20).

I propose that the same danger confronts the writing-process movement. Too many of the ultimate terms, those used again and again to justify this approach, are simply the obverse of traditional terms. "Product" is opposed by "process." "Assignment" is opposed by "choice." The "authority" of the teacher is set against the child's quasi-legal right to "ownership." But "the effort of thought," as Dewey would say, is to see these terms not as mutually exclusive choices, but as complementary principles.

## NATURE

Raymond Williams (1976), in his survey of "keywords" in Western thought, has claimed that "nature is perhaps the most complex word in the language" (184). Certainly, it is invoked regularly as the paradigm for child-centered language learning, or what is now called the "whole-language approach." For example, this is how one of the coeditors of a recent NCTE publication, *Observing the Language Learner* (Jaggar and Smith-Burke, 1985) describes the theme of the book: "A teacher's job is not to 'teach' children language, but, rather, to create an environment which will allow language learning to occur naturally." Almost all of the examples of children's writing that I have cited in this book seem to be the result of "natural" environments that the editors of *Observing the Language Learner* would endorse. The problem is the adjective. How can we determine what is "natural" and what is not when we are dealing with something as value-laden as language learning?

We can begin by distinguishing three different meanings of "natural" in this context. One we might call "natural-unforced": Children's learning should be natural in the sense that they participate in it willingly. They should be fully engaged because of their interest in the activity and not simply because they want to satisfy an external requirement or to avoid punishment. This meaning is useful as far as it goes. But children, particularly young children, adapt spontaneously to a range of social groups. The child of the alcoholic comes to see the alcoholic family as natural. I would imagine that the Puritan child participated willingly in a school dominated by rote learning and the *New England Primer* with its warnings of damnation. My first-grade daughter thinks it natural to complete worksheets where she is expected to find the drawing that is different and circle it. All of these "societies"—the alcoholic family, the Puritan classroom, the traditional first grade—may seem to us poor settings for learning, but, from the standpoint of participants, they often seem "natural."

But the real attraction of the term "natural" is that one can use it to argue without arguing. An appeal to nature is like an appeal to biological fact; the arguer seeks to transcend the debate about what is "good" and simply state what "is." It is to base a claim not on the shifting ground of opinion and debate, but on a seemingly firmer and unchanging reality. To paraphrase an old TV commercial, "You can't argue with Mother Nature." This line of argument is dangerous for two reasons. First, it may blind the proponent of the "natural" claim to the political or ideological reasons for an approach. It appears value-free when it is not. British critic Terry Eagleton (1983) comments on this problem:

*It is one of the functions of ideology to "naturalize" social reality, to make it seem as innocent and unchangeable as Nature itself. Ideology seeks to convert culture into nature, and the "natural" sign is one of its weapons. Saluting a flag, or agreeing that Western democracy represents the true meaning of the word "freedom" become the most obvious responses in the world. (135)*

Or, to offer another example, it was long thought that women "naturally" could not take on the jobs that men did or that blacks were "by nature" inferior to whites. It follows that most appeals to "nature" are really appeals to an unspecified and often objectionable set of values. They are rhetoric disguised as fact.

The second danger is identical to that connected with "choice" and "ownership." If the classroom is to be a "natural" environment, what authority do teachers have to shape that environment, to expect a certain kind of performance from children? Are their values less "natural" than those of the children? Do they denaturalize the classroom? There is an extraordinary tentativeness in much of the child-centered literature when it comes to describing what a teacher does. The teacher is not supposed to teach but to (and here there is a frantic search for a verb) "facilitate" learning. As we've already seen in the quotation from *Observing the Language Learner,* many educators speak of the need for teachers to create an *environment* (another key word in my opinion) that will take care of the actual teaching. But, as I have mentioned, teachers who create the interactive environments advocated by proponents of the writing process may actually exercise more influence than teachers in the traditional classroom. The writing conference, no matter how supportive and empathetic, is a powerful instrument for instruction, one in which the very questions asked imply a set of values. We're only fooling ourselves, Eagleton would argue, if we think that what we are doing is "natural."

In its second meaning, "natural" can refer to the inherent order of the universe. This is the meaning that Alexander Pope gave it in his couplet celebrating Sir Isaac Newton:

*Nature and Nature's laws lay hid in the night;*
*God said, Let Newton be! and all was light!*

Just as physical properties could be explained by natural laws, human growth followed a preordained path. Rousseau stated this general principle in *Emile* ([1762] 1979):

*Nature wants children to be children before becoming men. If we want to pervert the order, we shall produce precocious fruits which will be immature and insipid and not be long in rotting. We shall have young doctors [learned men] and old children. Childhood has its ways of seeing, thinking, and feeling which are proper to it. Nothing is less sensible than to substitute ours for theirs. . . . (90)*

It was apparently very common during the late 1700s for overeager tutors to have their young prodigies display their adultlike knowledge. Both Rousseau and William Wordsworth reacted to these displays with contempt and revulsion. The most caustic passage in Wordsworth's epic poem *The Prelude* ([1850] 1960) is a description of one of these prematurely wise children, "the monster birth/Engendered by these too industrious times." He continues:

*. . . 'tis a Child, no Child,*
*But a dwarf Man; in knowledge, virtue, skill;*
*In what he is not, and in what he is,*
*The noontide shadow of a man complete; (Book 5, lines 294–97)*

*He is a prodigy. His discourse moves slow,*
*Massy and ponderous as a prison door,*
*Tremendously embossed with terms of art;*
*Rank growth of propositions overruns*
*The Stripling's brain; the path in which he treads*
*Is chok'd with grammars. . . . (Book 5, lines 320–325)*

*. . . he must live*
*Knowing that he grows wiser every day,*
*Or else not live at all; and seeing, too,*
*Each little drop of wisdom as it falls*
*Into the dimpling cistern of the heart;*
*Meanwhile old Grandame Earth is grieved to find*
*The playthings, which her love designed for him,*
*Unthought of: in their woodland beds the flowers*
*Weep, and the river sides are all forlorn. (Book 5, lines 341–49)*

According to Rousseau, the fundamental error in this type of education was an overreliance on *words*. Children could learn the words, the "terms of art," the "rank growth of propositions," but they could not understand them because they could not connect this language to experience:

*Words, more words, always words. Among the various sciences that they boast of teaching their pupils, they are careful not to include those which would be truly useful to them. . . . Rather they choose those sciences one appears to know when one knows the terminology: heraldry, geography, chronology, languages, etc.—all studies so far from man, and especially from the child, that it would be a wonder if anything at all in them were of use to him a single time in his life. (108)*

The child taught the names of cities, states, and rivers learns not a description of the world, but names on a map. Rousseau recalls a geography textbook that began, "What is the world? It is a cardboard globe." Such, he concludes, is the "geography of children."

Rousseau's own scheme of education is often caricatured as permissive and laissez-faire. It is based on a conviction that children enter the world in a good and noble state, to which no additions would need to be made if we could *live* in a state of nature. However, since we don't live in a state of nature, since the child is destined to live with others, he (and, for Rousseau, it was a "he"—Sophie would be brought up quite differently) must be guided: "a man abandoned to himself in the midst of other men from birth would be the most disfigured of all" (37).

I can only outline the nature of this guidance here. There is a strong emphasis on physical activity. The very young Emile will not have strollers or padded bonnets; he will be taken regularly into fields and allowed to run. If he falls, "so much the better. That way he will learn how to get up sooner" (78). Rousseau boasts that his pupil will "often have bruises." Rousseau may also be the only major philosopher to speak of the value of throwing stones. This emphasis on physical strength and dexterity is matched by an emphasis on developing the capacity to perceive: "What becomes for us the art of reasoning, for them ought to be only the art of seeing" (145). He constantly is asking Emile to estimate sizes and distances. Nor are the other senses neglected; Rousseau spends more time developing Emile's sense of smell than he does teaching him to read.

When Rousseau does begin to teach Emile science, he strikes us as an eighteenth-century Mr. Wizard. To teach astronomy, he takes Emile out over the four seasons to show him how the sun rises at different points on the horizon. He sets up syphons to teach him hydrostatics. He describes an elaborate series of games with magnets used to teach how they work. "Be satisfied," he warns, "with presenting him with objects opportunely" (169). Anticipating the pragmatism of later educational reformers, he argues that knowledge should have utility. In a passage that could have come from William James (or John Dewey), Rousseau writes," 'What's it good for?' This is now [after age eight] the sacred word, the decisive word between him and me..." (179).

The emphasis on observation and perception is linked closely to a third meaning of "natural"—that which is not man-made. If nature is the god term, "society" becomes the term of rebuke. Nature is organic; society is mechanical and artificial. In the city, cut off from the redeeming and centering influence of the natural world, we are prey to pretense, opinion. Wordsworth paints a picture of a St. Bartholomew's fair in London that is positively disorienting and dehumanizing. Near the end of Book 7 of *The Prelude* (1960), he describes "This Parliament of monsters":

*...what a hell*
*for eyes and ears! What anarchy and din*
*Barbarian and infernal! 'Tis a dream,*
*Monstrous in colour, motion, shape, sight, sound.*
*(Book 7, lines 658–61)*

In this remarkable section, Wordsworth piles unnatural image upon unnatural image, until, almost in despair, he calls out, "Oh, blank confusion." He is able to reorient himself through the act of recollection, through a return to his "early converse with the works of God":

*By influence habitual to the mind*
*The Mountain's outline and its steady form*
*Gives a pure grandeur, and its presence shapes*
*The measure and the prospect of the soul*
*To majesty.* *(Book 7, lines 721–25)*

Childhood experience in the natural world thus provides an essential psychological resource that fortifies the individual. The images and feelings of childhood can be drawn upon to restore equanimity.

For both Wordsworth and Rousseau, the child's early education is presocial and rural. The city, in Wordsworth's words, is "a house of bondage." For Rousseau, cities are "the abyss of the human species. At the end of a few generations the races perish or degenerate. They must be renewed, and it is always the country which provides for this renewal" (59). The child is poorly equipped for civic life, according to Rousseau, because judgment is a capacity that must be learned. The child who adopts adult language and opinion without being able to judge them is extraordinarily vulnerable.

This general equation of rural life with the preservation of honesty and native intelligence has become part of American mythology, from *Huckleberry Finn* to *Mr. Smith Goes to Washington* to jokes about city folk asking Maine farmers for directions. It is also a particularly democratic view of learning. If the knowledge that matters must be obtained from institutions (that is, from the city), only an elite would have access to it. But the natural world is available to anyone. In the opening to *The Prelude*, after he has escaped that "house of bondage," the city, Wordsworth reclines under a tree:

*. . . sooth'd by a sense of touch*
*From the warm ground, that balanced me, else lost*
*Entirely, seeing nought, nought hearing, save*
*When here and there, about the grove of Oaks*
*Where was my bed, an acorn from the trees*
*Fell audibly, and with a startling sound.*
*(Book 1, lines 89–94)*

It is significant that Wordsworth begins his great poem, one that he hoped would take its place with the epics of Milton, with this seemingly insignificant detail: an acorn falling. Here, as elsewhere in the poem, he is inverting a scale of values; that which should be treasured is common to all:

*I yearn towards some philosophic Song*
*Of Truth that cherishes our daily life.*
*(Book 1, lines 230–31)*

Not coincidentally, both Wordsworth and Rousseau were deeply involved in the move toward democracy that culminated in the French Revolution. The earth was shifting, a "state of crisis" was at hand. Rousseau asks, when the revolution comes, "who can answer for what will become of you then?" (194). Those whose identities depended upon their positions in a crumbling world would be lost; only those with a more solid anchor, that of nature itself, could hope to survive.

This brief survey only hints at the richness of the Romantic view of education. But I hope that it at least suggests that "romantic" should not be used as a term of dismissal in discussing the education of children. In his comprehensive review of writing research, George Hillocks (1986) calls the "writing-process approach" the "natural-process" approach (thus joining two key words) and claims that it is a linear descendant of the educational approach described in *Emile*. But to what extent is this true? How much does the writing-process approach derive from these Romantic views, and where does it diverge?

If Rousseau could return to visit a writing-process classroom, my guess is that he would be appalled. He would find the focus on verbal learning, on reading and writing, oppressive and premature (he felt that, for children, books were "the instruments of their greatest misery" [116]). He would think classrooms too sedentary, too isolated from the natural world. He might even accuse process educators of violating his fundamental maxim—"Nature wants children to be children before being men" (90). He might consider the emphasis on the self-conscious awareness of the composing process to be highly unnatural. And he might judge the emphasis on revision to be exactly the kind of perversion that he and Wordsworth warned against, asking children to perform like adults.

In fact, the writing-process approach does diverge from the Romantic orientation in major ways. It views learning as "social" and not presocial; the emphasis on the classroom as community is strong. It rejects as extreme statements about the incapacity of the children to reason or make judgments—I suspect Rousseau wouldn't care for this book. But there are also some major similarities. The writing-process approach emphasizes writing that is the product of careful observation and is therefore rich in detail. Donald Graves (1983) stresses the value of "information" so strongly that it assumes an almost moral significance. For Graves, information is primarily detail gained from attention to our surroundings; by asking children to attend to this kind of information, we are asking them to do what Wordsworth attempted—to write, in their own way, a "Song/Of Truth that cherishes our daily life."

One standard complaint about the writing process is that it seems to focus on accounts of personal experience. If this is a weakness of the writing process approach, it is also a strength. Neil Postman, in his book, *Teaching as a Conserving Activity* (1979), argues that schools have a responsibility to counter the bias of the dominant culture, which he perceives to be the TV-video culture: "The school stands as the only mass medium capable of putting forward the case for what is not happening in the culture" (22). The case can be made that television tends to devalue, and even to replace, personal experience. Teachers of all grades hear students say that they cannot write about their lives because nothing ever happens—nothing, that is, remotely as exciting as what happens to characters on television. This is precisely the cultural message that writing-process teachers seek to countermand. Like Thoreau ([1854] 1983), we ask

*. . . of every writer, first or last, a simple and sincere account of his own life, and not merely what he has heard of other men's lives; some such*

*account as he would send to his kindred form, for if he has lived sincerely, it must have been in a distant land to me. (46)*

If the TV-video culture pushes children to be consumers, schools can stress that which is available for the looking, the natural world. My colleague Brenda Miller has noted that children often work on "holiday time"—their sense of expectation is governed by occasions when they will receive gifts. Miller noted that the teacher she observed, Pat McLure (of Chapter 6), regularly would plan activities that shifted the focus to natural time—the change in seasons, the birth and growth of animals.

The Romantic view of education is a hard sell. Those who sustain public education naturally expect schools to reflect and endorse their values. They are not likely to support an approach that seems to flout those values, dismissing them as oppressive. They have difficulty supporting such an approach, even if it only *appears* to view the child as the fixed point of attention. They will not be confident of an approach that is so squeamish about adult authority that the word "teach" has virtually disappeared from its lexicon. If the emphasis diverges too radically from societal expectations, the Romantic approach invites a countermovement stressing cultural knowledge and values. In fact, this reaction is occurring now under the banner of "cultural literacy." E. D. Hirsch's 1987 book of that title comes with endorsements from three of the most influential educational leaders in the country—William Bennett, Albert Shanker, and Bill Honig. The key word becomes "culture."

## CULTURE

Like "nature," "culture" is one of the most complex words in the language, which is hardly surprising since the two are often juxtaposed as opposites. There is that wonderful moment in *The African Queen* when Bogart justifies his drinking by saying, "It's human nature," whereupon Katherine Hepburn replies, "Human nature is what we're trying to overcome." That is, after all, what culture allows us to do.

The original meaning of "cultural" derives from the Latin *colere*, which had a range of meanings: inhabit, cultivate, protect, honor, and worship. The word "cult" retains the connection to worship. And the association with growing remains in terms like "throat culture" and "bacteria culture." In the eighteenth century, the word began to be used synonymously with "civilization," the universal secular process of human development. Raymond Williams (1976) notes a decisive shift in the meaning of the word at the end of the eighteenth century, when the concept of a monolithic culture shifted to "cultures"—"the specific and variable cultures of different nations and periods, but also the specific and variable cultures of social and economic groups within a nation" (79). The debate between advocates of "cultural literacy," on the one hand, and reformers like Rousseau, Wordsworth, Dickens, Whitehead, and, most extensively, John Dewey, on the other, rests not so much on the importance of "culture" but on the meaning each group attributes to the term.

I will focus on the cultural-literacy position of E. D. Hirsch, both because of its popularity and likely influence and because it represents the most recent example of a content-based approach arising in response to approaches based on "natural" human development. Since Dewey is the bête noire of those advocating cultural literacy, I'll cite briefly from his work to set off the debate.

Dewey was critical of content approaches because the argument for much content was, in his view, circular:

*Those who adhered to the established system needed merely a few high-sounding words to justify existing practices. The real work is done by habits so fixed as to be institutional. ([1938] 1963, 29)*

Grammar is taught because it has always been taught. "Great books" should be taught because they are great books. If something is a subject, it should be taught because it is a subject. In these content-oriented approaches, little attention is paid to the appropriateness or utility of knowledge for the children who are being taught:

*It is no reflection upon the nutritive quality of beefsteak that it is not fed to infants. It is not an invidious reflection upon trigonometry that we do not teach it in the first or fifth grade of school. It is not the subject* per se *that is educative or that is conducive to growth. There is no subject that is in and of itself, or without regard for the stage of growth attained by the learner, such that inherent educational value can be attributed to it. Failure to take into account adaptation to the need and capacities of individuals was the source of the idea that certain subjects and certain methods were intrinsically cultural or intrinsically good for mental discipline. ([1938] 1963, 44)*

The challenge for proponents of cultural literacy is to refute the charge of circularity (great books are great because they're great) and to demonstrate the positive consequences of a more content-oriented approach.

Hirsch, citing recent declines in standardized tests, particularly the SATs, argues that schools are not imparting the cultural knowledge necessary for students to be effective readers. Reading, he states, is not a contentless process but, rather, requires the application of cultural knowledge. Mark Twain, for example, assumed that Tom Sawyer's answer in church to the question "Who were the first two disciples?" would be riotously funny. But the humor of the passage relies on the reader understanding the silliness of Tom's answer, "David and Goliath." Without some knowledge of the Bible, the humor is lost.

Hirsch advocates teaching students this cultural content and even provides a list of almost four thousand terms that might serve as the core of instruction in cultural literacy. Like any list, his is subject to debate: why so few modern writers, why the absence of sports figures, why the absence of Latin American or Far Eastern writers? Yet, these debates, in a sense, prove one of Hirsch's points: An educational system must decide what is important. Vague appeals to diversity or pluralism can actually be ways of avoiding hard decisions while, at the same time, appearing tolerant and open. Other educational critics (Bloom, 1987; Sizer, 1984; Powell, Farrar, and Cohen, 1985), though differing on many issues, similarly criticize schools for failing to set priorities.

There is also a fundamental patriotic appeal in Hirsch's book. The existence of a national culture is, according to Hirsch, dependent upon a shared body of knowledge. A fragmented curriculum—one with no center—leads to a fragmented society without a common set of terms that allows individuals from different groups and different regions to talk to each other. The appeal of *Cultural Literacy* is similar to the appeal of movements to declare English the national language. Both speak to a desire for a unified culture.

However broad its appeal, Hirsch's plan suffers from two major flaws. First, he is extremely vague about how young children should be taught these key terms (it is important to know that he feels that they should be taught in grades 1 through 5). How, for example, should we teach children about Gresham's law? Hirsch implies that teaching children this cultural information should present no problem because young children naturally "absorb" information. But, historically, schemes to teach information to children regularly have run into the same problem: Children learn the names but not the significance of the names. The concepts (if they can be called that) are, as Whitehead contended, "inert."

The second major problem with cultural literacy, as Hirsch defines it, is the almost exclusive focus on information. To be culturally literate involves more than knowing key referents; it requires the ability to employ certain patterns of discourse, what Heath (1983) calls "ways with words." The children from working-class communities whom she studied often had difficulty in school, particularly relative to "mainstream" children, because they had no experience with the literate routines of the school. I've argued in this book that one key routine that forms the basis of informational writing is the identification-plus-attribute couplet that draws on bedtime-reading interactions.

Even for the college students whom I teach, the major problem is not so much the level of identification of cultural terms as a lack of awareness of discourse forms. One thing that I do is give them the opening paragraph to a Stephen Gould essay, "Were Dinosaurs Dumb?"

*When Muhammad Ali flunked his army intelligence test, he quipped (with a wit that belied his performance on the exam): "I only said I was the greatest; I never said I was the smartest." In our metaphors and fairy tales, size and power are almost always balanced by want of intelligence. Cunning is the refuge of the little guy. Think of Br'er Rabbit and Br'er Bear; David smiting Goliath with a slingshot; Jack chopping down the beanstalk. Slow wit is the tragic flaw of the giant. (1984, 418)*

This is a good example of a passage that assumes shared cultural knowledge (Jack and the Beanstalk; David and Goliath; the Uncle Remus tales). Gould also expects readers to know who Muhammad Ali is. The passage does indeed require a level of what Hirsch calls cultural literacy. But the difficulties that my students have with it do not relate to any of this cultural information.

I ask them to predict, from this opening, what Gould goes on to say in the essay. Most respond that he will answer the question about dinosaurs, but none can predict which way he will go. For me, and, I would guess, for most experienced readers, the opening suggests that Gould will show that dinosaurs were not dumb, that these myths are, well, myths. This is, in fact, Gould's position. But how do we make this guess? Gould's essay fits a pattern that we have seen before. A well-accepted position is put forward to be countered by a different, more interesting or more plausible position—in this case, that the brains of dinosaurs were not unusually small.

Hirsch's single-minded focus on information, on lists of cultural terms, leads him to absurd claims, similar to quick-fix vocabulary programs that promise to change your life. He states, for example, that:

*It should energize people to learn that only a few hundred pages of information stand between the literate and the illiterate, between dependence and autonomy. Moreover, the cost of recognizing this fact, if it is a cost at all, will be rather low—simply the demystification of literate culture. The benefit could be very great indeed—the achievement of significantly greater social and economic equity. (1987, 143)*

A big promise. But why aren't illiterates already energized by the availability of dictionaries? It is a cruel and false promise: Learn these terms, learn these words; they are the key to literacy. As Whitehead wrote in *The Aims of Education* (1949), "Culture is the activity of thought and the receptiveness to beauty and humane feelings. Scraps of information have nothing to do with it" (13).

The value—and appeal—of *Cultural Literacy* is its attack on instruction that pretends to be neutral, that stands for nothing. Hirsch shifts the fixed point of attention from the child to the democratic society, its shared knowledge and values, and the responsibility of schools to pass these on, for, if they don't, Hirsch warns, there is a "disintegration of cultural memory." Hirsch starts out so right and ends up so wrong. He reminds us of the historic role of schooling in uniting the various "cultures" in this country. But, in his reaction to the excesses of child-centered education, he is guilty of the same kind of extremism. Rejecting an approach that centers on the interests and experiences of the child, he advocates one that ignores them in favor of a predetermined, uniform curriculum. While he claims to offer a compromise, he really is presenting us with another version of either-or. To move beyond this unproductive polarizing, we need to turn once more to America's greatest educational philosopher—John Dewey.

## EXPERIENCE

John Dewey is often thought of as a twentieth-century educator. But he was born in 1859, during the presidency of William Buchanan, and his work was influenced profoundly by various social changes that occurred in the last half of the nineteenth century: the general acceptance of the theory of evolution, changes in industrial organization, the massive influx of immigrants, and the development of experimental methods in the sciences. This period also saw the transformation of the American educational system—schools serving an elite and dominated by a classical curriculum were replaced by institutions serving a far more varied population and attempting to seek out connections between the curriculum and the life experiences of students. Dewey usually is associated with "progressive" schools—and held responsible for their decline. Yet, in one of his last major books, *Experience and Education* ([1938] 1963), Dewey criticized progressive schools sharply for an approach to learning that was, in his opinion, almost as impoverished as the traditional approach that it was intended to replace.

In this section, I will try to show that Dewey provides the soundest philosophical position for understanding and defending the writing-process approach. To understand this philosophy, it is necessary to disentangle the real Dewey from the popularized versions of Dewey, the shorthand that equates Dewey with Rousseau and with a value-neutral curriculum built exclusively on the interests of the child.

First, there is a crucial difference between Dewey and Rousseau. While sympathetic to Rousseau's criticisms of the education of his day, Dewey rejects as "absurd" the position that "nature is supposed to furnish the law and end in development; ours is to follow and conform to her ways" ([1916] 1966, 112). Rousseau was "profoundly wrong" in stating that we can determine the goals of education simply by consulting nature; rather, it is "the office of the social medium [families, social organization, and preeminently, schools]...to direct growth through putting powers to the best possible use" (114). Dewey views the emphasis on nature as opposed to culture to be one more example of either-or; it is a protest against "attempts to force children directly into the mold of grown-up standards" (117).

But if the ends of education cannot be extracted from nature, where do they come from? Here, Dewey's answer is hardly different from Hirsch's. Children, according to Dewey, must be "initiated into the interests, purposes, information, skill, and practices of the mature members" ([1916] 1966, 3). For Dewey, experience is understood most broadly in terms of its continuity from generation to generation. Just as biological evolution is dependent on our genetic inheritance, our potential to evolve as a society depends on this transmission of culture:

*Society exists through a process of transmission quite as much as biological life. This transmission occurs by means of communication of habits of doing, thinking, and feeling from the older to the younger. Without this communication of ideals, hopes, expectations, standards, opinions, from those members who are passing out of group life to those who are coming into it, social life could not survive. (3)*

While this concept of transmission extends well beyond Hirsch's focus on information, it is hardly the statement of a formalist indifferent to what children learn.

Dewey's concept of transmission involves far more than children absorbing cultural information. Nor can it be understood as analogous to the physical process of handing something over, passing the torch, handing down an heirloom. Dewey explains his view of transmission in one centrally important paragraph in *Democracy and Education* ([1916] 1966):

*Society not only continues to exist* by *transmission,* by *communication, but it may fairly be said to exist* in *transmission,* in *communication. There is more than a verbal tie between the words common, community, and communication. Men live in a community in virtue of the things they have in common; and communication is the way in which they come to possess things in common. What they must have in common in order to form a community or society are aims, beliefs, aspirations, knowledge—a common understanding—like-mindedness as the sociologists would say. Such things cannot be passed physically from one to another like bricks, they cannot be shared as persons would share a pie by dividing it into physical pieces. The communication which insures participation in a common understanding is one which secures similar emotional and intellectual dispositions—like ways of responding to expectations and requirements. (4)*

If we are searching for the foundation of the writing process, this quotation certainly forms part of it. We transmit our culture to children not by handling something over to them, but by inviting and enabling their participation in communal action—we invite them to join the club. In an intriguing gloss on this passage, James Britton (1985) writes:

*In taking part in rule-governed behavior—and that might be a wine-and-cheese party, a debate, a game of volleyball—the novice, the individual learner, picks up the rules by responding to the behavior of others, a process precisely parallel to the mode by which the rules first came into existence. (74)*

Children learn society's rules tacitly; even the skilled language user could not formulate them. Children construct these rules as they are given demonstrations by more skilled members of the community and genuine opportunities to participate in activities.

For Dewey, in particular, this view of learning meant that the classroon should not be cut off from the wider community; instead, it should resemble that community.

Dewey clearly does not think that content or specific information is unimportant—he opposes exactly what Rousseau opposed: confusing the learning of names with actual learning. He tells the story of a visit to Moline, Illinois, where the superintendent told him that, every year, many children "were surprised to learn that the Mississippi river in their textbook had anything to do with the stream of water flowing past their homes" ([1900] 1956, 75). He is opposed to what Whitehead called inert ideas—"ideas that are merely received into the mind without being utilized, or tested, or thrown into fresh combinations" (3).

Dewey also criticizes the social attitudes fostered by instruction that aims solely to pass on information:

> *The mere absorption of facts and truths is so exclusively individual an affair that it tends naturally to pass into selfishness. There is no obvious social motive for the acquirement of mere learning, there is no clear social gain in success thereat. Indeed, almost the only measure of success is a competitive one, in the bad sense of that term—a comparison of results in recitation or in the examination to see which child has succeeded in getting ahead of others in storing up, in accumulating, the maximum of information. ([1900] 1956, 15)*

The same could be said for much current instruction in the language arts and reading. Listening to first graders talk about reading, I find that they rarely talk about what they like or even dislike; rather, the usual question seems to be "Which book are you on?" The only basis for book talk is competitive; a "good reader" is the child who is ahead in this basal-reader footrace.

To grasp what Dewey advocates, one must examine what he means by "experience"—no other concept is more central to his conception of education. In part, Dewey is drawing on a long-standing American distrust of the purely abstract and theoretical. This tendency was evident in the late 1830s to Tocqueville, who found that "those who cultivate the sciences amongst a democratic people are always afraid to losing their way in visionary speculation" ([1835, 1840] 1964, 149). They mistrusted systems and were reluctant to defer to the authority of others. Rather, they "adhere closely to facts, and study facts with their own senses."

The literary critic Phillip Rahv (1957) found the same tendency in American literature, calling it "the cult of experience."

Echoing Tocqueville, Rahv contends that American novelists exhibit, on the one hand, "a disinclination to thought and on the other, an intense predilection for the real: and the real appears as a vast phenomenology swept by waves of sensation and feeling" (361). The writers that Rahv criticizes view experience as the great teacher: It is by consulting the real, our reactions and perceptions in individual situations, that we are able to transcend the boundaries that have been set for us.

The preeminent illustration of this view of experience is surely Huckleberry Finn's decision not to turn in Jim. Huck has already written a note to Mrs. Watson, telling her where she can find Jim, her runaway slave:

*I felt good and all washed clean of sin for the first time I had ever felt so in my life, and I knowed I could pray now. But I didn't do it straight off, but laid the paper down and set there thinking—thinking how good it was all this happened so, and how near I come to being lost and going to Hell. And I went on thinking. And I got to thinking over our trip down the river; and I see Jim before me all the time: in the day and in the nighttime, sometimes moonlight, sometimes storms, and we a-floating along talking, and singing, and laughing. (Twain, [1885] 1979, 209)*

Huck goes on to think of Jim's acts of kindness during the trip, and, finally, he decides to tear up the note, saying, "All right then, I'll go to Hell."

In this great scene, Huck begins by adhering to the conventional moral and legal code, both of which ruled that, since Jim was a slave, Huck was duty-bound to turn him in. But Huck then turns to the experience of being with Jim, beginning with recollection and moving to an examination of that recollection. By being open to experience, to what Rahv disparagingly calls the realm of "sensation and feeling," Huck is able to transcend the moral code that prevents him from seeing Jim as a human being.

Dewey's theory thus has both stabilizing and destabilizing elements. As members of a community, we carry on traditions and values from one generation to the next, but these values are subject to the test of experience. As an evolutionist, Dewey claimed that we are living in a universe "with the lid off."

But the common definition of the word "experience" is so broad as to denote anything that happens to us—we have experiences by virtue simply of being alive. If the term is to have any utility or, as William James would say, "cash value," it must be delimited so that truly educational experiences can be distinguished from normal activities, which are sometimes aimless and often routine. Near the end of his career, after he had seen the inadequacy of many "progressive" schools, Dewey wrote *Experience and Education* ([1938] 1963), which is primarily an attempt to clarify the meaning of this key term.

One central criterion of truly educational experiences is continuity: Does an experience lead to subsequent educational experiences; does it open up new possibilities? Experiences can be interesting, even exciting, and yet be disconnected from anything that follows. Or they may involve students in routine activities (filling in worksheets) that don't grow out of earlier activities but duplicate them. This may seem like a self-evident principle, but it it one that schools regularly ignore. Various school subjects are often disconnected; teachers at various grades rarely discuss curriculum or student progress; universities often have little contact with schools (which, of course, does not stop professors from complaining about the schools).

The teacher is central to ensuring that experiences are continuous. Dewey was almost contemptuous of progressive schools that made the students' "freedom" an end in itself. The same can be said of the child's interests and desires. These are not ends but means; children who lack any possibility of choice—the children in the classes described by Goodlad—do not have the opportunity to learn in a purposeful way. But allowing them "freedom" to indulge inclinations is hardly enough. Dewey writes:

> *Impulses and desires that are not ordered by intelligence are under the control of accidental circumstance. . . . A person whose conduct is controlled in this way has at most only the illusion of freedom. Actually he is directed by forces over which he has no command. ([1938] 1963, 64–65)*

Interest and desires may be the "moving springs of action" (71), but they must be channelled into sustained, planned, purposeful activity if they are to be of lasting value. And the teacher has a critical role in this transformation. Put another way, Dewey is less concerned about students' freedom *from* direction and intervention than about their freedom *to* develop the attitudes, competences, and base of knowledge that will promote development.

Dewey clearly was bothered by the way his theories were used by progressive educators to justify a hands-off policy by teachers. This may have been due, in part, to a lack of clarity in his early writing, where the child regularly is described as reacting to the environment of the classroom. For Dewey, the teacher was a vital part of this environment, but the term itself suggests passivity—sunlight is part of a plant's environment, but it has no intentional relationship with the plant. Teachers, of course, do have an intentional role. If they are part of the environment, their part is uniquely important, because, to a considerable degree, they *create* the environment. In *Experience and Education*, Dewey stressed the active, intentional role of the teacher:

*The greater maturity of experience which should belong to the adult as educator puts him in a position to evaluate each experience of the young in a way in which the one having the less mature experience cannot do. . . . Failure by the teacher to take the moving force of an experience into account so as to judge and direct it on the ground of what it is moving into means disloyalty to the principle of experience itself. (38)*

He noted that, in many progressive schools, there was "uncertainty and laxity" in the selection and ordering of subject matter. He saw too much dependence on "improvisation":

*Improvisation that takes advantage of special occasions prevents teaching and learning from being stereotyped and dead. . . . But there is a decided difference between using [improvisations] in the development of a continuing line of activity and trusting them to provide the chief material in learning. (79)*

According to Dewey, it was the responsibility of the educator to determine the "line of activity":

*It thus becomes the office of the educator to select those things within the range of existing experiences that have the promise and potentiality of presenting new problems which by stimulating new ways of observation and judgment will expand the area of further experience. (75)*

Dewey's second major criterion is implicit in this discussion of continuity. Each experience involves an "interaction," or what Louise Rosenblatt would call a "transaction" (1978), in which the child brings his or her knowledge, wishes, purposes, and capacities to bear on a new problem, text, situation. Ideally, habitual patterns of response are not totally adequate to the interaction; the situation taxes these settled patterns. In Vygotsky's language, the child is working in a "zone of proximal development." The "undisciplined mind" simply ignores the problem, transforming the potentially puzzling into the routine:

*The undisciplined mind is adverse to suspense and intellectual hesitation; it is prone to assertion. It likes things undisturbed, settled, and treats them as such without due warrant. Familiarity, common repute, and congeniality to desire are the readily made measuring rods of truth. ([1916] 1966, 188)*

Just as scientific investigation (the paradigm for Dewey) proceeds by putting established truths constantly to the test of experimentation, the disciplined mind is open to the test of experience. The spirit is pragmatic in the sense that William James defined the term; theories are "limber" and "unstiffened." The attitude of the learner is one of "looking away from first things, principles, 'categories,' supposed necessities, and looking toward last things, fruits, consequences, facts" (James, [1907, 1954] 1968, 170). As befits the optimistic times in which Dewey and James wrote, the focus is on a future that will be an evolutionary advance on the present. And—for Dewey, in particular—democracy, by not restricting the individual to a class, or region, or an established and unquestioned set of beliefs, could provide the diversity of situations that promotes growth and respect for diversity itself.

But does any of this matter? Does this examination of Dewey, Rousseau, Hirsch, and others really shed any light on the teaching of writing, on the writing process? Am I violating the Jamesian motto by looking for antecedents rather than facts and consequences; by emphasizing the retrospective over the prospective view? Yet Dewey himself emphasized pragmatic reasons for examining the past: Just as memories of the past must guide individuals' present actions, so the issues and problems of social life are in intimate connection with those of the past.

My reading of Dewey has been prompted by incidents in my past, most particularly, stories that my mother told of attending Ohio State's College of Education in the 1930s. One of her classes filled a lecture hall—600 students listening to lectures from the "Dewey man" at Ohio State. Over fifty years later, she could still recapture the excitement of that class. Her stories caused me to wonder how Dewey could have been so central to teacher education in the Thirties yet be so peripheral today. Is this just one more example of another, very American, tendency—our readiness to forget the past, to believe that we begin each waking day anew, with the slate wiped clean? Is it one more example of the discontinuities about which Dewey warned?

I have tried to show in this last chapter that Dewey articulated many of the cardinal principles of the writing process: the constructive model of thought; the primacy of experience; the social nature of learning; the relationship of classroom learning to democratic values. He also provided a pertinent warning about defining the "writing-process" or the "whole-language" approach in such a way that "choice" or "student centered" become the new god terms. Choice, while essential, says little about objectives or goals for learning; it can say nothing about the ways in which we evaluate choices. Choice is a means rather than an end. In the same way, child-centered education easily can ignore the goals of education, which cannot be determined by focusing exclusively on the child's interests and abilities. The progressive movement lost public support because it was perceived as permissive, directionless, and lacking in rigor. The same mistakes should not be repeated.

But Dewey is more than a Cassandra. He reminds us of the complexity of teaching: "The road of the new education is not an easier road to follow than the old road but a more strenuous and difficult one" ([1938] 1963, 90). Strenuous and difficult because it refuses to fall into the trap of either-or, because it requires teachers to become dialecticians and not "true believers."

It was F. Scott Fitzgerald who wrote that "the test of a first-rate intelligence is the ability to hold two opposed ideas in the mind at the same time, and still retain the ability to function" (1931, 69). This is the intelligence that Dewey expects of teachers: an ability to view both the ends of education—the complex of social and intellectual competences that the child needs for full participation in a democratic society—and the means of education—the interests, capabilities, and purposes that the child brings to a learning situation. The teacher must consider both parts of the interaction, even though it is far easier to emphasize one as *opposed* to the other, as Hirsch does in *Cultural Literacy*.

As distant as Dewey's writing often seems, he clearly understands the "feel" of teaching. If learning requires an openness to experience, a capacity for intellectual hesitation, a willingness to modify beliefs on the basis of careful observations, so does teaching. In a deeply moving portrait of an eleventh-grade teacher, Nancy Wilson describes her own preconceptions about teaching and how her observations dispelled them:

*Before I watched Audre teach, I thought other teachers—the ones I passed in the hall—moved smoothly from one high point to another, never breaking step, never doubting direction or losing sight of goals or wondering if their students were learning anything at all. My own teaching, of course, was seldom so smooth. I kept teaching journals filled with doubts and questions, seesawing between elation and despair. But surely the teacher next door rode a steadier course?*

*Audre's classroom, with its ups and downs; her journals, with their honest recording of highs and lows; her raging, her laughter, and her tears were a revelation to me. Reading her journals and observing her classroom,*

*I found, as in the messy manuscripts of published writers, evidence of a process more complex but, in the end, more worthy of respect than the smooth sequences I had expected to see. (Perl and Wilson, 1986, 37)*

This is Dewey's "strenuous and difficult road," a road that cannot be mapped once and for all because the terrain keeps shifting. It is a kind of teaching that can never fit management systems or step-by-step versions of the writing process that promise to take the anxiety (and, inevitably, the joy) out of our work. It is a strenuous and difficult craft because it can never be mastered—we never believe completely that we know what we're doing.

Dewey, of course, provides no system. He defines the complexity of our task, a complexity that can be illustrated in one final key word—"individual." The word originally meant "indivisible," and, until the eighteenth century, it was used to mean an individual member *of a group*. At that point, it began to be used to indicate "uniqueness," that which distinguishes the individual *from* the group or other individuals. For Dewey, the drama of education, and of democracy itself, arose from this double meaning—the relationship of "I" to "we."

# Epilogue: By Sawlor's Lake

As I finished writing this book, I made a small discovery. I was reading Dykhuizen's biography of John Dewey, and among the illustrations was a photograph of Dewey working on the open porch of a cabin on Sawlor's Lake in Hubbards, Nova Scotia. It must have been warm that day, because Dewey was wearing no shirt as he sat in his chair of rough birch logs and worked away at his upright Royal typewriter. This was his summer home for a number of years in the Forties, and some of his most important later work was done on that porch.

I was struck by the picture because one of my doctoral students, Lorri Neilsen, lived in Hubbards, and we had spoken frequently about Dewey's work, never guessing that Dewey had lived just down the road from her. I sent off photocopies of the cabin photographs to Lorri, and she and her husband, Allan, promised to try to locate the cabin.

In February of 1988, after delivering a completed draft of this book to Heinemann, I visited Lorri and Allan in Hubbards. Near their house, Allan pulled off the highway saying, "There's something I want to show you." We drove down a narrow, unplowed road to near the lake's edge and then walked to the shore. The lake was frozen, and the wind coming off it was bitter. The cabins were boarded up and would remain so for four months.

"We're thinking it could be this one," Allan said. "But the location of the porch doesn't quite fit the picture. Who knows, some later owner could have redone the porch." The cabin was old and weather-beaten in a comfortable sort of way. In my mind, I was sure that we had found the right place. Dewey had walked this ground before we did.

But, then, he'd always been there ahead of us. At the turn of the century, he wrote in his book *The School and Society* ([1900] 1956):

*We hear much nowadays about the cultivation of the child's "imagination." Then we undo much of our talk and work by the belief that the imagination is some special part of the child that finds its satisfaction in one particular direction—generally speaking, that of the unreal and make-believe, of myth and made-up story. Why are we so hard of heart and so slow to believe? The imagination is the medium in which the child lives. . . . If we once believe in life and in the life of the child, then will all occupations and uses spoken of, then will all history and science, become instruments of appeal and materials of culture to his imagination. . . . (60–61)*

We have here the theme of this book. He's walked this ground before.

# Bibliography

Allard, Harry. 1981. *There's a Party at Mona's Tonight*. New York: Doubleday.

Allard, Harry, and James Marshall. 1981. *The Stupids Die*. Boston: Houghton Mifflin.

Applebee, Arthur. 1984. *Contexts for Learning to Write*. Norwood, N.J.: Ablex.

Applebee, Arthur, and Judith Langer. 1983. "Instructional Scaffolding: Reading and Writing as Natural Language." In *Composing and Comprehending*, ed. Julie Jensen. Urbana, Ill.: National Council for Research in English/ERIC.

Atwell, Nancie. 1987. *In the Middle: Writing, Reading, and Learning with Adolescents*. Portsmouth, N.H.: Boynton/Cook.

Barnes, Douglas. 1976. *From Communication to Curriculum*. Harmondsworth, England: Penguin.

Bartlett, John. 1968. *Familiar Quotations*. 14th ed. Boston: Little, Brown.

Benedict, Susan. 1985. "Emily Dickinson's Room is as Old as Grandfather Frog: Developing Basic Skills." In *Breaking Ground: Teachers Relate Reading and Writing in the Elementary School*, ed. Jane Hansen, Thomas Newkirk, and Donald Graves. Portsmouth, N.H.: Heinemann.

Bereiter, Carl. 1980. "Development in Writing." In *Cognitive Processes in Writing*, ed. L. Gregg and E. Steinberg. Hillsdale, N.J.: Lawrence Erlbaum.

Bereiter, Carl, and Marlene Scardamalia. 1979. "From Conversation to Composition." In vol. 1 of *Advances in Instructional Psychology*, ed. Ronald Glaser. Hillsdale, N.J.: Lawrence Erlbaum.

Berlin, Isaiah. 1970. *The Hedgehog and the Fox*. New York: Simon and Schuster.

Berthoff, Ann. 1984. "Is Teaching Still Possible? Writing, Meaning, and Higher Order Reasoning." *College English* 46: 743–55.

Bissex, Glenda. 1980. *GNYS AT WRK: A Child Learns to Write and Read*. Cambridge: Harvard University Press.

Bloom, Allan. 1987. *The Closing of the American Mind*. New York: Simon and Schuster.

Bloom, Benjamin, et al. 1956. *The Taxonomy of Educational Objectives: The Cognitive Domain.* London: Longman.

Borges, Jorge Luis. 1953. "El Idioma Analitico De John Wilkins." In *Otras Inquisiciones.* Buenos Aires: Emece.

Borke, Helen. 1971. "Interpersonal Perception of Young Children: Egocentrism or Empathy." *Developmental Psychology* 5:263–69.

Brannon, Lil, and C. H. Knoblauch. 1982. "On Students' Rights to Their Own Texts: A Model of Teacher Response." *College Composition and Communication* 33:157–66.

Bridge, Susan. 1988. "Squeezing from the Middle of the Tube." In *Understanding Writing: Ways of Observing, Learning, and Teaching*, 2nd ed., ed. Thomas Newkirk and Nancie Atwell. Portsmouth, N.H.: Heinemann.

Britton, James. 1970. *Language and Learning.* Harmondsworth, England: Penguin.

———. 1985. "Research Currents: Second Thoughts on Learning." *Language Arts* 62, no. 1 (January):72–77.

Britton, James, et al. 1975. *The Development of Writing Abilities, 11–18.* London: Macmillan.

Bruner, Jerome. 1983. *Child's Talk.* New York: Norton.

Calkins, Lucy. 1983. *Lessons from a Child.* Portsmouth, N.H.: Heinemann.

———. 1986. *The Art of Teaching Writing.* Portsmouth, N.H.: Heinemann.

Cassirer, Ernst. 1984. "From *Language and Myth.*" In *Reclaiming the Imagination: Philosophical Perspectives for Teachers of Writing*, ed. Ann Berthoff. Portsmouth, N.H.: Boynton/Cook.

Cazden, Courtney. 1982. "Adult Assistance to Language Development: Scaffolds, Models, and Direct Instruction." In *Developing Literacy: Young Children's Use of Language*, ed. R. Parker and F. Davis. Newark, Del.: International Reading Association.

Chittenden, Linda. 1982. "What If All The Whales Are Gone Before We Become Friends?" In *What's Going On? Language/Learning Episodes in British and American Classrooms 4–13*, ed. Mary Barr, Pat D'Arcy, and Mary Healey. Portsmouth, N.H.: Boynton/Cook.

Christensen, Francis. 1967. *Notes Towards a New Rhetoric.* New York: Harper and Row.

Clay, Marie. 1975. *What Did I Write?* Portsmouth, N.H.: Heinemann.

Cole, Michael, and Roy Andrade. 1982. "The Influence of Schooling on Concept Formation: Some Preliminary Conclusions." *Quarterly Newsletter of the Laboratory of Comparative Human Cognition* 4:19–26.

Coleridge, Samuel Taylor. [1918] 1950. *The Portable Coleridge.* New York: Vintage.

Coles, Robert. 1981. "How Do You Measure a Child's Level of Morality?" *Learning* 10 (July/August):70–71.

Dewey, John. [1902, 1900] 1956. *The Child and the Curriculum/The School and Society.* Chicago: University of Chicago Press.

———. [1916] 1966. *Democracy and Education.* New York: The Free Press.

———. [1938] 1963. *Experience and Education.* New York: Macmillan.

Donaldson, Margaret. 1978. *Children's Minds.* New York: Norton.

Duncan, H. F., M. Gourlay, and W. Hudson. 1973. *A Study of Pictorial Perception Among Bantu and White Primary School Children in South Africa.* Johannesburg: Witwatersrand University Press.

Dyson, Ann. 1986. "Transitions and Tensions: Interrelationships between the Drawing, Talking, and Dictating of Young Children." *Research in the Teaching of Writing* 20:279–409.

Eagleton, Terry. 1983. *Literary Theory.* Minneapolis: University of Minnesota Press.

Eisner, Elliot. 1983. "On the Relationship of Conception to Representation." *Art Education* 36 (March):22–25.

Emerson, Ralph Waldo. [1841] 1965. "Self-Reliance." In *Selected Writings of Ralph Waldo Emerson.* New York: New American Library.

Emig, Janet. 1971. *The Composing Processes of Twelfth Graders.* Urbana, Ill.: National Council of Teachers of English.

Fabre, J. Henri. [1913] 1964. *The Insect World.* Greenwich, Conn.: Fawcett.

Ferreiro, Emilia, and Ana Teberosky. 1982. *Literacy Before Schooling.* Portsmouth, N.H.: Heinemann.

Fitzgerald, F. Scott. 1931. *The Crack-Up.* New York: New Directions.

Fox, Mem. 1988. "The Fox in Possum's Clothing: The Teacher Disguised as Writer, in Hot Pursuit of Literacy." In *Understanding Writing: Ways of Observing, Learning and Teaching*, 2nd ed., ed. Thomas Newkirk and Nancie Atwell. Portsmouth, N.H.: Heinemann.

Fujiawa, Gyo. 1978. *Baby Animals.* New York: Putnam.

Gardner, Howard. 1980. *Artful Scribbles.* New York: Basic Books.

———. 1983. *Frames of Mind: The Theory of Multiple Intelligences.* New York: Basic Books.

Gilligan, Carol. 1982. *In a Different Voice: Psychological Theory and Women's Development*. Cambridge: Harvard University Press.

Goffman, Erving. 1976. "Replies and Responses." *Language in Society* 5 (December):257–313.

Goodlad, John I. 1984. *A Place Called School: Prospects for the Future*. New York: McGraw-Hill.

Goodnow, Jacqueline. 1977. *Children Drawing*. Cambridge: Harvard University Press.

Goody, Jack. 1977. *The Domestication of the Savage Mind*. Cambridge, England: Cambridge University Press.

Gould, Stephen J. 1984. "Were Dinosaurs Dumb? In *The Contemporary Essay*, ed. Donald Hall. New York: St. Martin's Press.

Graves, Donald. 1978. "A Two-Year Case Study Observing the Development of Primary Children's Composing, Spelling, and Motor Behaviors During the Writing Process." Unpublished proposal submitted to the National Institute of Education.

———. 1982. *A Case Study Observing the Development of Primary Children's Composing, Spelling, and Motor Behaviors During the Writing Process*. NIE–G–78–0174. Washington, D.C.: National Institute of Education.

———. 1983. *Writing: Teachers and Children at Work*. Portsmouth, N.H.: Heinemann.

Graves, Donald, and Jane Hansen. 1983. "The Author's Chair." In *Composing and Comprehending*, ed. Julie Jensen. Urbana, Ill: National Council for Research in English/ERIC.

Greene, Jennifer. 1985. "Children's Writing in an Elementary School Postal System." In *Children's Early Writing Development*, ed. Marcia Farr. Norwood, N.J.: Ablex.

Gross, Larry. 1974. "Modes of Communication and the Acquisition of Symbolic Competence." In *Media and Symbols: The Forms of Expression, Communication, and Education*, ed. David Olson. Part 1 of the 73rd Yearbook of the National Society for the Study of Education. Chicago: University of Chicago Press.

Halliday, Michael. 1975. *Learning How to Mean: Explorations in the Development of Language*. Baltimore: E. Arnold.

Hansen, Jane. 1987. *When Writers Read*. Portsmouth, N.H.: Heinemann.

Harste, Jerome, Virginia Woodward, and Carolyn Burke. 1984. *Language Stories and Literacy Lessons*. Portsmouth, N.H.: Heinemann.

Heath, Shirley. 1982. "What No Bedtime Story Means: Narrative Skills at Home and School." *Language in Society* 11:49–76.

———. 1983. *Ways with Words: Language, Life, and Work in Communities and Classrooms*. Cambridge, England: Cambridge University Press.

Hilgers, Thomas. 1986. "How Children Change as Evaluators of Writing: Four Three-Year Case Studies." *Research in the Teaching of Writing* 20:36–55.

Hilliker, Judith. 1988. "Labelling to Beginning Narrative." In *Understanding Writing: Ways of Observing, Learning, and Teaching*, 2nd ed., ed. Thomas Newkirk and Nancie Atwell. Portsmouth, N.H.: Heinemann.

Hillocks, George. 1986. *Research on Written Composition: New Directions for Teaching*. Urbana, Ill.: National Council of Teachers of English.

Hirsch, E. D., Jr. 1984. "'English' and the Perils of Formalism." *American Scholar* 53:369–80.

———. 1987. *Cultural Literacy: What Every American Needs to Know*. Boston: Houghton Mifflin.

Hubbard, Ruth. 1987. "Transferring Images: Not Just Glued on the Page." *Young Children* 42:60–67.

———. 1988. "Authors of Pictures, Draughtsmen of Words." Ph.D. diss., Education Department, University of New Hampshire, Durham, N.H.

Huxley, Aldous. [1931] 1959. "Selected Snobberies." In *Music at Night and Other Essays*. New York: Harper and Row.

Isaacs, Susan. 1929. *Intellectual Growth in Young Children*. New York: Schocken.

Jaggar, Angela, and M. Trika Smith-Burke, eds. 1985. *Observing the Language Learner*. Newark, Del., and Urbana, Ill.: International Reading Association and National Council of Teachers of English.

James, William. [1907, 1954] 1968. "What Pragmatism Means." In *American Thought: Civil War to World War I*, ed. Perry Miller. New York: Holt.

Karelitz, Ellen Blackburn. 1988. "Note Writing: A Neglected Genre." In *Understanding Writing: Ways of Observing, Learning, and Teaching*, 2nd ed., ed. Thomas Newkirk and Nancie Atwell. Portsmouth, N.H.: Heinemann.

Keller, Helen. 1954. *The Story of My Life*. New York: Doubleday.

Kellogg, Rhoda. 1970. *Analyzing Children's Drawings*. Palo Alto, Calif.: Mayfield.

Kinneavy, James. 1972. *A Theory of Discourse*. Englewood Cliffs, N.J.: Prentice-Hall.

Knoblauch, C. H., and Lil Brannon. 1984. *Rhetorical Traditions and the Teaching of Writing*. Portsmouth, N.H.: Boynton/Cook.

Kohlberg, Lawrence. 1977. *Assessing Moral Stages: A Manual.* Cambridge: Harvard University Press.

Lindberg, Marlene. 1988. "The Development and Field Testing of a Kindergarten Writing Assessment Procedure." Ph.D. diss., Department of Psychology, University of Hawaii, Honolulu, Hawaii.

Loban, Walter. 1976. *Language Development: Kindergarten Through Grade Twelve.* Urbana, Ill.: National Council of Teachers of English.

Lunsford, Andrea. 1978. "Cognitive Development and the Basic Writer." *College English* 41:38–47.

Martin, Bill, and John Archambault. 1986. *Barn Dance!* New York: Henry Holt.

Michaels, Sarah. 1981. "Sharing Time: Children's Narrative Styles and Differential Access to Literacy." *Language in Society* 10 (December): 423–42.

Moffett, James. 1968. *Teaching the Universe of Discourse.* Boston: Houghton Mifflin.

Moffett, J., and Wagner, B. 1984. *Student Centered Language Arts and Reading, K–13.* 3rd ed. Boston: Houghton Mifflin.

Murray, Donald. [1972] 1982. "Teach Writing as a Process Not Product." In *Learning by Teaching: Selected Articles on Writing and Teaching*. Portsmouth, N.H.: Boynton/Cook.

———. [1978] 1982. "Write Before Writing." In *Learning by Teaching: Selected Articles on Writing and Teaching*. Portsmouth, N.H.: Boynton/Cook.

———. 1980. "Writing as Process: How Writing Finds Its Own Meaning." In *Eight Approaches to Teaching Composition*, ed. Timothy R. Donovan and Ben W. McClelland. Urbana, Ill.: National Council of Teachers of English.

———. 1984. *Write to Learn.* New York: Holt, Rinehart & Winston.

National Assessment of Educational Progress. 1981. *Reading, Writing, and Thinking*. Denver: Educational Commission of the States.

National Commission on Excellence in Education. 1983. *A Nation at Risk: Report of the President's Commission.* Washington, D.C.: U.S. Government Printing Office.

Newkirk, Thomas. 1987. "The Non-narrative Writing of Young Children." *Research in the Teaching of English* 21, no. 1:121–44.

———. 1988. "Young Writers as Critical Readers." In *Understanding Writing: Ways of Observing, Learning, and Teaching*, 2nd ed., ed. Thomas Newkirk and Nancie Atwell. Portsmouth, N.H.: Heinemann.

Ninio, Anat. 1980. "Ostensive Definition in Vocabulary Teaching." *Journal of Child Language* 7:565–73.

Ninio, Anat, and Jerome Bruner. 1978. "The Achievement and Antecedents of Labelling." *Journal of Child Language* 5:1–15.

Olson, David. 1977. "From Utterance to Text: The Bias of Language in Speech and Writing." *Harvard Educational Review* 47:257–81.

Ong, Walter. 1981. "Literacy and Orality in Our Times." In *The Writing Teachers' Sourcebook*, ed. Gary Tate and Edward P. J. Corbett. New York: Oxford University Press.

Perl, Sondra, and Nancy Wilson. 1986. *Through Teachers' Eyes: Portraits of Writing Teachers at Work*. Portsmouth, N.H.: Heinemann.

Philips, Susan. 1972. "Participant Structures and Communicative Competence." In *Functions of Language in the Classroom*, ed. Courtney Cazden, Vera John, and Dell Hymes. New York: Teachers College Press.

Plato. 1973. *The Phaedrus*. Trans. Walter Hamilton. Harmondsworth, England: Penguin.

Polanyi, Michael. 1958. *Personal Knowledge: Towards a Post-Critical Philosophy*. Chicago: University of Chicago Press.

Post, Emily. 1922. *Etiquette*. 14th ed. New York: Funk and Wagnalls.

Postman, Neil. 1979. *Teaching as a Conserving Activity*. New York: Delta Books.

Powell, Arthur G., Eleanor Farrar, and David Cohen. 1985. *The Shopping Mall School: Winners and Losers in the Educational Marketplace*. Boston: Houghton Mifflin.

Rahv, Phillip. 1957. "The Cult of Experience in American Writing." In *Literature in America*, ed. Phillip Rahv. Cleveland: World Publishing.

Ratner, N., and Jerome Bruner. 1978. "Games, Social Exchanges and the Acquisition of Language." *Journal of Child Language* 5:391–401.

Rodriguez, Richard. 1981. *Hunger of Memory: The Education of Richard Rodriguez*. Boston: Godine.

Rosen, Harold, and Connie Rosen. 1973. *The Language of Primary School Children*. Harmondsworth, England: Penguin.

Rosenblatt, Louise. 1978. *The Reader, the Text, and the Poem*. Carbondale, Ill.: Southern Illinois University Press.

Rousseau, Jean-Jacques. [1762] 1979. *Emile, or On Education*, trans. Allan Bloom. New York: Basic Books.

Scardamalia, Marlene. 1981. "How Children Cope with the Cognitive Demands of Writing." In *Writing: The Nature,*

*Development, and Teaching of Written Communication*, Vol. 2, ed. Carl Fredrickson and Joseph Dominic. Hillsdale, N.J.: Lawrence Erlbaum.

Scarry, Richard. 1971. *Things to Know*. New York: Golden Press.

Scollon, Michael, and Suzanne Scollon. 1979. *The Literate Two-Year-Old: The Fictionalization of Self.* Austin, Tex.: Southeast Regional Laboratory.

Searle, Dennis. 1984. "Scaffolding: Who's Building Whose Building?" *Language Arts* 61:480–83.

Searle, John. 1970. *Speech Acts*. Cambridge, England: Cambridge University Press.

Shaughnessy, Mina. 1977. *Errors and Expectations: A Guide for the Teacher of Basic Writing*. New York: Oxford University Press.

*Shoelace Page-A-Day Calendar 1987*. 1987. New York: Workman Publishing.

Sizer, Theodore. 1984. *Horace's Compromise: The Dilemma of the American High School*. Boston: Houghton Mifflin.

*Skillpack: Ride the Sunrise (Level 12)*. 1985. Lexington, Mass.: Ginn.

Smith, Frank. 1981. "Demonstrations, Engagement, and Sensitivity: A Revised Approach to Language Learning." *Language Arts*. 58:103–12.

——— 1983. *Essays into Literacy*. Portsmouth, N.H.: Heinemann.

Smith, Nila. 1965. *American Reading Instruction*. Newark, Del.: International Reading Association.

Snow, Catherine. 1983. "Literacy and Language: Relationships during the Preschool Year." *Harvard Educational Review* 53:165–89.

Sowers, Susan. 1985a. "Learning to Write in the Workshop: A Study in Grades One through Four." In *Advances in Writing Research: Children's Early Writing Development*, ed. Marcia Farr. Norwood, N.J.: Ablex.

———. 1985b. "The Story and the All-About Book." In *Breaking Ground: Teachers Relate Reading and Writing in the Elementary School*, ed. Jane Hansen, Thomas Newkirk, and Donald Graves. Portsmouth, N.H.: Heinemann.

———. 1988. "Reflect, Expand, Select: Three Responses in the Writing Conference." In *Understanding Writing: Ways of Observing, Learning, and Teaching*, 2nd ed., ed. Thomas Newkirk and Nancie Atwell. Portsmouth, N.H.: Heinemann.

Staton, Jana. 1980. "Writing and Counseling: Using a Dialogue Journal." *Language Arts* 57:514–18.

———. 1981. "*It's Not Gonna Come Down in One Little Sentence*": *A Study of Discourse in Dialogue Journal Writing*. Washington,

D.C.: Center for Applied Linguistics.

Stotsky, Sandra. 1984. "A Proposal for Improving High School Students' Ability to Read and Write Expository Prose." *Journal of Reading* 28:4–7.

"Talk of the Town." 1985. *New Yorker*, October 14:33.

Taylor, Denny. 1983. *Family Literacy: Young Children Learning to Read and Write*. Portsmouth, N.H.: Heinemann.

Thoreau, Henry David. [1854] 1983. *Walden and Civil Disobedience*. Harmondsworth, England: Penguin.

Tocqueville, Alexis de. [1835, 1840] 1964. *Democracy in America*, trans. Henry Reeve. New York: Washington Square Press.

Toulmin, Stephen. 1969. *The Uses of Argument*. Cambridge, England: Cambridge University Press.

Twain, Mark. [1885] 1979. *Adventures of Tom Sawyer and Huckleberry Finn*. New York: New American Library.

Vygotsky, Lev. 1962. *Thought and Language*. Cambridge, Mass.: MIT Press.

———. 1978. *Mind in Society: The Development of Higher Psychological Processes*, ed. Silvia Scribner and Michael Cole. Cambridge: Harvard University Press.

Weaver, Richard. 1953. *The Ethics of Rhetoric*. Chicago; Regnery.

Wells, Gordon. 1986. *The Meaning Makers: Children Learning Language and Using Language to Learn*. Portsmouth, N.H.: Heinemann.

Whitehead, Alfred North. 1949. *The Aims of Education*. New York: New American Library.

Wilde, Jack. 1988. "The Written Report: Old Wine in New Bottles." In *Understanding Writing: Ways of Observing, Learning, and Teaching*, 2nd ed., ed. Thomas Newkirk and Nancie Atwell. Portsmouth, N.H.: Heinemann.

Williams, Raymond. 1976. *Keywords: A Vocabulary of Culture and Society*. New York: Oxford University Press.

Wood, D., J. Bruner, and G. Ross. 1976. "The Role of Tutoring in Problem-solving." *Journal of Child Psychology and Psychiatry* 17:89–100.

Wordsworth, William. [1850] 1960. *The Prelude, or Growth of a Poet's Mind*. London: Oxford University Press.

Zinsser, William. 1980. *On Writing Well: An Informal Guide to Writing Nonfiction*. 2nd ed. New York: Harper and Row.

# Index